D0759814

ANTHOLOGY OF
GERMAN EXPRESSIONIST DRAMA

ANTHOLOGY OF GERMAN EXPRESSIONIST DRAMA

A Prelude to the Absurd

REVISED AND
ABRIDGED EDITION

EDITED BY
Walter H. Sokel

Cornell University Press

ITHACA AND LONDON

First published Cornell Paperbacks, 1984.
Published in the United Kingdom by
Cornell University Press Ltd., London.

Original edition published by Anchor Books, 1963, under the title
Anthology of German Expressionist Drama: A Prelude to the Absurd

International Standard Book Number 0-8014-9296-3
Library of Congress Catalog Card Number 84-45197
Printed in the United States of America

CONTENTS

ACKNOWLEDGMENTS

I wish to express my most sincere thanks to: Professor Eric Bentley, for having originally suggested the idea of doing this anthology and for his most helpful advice at all stages of its compilation; Pyke Johnson, for his splendid encouragement of this task, his admirable patience with the many problems attendant upon it, and his extremely valuable suggestions; Kurt Pinthus, for sharing his rich memories of the Expressionist period with me and, specifically, for allowing me to use a rare copy of the original edition of Walter Hasenclever's *Die Menschen*; Helen Printz, for her excellent suggestions in the renditions into English of several of these plays and especially for her aptness in finding proper rhyme words in some of the poetry; Lore Taussig, for her valuable editorial assistance; Molly Yeager, for her wonderful attention to the manuscript, for her untiring devotion to the many chores connected with this undertaking, and for always amiable cooperation. Above all, I wish to thank my wife, Jacqueline, for her wonderful readiness to live with the often painful labors involved in this work, for providing the atmosphere conducive to its materialization, and for her devoted participation in every phase.

Acknowledgment is made to the following publishers and owners of copyrighted material which appears in this volume:

CROWN PUBLISHERS, INC.: "Epilogue to the Actor," by Paul Kornfeld, translated by Joseph Bernstein, from *Actors on Acting*, edited by Toby Cole and Helen Krich Chinoy. Copyright 1949, 1954, © 1970 by Toby Cole and Helen Krich Chinoy. Used by permission of Crown Publishers, Inc.

IRMELA FLIEDNER: *Cry in the Street*, by Rolf Lauckner.

MME. EDITH HASENCLEVER: *Humanity*, by Walter Hasenclever.

Walter Huder, Propyläen Verlag, Akademie der Kunste: *Alkibiades Saved* and excerpt from *Man in the Tunnel*, by Georg Kaiser. Originally published by Walter Huder (Frankfurt, Berlin, Vienna: Propyläen, 1971).

Verlagsgruppe Langen-Müller/Herbig, Munich: *Murderer the Women's Hope* and *Job*, by Oskar Kokoschka.

Hermann Luchterhand Verlag, Cologne: *The Strongbox*, by Carl Sternheim.

Reinhard M. Sorge and Johannes Sorge: *The Beggar*, by Reinhard Sorge.

EDITOR'S NOTE

Bertolt Brecht's *Baal*, translated by Eric Bentley and Martin Esslin, appeared in the original edition of this work, published in 1963 by Anchor Books. Owing to copyright restrictions, it could not be included in this edition.

W.H.S.

April 1984

INTRODUCTION

Although the term Expressionism had, as a literary term, already been in use in English-speaking countries by the middle of the nineteenth century, it was employed by the French painter Hervé in 1901 to serve as a common denominator for the art of Van Gogh, Cézanne, and Matisse. As such, the term was imported into German art criticism and used by the influential aesthetician Worringer in 1911 to designate one of the forms of "abstraction." A few years later, the critic and playwright Hermann Bahr popularized it as a term designating a new type of literature that had sprung up in German-speaking countries around 1910 and was to flourish into the twenties.

Marked individual differences existed among the poets and playwrights of the new generation. Yet enough common features seemed to unite them to enable critics, editors, and scholars to feel justified in applying the term Expressionism, and so to stamp them as a group. The unifying features were seen to be revolt, distortion, boldness of innovation. The novelty of this literature was especially striking in lyric poetry and the drama. The new playwrights—Sorge, Kornfeld, Hasenclever, Barlach, Sternheim, Kaiser, Werfel, Kokoschka, Goering, Goll, Csokor, Bronnen, Toller, Wolff, Brecht, and many others—despite profound differences in spirit and form, seemed to have this in common: they rebelled against propriety and "common sense," against authority and convention in art and in life. They rejected the tradition of the "well-made play," and the canons of plausibility and "good taste" in art. They openly defied the ideal of objective recording of everyday life, on which "realistic" theater since Scribe and Ibsen had been based; but they likewise turned against the disdainful aloofness from contemporary urban reality that characterized those who sought to revive the romanticism or neoclassicism of the past. Along with the dominant art of bourgeois society, they rejected, unmasked, and caricatured its mores and institutions. They stood in opposition to the prevailing temper of Wilhelminian Germany and Hapsburg Austria, in which they had grown up, and many identified themselves with, and even participated in, the opposition to World War I and the revolutions of 1918 and 1919. They constituted not merely an aesthetic but also an ethical, social, and sometimes even political revolt. Although there were strong Nietzschean and futurist influences on Expressionism, especially in its initial phase, full-fledged Expressionism was largely allied with pacifism, humanitarianism, Socialism, and progressive school reform. However, since this revolt was in many cases neither specific nor rational, but vague and emotional, we find the paradoxical fact that the same movement numbered among its ranks some who afterward were to contribute their support to National Socialism or Communism. Still, the majority of Expressionists, insofar as they survived World War I at all, were to perish as victims of Nazism or survive it in exile, outlawed in their native lands and branded as "degenerates" together with Picasso, Chagall, and other leading figures of the international revolution in the arts.

Expressionism was part and parcel of the international movement of experimentation in the arts which, with antecedents in symbolism and romanticism, has characterized our century. The Expressionists were allies and spiritual kinsmen of the Cubists and Surrealists of France, the Futurists of Italy and Russia, and the one-man revolution called James Joyce. The Expressionist Yvan Goll had close personal connections with Apollinaire (whom he greatly admired), Cocteau, and Jules Romains in Paris, and with James Joyce in Zurich. Herwarth Walden's journal *Der Sturm* published Marinetti's manifesto of Futurism in its pages, and spread the fame and cult of Picasso several years before World War I.

Striking parallels in structure, tone, and theme are found between German Expressionism and the early plays of O'Neill, especially *Emperor Jones, The Hairy Ape,* and *The Great God Brown.* These parallels derive from common indebtedness to Strindberg. The Expressionists in general were deeply influenced by Dostoevski, Nietzsche, Walt Whitman, and Rimbaud; the dramatists in particular by Strindberg, Büchner, and Wedekind. In the years immediately preceding World War I, Strindberg was the most frequently performed playwright on the German and Austrian stage. The young playwrights who were to shape Expressionist drama devoured his works and received decisive inspiration from his experimental "dream plays"—*To Damascus* (1898–1904), *A Dream Play* (1902), and *The Ghost Sonata* (1907).

The German Expressionists in turn influenced the American Expressionism of the theater of the twenties, and the so-called Theater of the Absurd of our own day. As for the latter, Martin Esslin, in his excellent work on the subject, counts the Expressionists among the forerunners of the contemporary revolution in the theater. To be sure, the influence is hardly direct. Yvan Goll, who made his home in Paris, had considerable prestige in France, but more on account of his poetry than for his Expressionist-Surrealist plays of the late teens and early twenties. The influence of the Expressionist Georg Kaiser, who died in exile in Switzerland in 1945, can be detected in the Swiss-German playwrights Max Frisch and Friedrich Dürrenmatt. But on the whole the heritage of Expressionism was transmitted to contemporary avant-garde playwrights through two German authors—Franz Kafka and Bertolt Brecht. Through his friendship with Max Brod, Kafka had personal ties with the Expressionists, and one of their most active publishers, Kurt Wolff, launched Kafka's literary career. More important, there are close structural and thematic connections between Kafka and the Expressionists, which will be touched upon below. Bert Brecht grew out of Expressionism, where the roots of the Epic Theater can be found. While Brecht had nothing but sardonic contempt for the hymnic-naïve and sentimental aspect of Expressionism (pouring his scorn on the movement in one of his versions of *Baal*), he acknowledged his gratitude and respect to Georg Kaiser. One of Brecht's *Calendar Tales* (*Kalendergeschichten*) is based on the Kaiser play in this anthology.

What was Expressionism? Any answer would necessarily

have to be inadequate, because the question assumes as a single fact what is actually a convenient term for designating a richly varied period in the history of drama. Expressionism was not a program guiding individual authors as they wrote their works. It was a term applied by critics, editors, anthologists, and historians of literature in dealing with a group of authors. The term was used after the fact. Most of the authors usually called Expressionist felt that they were expressing themselves in new ways, and they groped for new terms to define their feeling. However, they rarely applied the term Expressionist to themselves.

An "ism" is a convenience making rational discourse about the phenomena of cultural history easier, or even possible. Too many individual variations exist to permit us to expect hard-and-fast definitions. There are as many styles as there are individual authors or, more accurately still, individual works. It has recently become the fashion among German critics to deny altogether, or at least to doubt, the legitimacy of such generic terms as Expressionism. Such an extreme position, however, would unnecessarily impoverish our intellectual discourse; for terms that denote, however approximately, common elements in a literary period can serve a useful function, provided we keep in mind their limitations. There were some significant things that most Expressionist plays had in common, and that distinguished them from "well-made" plays, or realistic and Naturalistic plays, or plays of the classical tradition. To blind our eyes to this fact, from fear of generalization, would be as naïve as to expect that each play called Expressionist must in every respect conform to all the other plays of this group, or must in every respect differ from all the works of other periods and movements. The following is not to be interpreted as a definition of Expressionist drama but as an orientation to an extremely interesting, vital, and seminal phase in the history of the theater, for which the term Expressionism will be used.

What strikes one first about Expressionist plays is an extremism of theme, language, stagecraft, mixed with many features of realistic or classical drama. There are in these plays elements of distortion, exaggeration, grotesqueness, and implausibility that clearly anticipate the alienating effects encountered in the avant garde theater of our own time. We witness bizarre events. For example, we see a murdered man reappearing in the modern metropolis carrying his head in a sack, brought to court, and condemned as his own murderer. A woman floats out the window of her lover's apartment. A poodle changes into a psychologist. A cuckolded husband grows antlers on his head. A group of airplane pilots suddenly appears in a café, reciting verses in the style of Greek tragedy, and a group of prostitutes and their lovers engage in a stylized orgy while a literary conversation takes place in another section of the café. Plots are disjointed and confusing, or cease to be recognizable as such. Dialogue suddenly changes from prose to hymnic poetry and rhapsodic monologue, completely interrupting the action. Lyrical passages alternate with obscenities and curses. Characters speak past rather than to each other. Language tends to be reduced, in some plays, to two- and one-word sentences (the "telegraphic style"), to expletives, gestures, pantomime.

Some of these developments were simply an intensification of Naturalism. The Naturalists, in the wake of Ibsen, had brought to the stage subject matter which the "well-made play" of the Victorian era carefully avoided, and their language, especially in German Naturalism, increasingly flaunted an emotional directness that made the linguistic innovations of the Expressionists possible. Ibsen had made syphilis the theme of tragedy; Strindberg, in his Naturalistic phase, introduced the strait jacket on the stage; Schnitzler made sexual intercourse the structural center of each scene in his *La Ronde*; Hauptmann, in his *The Weavers*, made workers' dialect the language of tragedy. At first glance, an Expressionist play like Arnolt Bronnen's *Patricide*, in which a high-school boy has sexual intercourse with his mother on stage and mortally stabs his father, seems simply an extreme development of Naturalism, foreshadowing and even outdoing Tennessee Williams. But in spite of the play's many resemblances to extreme Naturalism, the spirit in which *Patricide* was written was diametrically opposed to Naturalism. In his autobiography, *Arnolt Bronnen Goes on Record* (*Arnolt Bronnen Gibt zu Protokoll*, 1954), Bronnen tells us that he wrote down not what he observed but what he felt and suffered; he not only dramatized the Freudian Oedipus complex in its primitive essence, he also exemplified the Freudian view of the artist—he had sublimated his misery into a dream and projected this dream on paper. With this, the keynote of Expressionism is struck: subjectivism. Dream became literature.

The extremism and distortion of Expressionist drama derive from its closeness to the dream. In its crude aspects, Expressionism is dramatized daydream and fantasy. In its subtler and more interesting examples, Expressionism parallels the concealing symbolism and subliminal suggestiveness of night dreams. Strindberg called the experimental plays he wrote when he passed beyond Naturalism "dream plays." In them projection and embodiment of psychic forces take the place of imitation of external facts; association of ideas supplants construction of plot based on logical connection of cause and effect. The old structural principle of causal interrelation between character, incident, and action gives way to a new structural pattern, closer to music than to drama—the presentation and variation of a theme.

Strindberg's "dream plays" became the inspiration of the Expressionists. Unlike the French Surrealists of the twenties and thirties, the Expressionists rarely reproduced actual dreams. Rather, the structure of many of their plays resembled, in some respects, the pattern of the human mind in dream and reverie. The influence of Strindberg coincided with that of psychoanalysis (Freud's *Interpretation of Dreams* appeared two years before *A Dream Play*). Psychoanalysis had decisive significance for Expressionism. But even before Freud, the intellectual atmosphere in the wake of Romanticism, and German philosophy from Schelling to Schopenhauer and Nietzsche, had given intimations of the concept of the subconscious. Even those Expressionists who were not conversant with the actual works of Freud and Jung could not help but be familiar with the climate of thought that had given rise to psychoanalysis in the first place.

Dream effects were achieved in a variety of ways. A comparison of two examples—the first act of Reinhard Sorge's *The Beggar* and Oskar Kokoschka's play *Job*—might illustrate the range. The choice of these two playwrights has special relevance, since they introduced full-fledged Expressionism to the German theater. Kokoschka, more famous as a painter, wrote the first Expressionist play, *Murderer the Women's Hope*, in 1907; Sorge composed *The Beggar* in 1911.

Sorge achieves dreamlike effects by scenic arrangements, light, the grouping of characters, and speech variations. Floodlight takes the place of stream of consciousness. The wandering of the floodlight over the stage, illuminating now one and now another section, symbolizes the process of the mind itself. When the latent substratum emerges, the center of the stage is obscured while a particular corner—significantly supplied with couches or benches—is highlighted. When the mind shifts back to the surface plot, the corner sinks into darkness, while the center is illuminated. The corner scenes, so puzzlingly unrelated to the main-action center stage, can now be seen as only apparently unrelated. These scenes function as symbolically disguised commentary and reflection on the themes discussed in the center, and in that lies their dreamlike quality.

This relationship between scenic interludes and main dialogue or plot was a radical extension of the multiple-plot structure of Shakespeare's plays, which had inspired not only Sorge but all those who, since the Storm and Stress of the eighteenth century, had rebelled against the neo-classicist unities and their modern successor, the "well-made play," with its neat logic and economy of plot. Those for whom theater meant more than drama and dramatic plot, for whom theater was play, show, and vision of the world, had to hark back to Shakespeare and beyond. The Expressionists benefited greatly from Max Reinhardt's imaginative stagings of

Shakespeare and Strindberg, and from the general advances in stagecraft, especially lighting effects, associated with this master showman of the Berlin theater.

The historic importance of Sorge's play lies in its attempt to create on the stage something that happened to be akin to the interior monologue in the novel. This approach leads to musical, rather than dramatic, structure. Expressionist drama is theme-centered rather than plot- or conflict-centered. This factor constitutes the most marked break with the tradition of the "well-made play." The first impression given by Sorge's *The Beggar*, for instance, is one of bewildering formlessness. The play flies in the face of the plot-centered tradition of drama with which we are most familiar. Yet a closer examination of the play reveals the opposite of formlessness—careful craftsmanship and richly interwoven texture, at least in the first three acts, the bulk of the play. The intricate arrangement of themes closely corresponds to the composition of a symphony rather than a drama in the traditional sense. The interludes of the first act echo the foreground theme in choral variations. The Prostitute interlude represents a counterpoint to the Girl theme. The Poet's visionary speech finds its exact counterpoint in the Father's enraptured vision in the second act. The insane Father's engineering "mission," which dominates Acts II and III, is the contrapuntal theme to the Son's poetic mission in Act I.

These few examples should help dispel the widespread notion that Expressionism was necessarily formless. The subtle musical structure of *The Beggar*, or the classically polished, lyrical grotesqueries of Kokoschka, show that the abandonment of a logical, unified plot does not mean the abandonment of theatrical form. Like abstract paintings or like *Finnegans Wake*, the experimental plays of Expressionism did not necessarily renounce aesthetic form and inner coherence merely because these offered greater obstacles to immediate appreciation.

In his play *Sphinx and Strawman* (*Sphinx und Strohmann*), performed by the Zurich Dadaists in 1917, the Austrian painter Oskar Kokoschka developed a kind of dream play

which differed from Strindberg's and Sorge's type. He deep-
ened, expanded, and changed this play from prose into poetry
of classical smoothness and elegance, and so gave birth to his
finest poetic achievement—*Job*, which created a theater scandal at its performance in 1919. Like Sorge, Kokoschka trans-
forms aspects of the dream process into theater. His play
revolves about the projection of psychic processes into visual
terms. Unlike Sorge, Kokoschka relies less on light effects
and stage division than on the transformation of metaphors, of
figures of speech, into stage images. Job's tragedy consists
in having his head turned by woman. The author shows this
literally happening on the stage. In his helpless anxiety over
his wife Anima, Job twists his head and cannot set it straight
again. As his wife flagrantly deceives him, antlers grow on
his head and become the clothestree for his wife's and her
lover's undergarments. The metaphors contained in the figures of speech—"she turns his head," "she puts horns on
him"—become dramatic image, visual fact. Intimately related
to the dream and the workings of the human subconscious,
as expounded by Freud in his *Interpretation of Dreams* and
Wit and Its Relation to the Unconscious, Kokoschka's method
constitutes the dramatic parallel to Kafka's art of projecting
the repressed content of the mind into mysterious events.
In Kokoschka's play, the projection of psychic situations into
symbolic images, an essential function of the subconscious
mind, becomes action on the stage. This principle offered
Kokoschka, and Goll after him, a means of returning to the
ancient nature of the theater as magic show, as visual and
pantomimic liberation from the confining fetters of realism and
propriety. As Esslin has pointed out, it is precisely this triumph of the image, this staging of the metaphor, which makes
for the dramatic poetry in the works of Beckett, Ionesco,
and Genet. The ash cans in which the senescent parents in
Beckett's *Endgame* spend their lives, the audience of empty
chairs in Ionesco's *The Chairs*, or the transformation of human
beings into rhinoceros in his *The Rhinceros*—such central
stage images of the Theater of the Absurd are born of the
same kind of inspiration as Job's twisted head or the Chagal-

lian heroine floating out the window in Goll's *The Immortal One*. This particular form of Expressionist dream play not only points ahead to the avant-garde theater of our day, but also re-establishes connections with the ancient mainstream of European theater, which the "well-made" respectable play of the modern era had repudiated. Cabaret and circus, *commedia dell'arte*, Passion and miracle play, and above all, the magic farce of the Vienna popular theater, which flowered in Mozart's and Schikaneder's *Magic Flute*, the whole baroque delight in the *spectaculum mundi*, contributed to that feast of theatricality and poetry—Kokoschka's *Job*.

In Georg Kaiser's play, *Alkibiades Saved*, a figure of speech becomes event and forms the brilliantly ironic plot.[1] Kaiser's drama is a spectacle showing how "the thorn in the flesh" gives rise to Platonism, idealism, and spirituality. By preventing Sokrates from engaging in normal physical activity, the thorn lodged in his foot forces him to question and subvert the athletic-heroic values of his civilization and replace them with new values of intellect and spirit. The process of sublimation is acted out before our eyes. No one of the Athenians (except Sokrates himself and Xantippe, his wife) knows of the thorn, the invisible wound that makes Sokrates the subverter and scandalizer of the old and the prophet of a new civilization. But for us, the spectators, the invisible is visualized, the spiritual and psychological problem is projected into a vividly concrete, physical happening.

The projection of abstract idea and psychic situations into symbolic images and happenings is one of the most basic features of Expressionist drama. Consequently, language loses the pre-eminent rank it held in traditional drama. Dynamic utilization of setting and stage (in *The Beggar*, for instance, the walls of the living room literally widen and part to let in the cosmos) expresses many things formerly expressed by language, or not expressed at all. Broad gestures, uninhibited overacting, as demanded by Kornfeld, the return to mask, buskin, and chanting—these are the demands made by Ex-

[1]For the spelling in this play, see note on title page of the play.

pressionist theory and frequently exhibited by Expressionist practice. An immediate appeal is made to the audience's visual sense rather than to its conceptual thought. The memory of empirical reality, with its demand for causal logic and plausibility, is suspended.

The single emotional word replaces the involved conceptual sentence as the basic unit of Expressionist language. Repetition, variation, modulating echo, and contrapuntal clash of single words are essential parts of Expressionist dialogue. The Expressionists utilize to their fullest extent the expressive possibilities of punctuation. Punctuation becomes one of the tools of visualization and attains a crucial role. The accumulation of exclamation points, or the linking of exclamation point and question mark, as in Kaiser and Sorge, and punctuation in general, are transformed on the stage into inflection and gesture and thereby augment and even create the emotional impact of their language. Punctuation becomes one of the primary tools of visualization and assumes a significance unknown in traditional drama. Concomitantly, the demands made upon the vocal apparatus and bodily effort of the actors greatly transcend those of traditional plays. As Kornfeld's essay shows, Expressionism stands at the opposite pole of Stanislawski. The Expressionist actor stands somewhere between actor, singer, and mime. Frequently his greatest impact must come from his stage presence rather than his speech. Sokrates, in Kaiser's play, dominates the scene in which he refuses the wreath simply by the visual contrast between his massive silence and static presence, and the frantic verbosity of the others. At the banquet, his presence falls like a shadow over the revellers. The chill that overtakes them is conveyed by Sokrates' silences more than by his words. Bereft of the customary support of dialogue, the actor has to rely on the resources of his body to a much greater degree than in conventional plays, in which dialogue is the primary, and often exclusive, means by which meaning is conveyed.

Expressionist drama employs silence more frequently and more strategically than conventional drama, extending and further developing a tendency initiated by realism and Naturalism in their revolt against language-centered classical drama. Brecht in *Baal*, Kaiser, and Hasenclever use silence as a counterpoint to the meaning of the spoken dialogue. Words and pauses together form a kind of linguistic chiaroscuro, counterpart to the visible chiaroscuro of illumination and dimness or darkness on Sorge's stage. The deliberate use of the pause as a significant means of expression (indicated on the printed page by the abundance of dots and dashes in Expressionist plays) reveals most clearly the kinship between Expressionist drama and music. Dots and dashes are the equivalents of pauses in musical scores. The pause is an essential part of the Expressionist attempt to create or re-create a theater of depths inaccessible to conceptual speech, a "super-drama," as Yvan Goll calls it, conveying a "surreality" which is to empirical reality what depth is to surface. Such a theater would be a "total work of art," like the drama of the Greeks. It would restore the theater as cult. While the Expressionists sought to restore theater as cult, Brecht, going beyond Expressionism, sought to develop theater as seminar and laboratory. Both were equally opposed to the "culinary" theater of mere entertainment and commercial profit.

The displacement of conceptual language by exclamation and pantomime reached an extreme point in Walter Hasenclever's *Humanity (Die Menschen)*, in 1918. The early silent films with their exaggerated gestures and miming influenced Hasenclever's modern Passion play. The mixture of sentimental pathos, social protest, and grotesqueness characteristic of the silent films is found here, too. Attracted by the new medium, Hasenclever, soon after *Humanity*, wrote the scenario of the film *Plague (Pest)* in 1920. The possibilities of the film intrigued other Expressionists as well. Yvan Goll celebrated Charlie Chaplin, along with Apollinaire one of his most decisive influences, in his scenario *Chaplinade*. The great film *The Cabinet of Dr. Caligari* (1919), which ushered in the classical period of the German film, was an excellent example of pure Expressionist theater on the screen. Fritz Lang's film *Metropolis* (1926) continued Expressionism in the German movies.

Because of its subjectivism, Expressionist drama does not allow genuine conflict to arise. With few exceptions, Expressionist drama conforms to an "epic" or narrative, rather than to a strictly dramatic pattern. It is not based upon the clash of independently motivated characters, but upon the showing and telling of themes. Ultimately its structure can be traced to the Christian miracle and Passion plays. The content of Expressionist drama is, of course, frequently the opposite of Christian: glorification of murder, blasphemy, pederasty, and vigorous anti-theism (a term more fitting than atheism in the context of Expressionism). Yet even though content may differ profoundly, structural pattern may be similar. The protagonist in Expressionist plays usually serves as an existential example, a paragon, very much like Christ in the Passion plays. The other "characters" are not so much characters as functions in his mission or martyrdom. They represent his opportunities, obstacles, parallels, variations, and counterpoints. Genuine antagonists do not exist. There are antagonistic characters, usually philistines, materialists, often scientists or engineers, moralists and sentimentalists. However, these antagonistic characters do not act as independent personalities motivated by aims of their own, but as foils to the protagonist. They do not carry the action forward. They are closer to the tempting devil in miracle plays or to Goethe's Mephistopheles than to Claudius in *Hamlet*.

The absence of conflict determines the pageant or pilgrimage-type structure of many full-length Expressionist plays, such as Hasenclever's *Humanity* and Brecht's *Baal*. A loosely connected "life story," a series of "stations," pictures, and situations takes the place of a well-knit plot. The major influences for this truly epic or narrative character of Expressionist drama are the Christian Passion play and Goethe's *Faust*, both of which deeply influenced Strindberg, and with him the Expressionists; Shakespeare; Storm and Stress playwrights like Lenz; Büchner (especially in his *Wozzeck*); and the modern cabaret, with its brief skits and numbers. From this type of Expressionist play, the left-wing director Erwin Piscator, Lion Feuchtwanger, and Bertolt Brecht developed

in the twenties what is now known as the Epic Theater. Both
Expressionism and Brecht's Epic Theater emphasized theater
as "show" or demonstration rather than as drama without
emphasis on action and suspense. The difference was that
most Expressionists (although by no means all) sought to appeal to the emotions, while Brecht's Epic Theater tried to
appeal to the critical intellect of its audience.

Kaiser's dramas offer by their taut construction a remarkable contrast to the "epic" looseness and disconnectedness of
many Expressionist plays. "Writing a drama" meant for him
"thinking a thought through to its conclusion." He compared
dramas to "geometric problems" and considered Plato's dialogues perfect models for playwrights. However, subjectivism
also formed the basis of Kaiser's work. It was a symptom of this
subjectivism that Kaiser admired Plato as a "dramatist." For
Plato's dialogues fail to present genuine conflict and dramatic
encounter of ideas. They are not true dialogues, but thinly
veiled monologues. Significantly, Kaiser noted and praised
not the dramatic but the visionary quality of Plato's work.
As Professor Wolfgang Paulsen pointed out in his recent work
on Kaiser (Tübingen, 1960), Kaiser, unlike Shaw, was not
a truly "dialectical" playwright. At best he dramatized an-
titheses, embodied in different characters, as he did in the
Billionaire's Son and the Engineer of his famous *Gas I* (1918).
Many of his plays even lack such an antithesis. Sokrates, in
Alkibiades Saved, for example, has no real antagonists waging
a real conflict against him. All action comes from Sokrates;
the others merely react against him. They are blindly caught
in a problem of which Sokrates alone is aware, and which is
his own creation. Actually, it is not Sokrates, the character,
but Sokrates' idea, to which the thorn in his foot gave rise,
that moves the action, until nearly the end. The other characters, with the exception of the judges, are pawns in Sokrates'
great enterprise of "saving Alkibiades," the tragic irony of
which he alone can see. While more subtly expressed than
in the works of other Expressionists, subjectivism informed
Kaiser's dramas as much as it did theirs.

Subjectivism in Expressionist dramas entailed not only the

absence of genuine conflict but of all real touch and communication between human beings. The most powerful example is Brecht's *In the Swamp* (*Im Dickicht der Städte*) (1922), which came at the end of the Expressionist period. With the formulation, in theatrical terms, of the breakdown of human communication, Expressionist drama foreshadowed French Existentialism and almost all the serious literature of our time.

Expressionism had two faces: With one of these it looked back to Romanticism; with the other it looked forward to what is most significant and new in the theater of our own time. It was the positive content given to "mission" in Expressionist plays that harked back to Romanticism. It was the parody of "mission" that pointed to the future. What was the content of the Expressionists' "mission"? The Poet in Sorge's *The Beggar* proclaimed that his new theater would regenerate and redeem the world. Kaiser defined drama as "vision." The content of the vision was "the regeneration of man" ("*die Erneuerung des Menschen*").

With their concept of the writer as visionary and savior, the Expressionists renewed the old dream of Romanticism. Shelley's definition of the poets as "unacknowledged legislators of the world" could have been their motto. The mission themes of Expressionist plays projected the author's romantic self-pity and isolation in the modern world, as well as their equally romantic self-glorification, their dream of changing the world into a place in which they would feel at home.

There was another side to Expressionism, the counterpart of the idealism contained in its "mission" themes: the acid and macabre presentation of a meaningless, insanely materialistic world. It is in this respect that Expressionism shows an amazing relevance today. The insane Father in Sorge's *The Beggar*, the engineer who draws blueprints of fantastic machines he imagines having "seen" on Mars, strikes us as a truer, more convincing figure than the idealistic Son who hopes to save the world by poetry. The Father resembles the Engineer in Kaiser's *Gas I*, who, after a devastating explosion, calls upon the workers to push ahead from "explosion to explosion" to the conquest of the universe. In our age, shadowed by mushroom clouds and moon rockets, the technocratic nightmares of the Expressionists appear astonishingly prophetic, and much more realistic than at the time they were conceived. Distortion served the Expressionists as an X-ray eye for detecting the dynamic essence of their time, the direction in which history was moving. In caricature and nightmare they approached the truth. Their idealism, on the other hand, was a desperate attempt at self-deception, protecting them from the truth.

Kaiser's brilliant tour de force, *Alkibiades Saved*, amounts to a clear statement of the irony and paradox underlying the Expressionist position. Sokrates' mission is to endure suffering and court the death penalty in order to save Greece from absurdity. Only Sokrates, the intellectual, knows the trivial accident—the thorn in his foot—to which the hero, Alkibiades, owes his life, and the country its victory. If Sokrates discloses the absurd secret, the hero would become a laughingstock, and faith in history and human gestures would be shattered. Civilization could not withstand such a shock. Better to interpose new values, a new "message" between the traditional hero worship and the absurdity of truth than to allow truth to make all messages ridiculous. Subversive as these new values of intellect may be, they serve as a screen between man and the devastating insight into the absurdity of his existence.

This is the crux of the Expressionist sense of "mission": it is a last barrier, frantically held, against absurdity. Its ecstatic humanism is the surface froth. But beneath it lies a cynical, bitter, and sardonic spirit. This spirit informed some of the finest and most brilliant works of Expressionism, from Carl Sternheim to Bert Brecht. The parodying of the sense of mission, or, rather, the demonstration of its absurdity, lies at the heart of Sternheim's comedies and Brecht's earlier plays.

Carl Sternheim's comedies of "the heroic life of the bourgeoisie" lack the dreamlike distortions of much of Expressionist drama. Their hilarious caricatures and farcical situations remind one at first glance of conventional comedy. However, if we look a little closer, we discover qualities that profoundly distinguish Sternheim's comedies from the traditional type and make them the nearest counterpart to the grimly sardonic drawings of George Grosz.

There are not in Sternheim's comedies, as there are in Molière's, characters with moderate points of view, representing common sense—i.e., the common ground shared by author and audience. Sternheim fails to supply us with the convenient yardstick by which we can judge, while feeling comfortably above them, the comic characters as eccentrics. In Sternheim it is not the characters, but the world that has lost its center. His characters demonstrate a process that defines the whole of bourgeois society, and that might be called a quiet pandemonium of cold-blooded, insidious inhumanity. In *The Strongbox*, faith in securities, the new "soul of man," triumphs effortlessly over the older romantic, sensuous, and sentimental nature of man. But Sternheim does not weep for the lost glory of romantic man. He, too, is shown to be a self-drugging fraud. The aesthete and lover Silkenband is even phonier and more absurd than the tough-minded Professor Krull, with his monomaniac obsession with the security contained in the strongbox. Sternheim's characters function grotesquely in a world become demonic through what is supposed to be most commonplace and sober in it—its monetary system. Instead of making love to his beautiful young wife, the materialistic professor locks himself in with the strongbox, counting the maiden aunt's securities, listing and relisting their numbers, and figuring their values. Yet neither does Sternheim hold any brief for the neglected young beauty, who turns out to be engaged in a ruthless struggle for power with her shrewd and terrifying spinster aunt. No single value is more rational than any other; beauty and art, romantic love, sensuality, legacy-hunting, and financial fever—all are absurd.

Sternheim's characters are "soulless" in the literal sense—they have no stable permanent core of personality. They are completely identified with their maneuvers and obsessions—their "masks." Many of Sternheim's comedies deal with a bourgeois family called Maske. The name symbolizes modern man's essence, which Sternheim "unmasks." The modern bourgeois's essence is his mask—his veneer, as in Dickens' Mr. and Mrs. Veneering, who foreshadow Sternheim's ruthless characters not only in their go-getting cold-bloodedness but even in their peculiarly staccato baldness of diction, which perfectly expresses their cold-blooded spirit. Yet the obsessions of these characters are not the idiosyncrasies of individual eccentrics nor the embodiments of timeless vices familiar to us from Molière. They embody the obsession of society and the absurdity of the human condition itself. Lacking a stable center at his core, man in Sternheim is denatured.

Sternheim's "comedy" has a mission as its plot—the old aunt's strongbox pulls all men away from sexuality and passion to its own cold self. Not plot, but theme, is the center of interest. If the plot were the main interest—in other words, if Sternheim had written a traditional comedy about greed—the question of whether or not Professor Krull would inherit the strongbox would be left in suspense until as near the end as possible. Instead, the disclosure of the aunt's will, which bequeaths the contents of the box to the Church, is put near the middle of the play. The play ends not with the ironic punishment and just comeuppance of a greedy and neglectful husband, but with a new convert to mammonism. Capitalism, as the modern truth, replaces the older "truths" of chivalrous mummery and romance, or bohemian idealism. However, the "mission" of capitalism is patently absurd, too, since we know that the securities in the strongbox will never belong to their worshipers. The strongbox becomes a symbol of absurdity, like the Mars machines "seen" by the Father in Sorge's play. An absurd mission, seriously and consistently engaged in, reveals the absurdity of the world.

Something should be said about the selection and its arrangement. I deemed it essential to provide some theoretical background to give the reader an idea of the atmosphere and the aims that animated the literary climate called Expression-

ism. Therefore, I chose a few quasi-theoretical pronounce-
ments to preface the collection of plays.

The first of these four manifestoes, Ludwig Rubiner's "Man
in the Center," shows Expressionism as more than an innovation of form or a merely aesthetic-literary movement. It shows
the vague but intense general spirit of revolt underlying the
literary and artistic experiments. Rubiner was a revolutionary
intellectual, deeply influenced by Russian civilization, an out-
and-out opponent of war, and an outstanding representative
of the political radicals and utopianism that characterized the
intellectual temper in the last stages of World War I and at
the beginning of the "democratic and socialist" Weimar Re-
public. Before his death in 1920, Rubiner joined the Com-
munist movement.

The three following essays, by Paul Kornfeld, Yvan Goll,
and Georg Kaiser, are more directly concerned with drama.
They are given in chronological order. Insofar as a basic
manifesto of Expressionist theater can be said to exist, it was
provided by Kornfeld. His "Epilogue to the Actor," appended
to his play *The Seduction* (*Die Verführung*) (1913), clearly
shows the anti-Stanislawski attitude of Expressionism, its complete opposition to the Method, attendant upon the Expressionist repudiation of the principles of realism and mimesis
in art. At the same time, Kornfeld's essay shows that this
break meant, in the eyes of those who made it, nothing really
new, but was a rejuvenation of the ancient and universal
tradition of theater as opposed to the "well-made play" of recent times. The same tendency manifests itself in Yvan Goll's
ambitious program of "The Superdrama." The curious combi-
nation of spiritual idealism and one-upmanship, of Platonism
and modernity, characteristic of so much of Expressionism is
best conveyed by Kaiser's declaration in "Man in the Tunnel."

Last but not least, the manifestoes have been chosen to
give the reader a taste of Expressionist prose style, especially
in the case of Rubiner and Kaiser. For it is through the style
that the ideas become meaningful.

The plays are arranged, on the whole, chronologically, to

show development within Expressionism. My criteria for selection were threefold: dramatic or aesthetic quality and impact; representation of the extremes of stylistic and thematic diversity of Expressionism; connection with previous or following developments in Western theater, especially with the contemporary *avant-garde*. Not every play demonstrates the first of these criteria.

Kokoschka's early play, *Murderer the Women's Hope*, with which Expressionist drama begins, shows the return to myth enactment in the theater, which Yvan Goll's manifesto demanded eleven years later.

Sorge's *The Beggar* not only initiated full-fledged German Expressionism, but is one of the most impressive examples of the Strindbergian and Nietzschean influence, the musical-symphonic structure of many Expressionist plays, and the imaginative use of modern stage techniques, especially the utilization of new lighting devices. In the last particularly, the great debt of Expressionism to experimental-theater directors like Max Reinhardt is most evident.

Carl Sternheim represents the sardonic and nihilistic spirit of Expressionist caricature and shows the influence of Frank Wedekind on the one hand and, on the other, points to future developments in literature and art (Dadaism, Bert Brecht, George Grosz).

Oskar Kokoschka's *Job* provoked a theater scandal. This play displays the dreamlike, magical, and Surrealistic poetry of Expressionist theater and its peculiarly subjective use of myth and Biblical and literary allusions. (It is interesting to compare Kokoschka's *Job* and MacLeish's version, where myth is modernized, but conforms faithfully to the original pattern; the subjectivist character of the Expressionist play becomes even more striking.)

Georg Kaiser's *Alkibiades Saved* shows the same subjective use of historical material. Furthermore, it represents one of the most brilliant works of Expressionism, illustrating both the Platonic tendency and the basic cultural problem of which Expressionism was one manifestation. I chose this play by Kaiser instead of his more famous *Gas* trilogy or *From Morn to Midnight* because they are available in several English versions.

Walter Hasenclever's *Humanity* represents the most extreme form of the Expressionist reduction of language and its approximation to pure pantomime and silent film. It is also a most convincing example of the melodramatic pathos common to much of Expressionism, and it exemplifies the Passion-play structure, as does Brecht's *Baal*, for all their differences in spirit. Hasenclever's work is also a good example of the great unevenness that often prevails within individual Expressionist works—cheap banality standing next to grotesque power.

Yvan Goll's fantasy *The Immortal One* shows the transition from Expressionism to Dadaism and Surrealism. The kinship to Chaplin's and Chagall's art is striking. Although the two plays, *The Immortals*, of which our example is the first, are actually too light and tender to be suitable illustrations of Goll's theory of the Superdrama, the very lightness of the Goll selection enables it to serve as a good antidote to the somber and serious tone that pervades so much of the movement.

Rolf Lauckner is very little known. His vignette, taken from a series of dramatic vignettes called *Cry in the Street* (*Schrei aus der Strasse*), conveys a peculiar, eerie power, macabre humor, and insight into the "periphery" of human existence. In this work, we clearly see the link between Expressionism and naturalistic realism: it lies in the exploration of marginal human situations.

I regret that limitations of space have compelled me to exclude four authors whom I would have liked to bring to the English-speaking public in this volume. They are Ernst Barlach, Franz Th. Csokor, Ernst Toller, and Franz Werfel. My choice was a difficult one. Not all major Expressionists could be included. What determined my choice ultimately was the criteria I mentioned above, which, *mutatis mutandis*, I felt were best served by including those plays that were finally chosen.

I hope that this selection will give the reader an experience of Expressionist drama that he will find meaningful per se, and that will add to his understanding of the twentieth-century revolution in the theater.

WALTER H. SOKEL

Columbia University
October, 1962 (rev. 1984)

THE THEORY

MAN IN THE CENTER*

by Ludwig Rubiner

Translated by Walter H. Sokel

I know some things which I am no longer ready to discuss. I know that life can have only a moral purpose: Intensity, the roaming fire of intensity, the burstings, splittings, explosions of intensity. Intensity overshooting its mark, intensity killing, intensity begetting the unforgettables in a single—everlasting —second. I know the cracking of the earth's crust; I know dust flying out and scattering; I know ancient layers of filth cracking in two. The fiery hissing of spirit bubbles out of these. I know that evolution does not exist. I know that the multiplication of masses does not alter the motivation for such multiplication. . . . I know for us are left only catastrophes, conflagrations, explosions, leaps from high towers, light, violent laying about oneself, the cries of runners gone amuck. These are our memories, filtered a thousand times, our memories of spirit bursting forth from the glaciering abyss of catastrophe. Life has only moral purpose: to rip away from these memories the new gentle sweetnesses of the recent past. To cast out the complacency and security of feeling oneself swept away by environment. We want to bring, for one brief moment, intensity into human life: We want to arouse by means of heart-shaking assaults, terrors, threats, the individual's awareness of his responsibility in the community!

Who are our comrades? Prostitutes, poets, sub-proletarians, collectors of lost objects, thieves on favorable occasions, idlers,

* From "Der Mensch in der Mitte," in *Politische Aktionsbiblio-thek*, Vol. II, 1917.

lovers in the middle of embrace, religious lunatics, drunks, chain smokers, the unemployed, gluttons, jailbirds, burglars, critics, somnivolents, rabble. And, at certain moments, all the women in the world. We are the scum, the offal, the despised. We are the holy mob.

We do not want to work because work is too slow. We are intractable about progress; progress does not exist for us. We believe in miracle. We believe in the expulsion of all flux in us. We believe in fiery spirit suddenly consuming us. We believe in a single moment's eternal fulfillment. For our whole life long, we search for the glow from conflagrations on the horizons of our memory, we rush after every hue. We wish to penetrate alien spaces, we desire to enter into bodies of strangers, to metamorphose into organ sounds and the vibration of instruments; we want to slip through all cellular clusters of music, out and in, in and out, like lightning strokes.

We light a cigarette, we fit ourselves into a new coat, we drink schnapps, women with come-hither eyes and tangled arms let themselves drop into the water. Or women commit arson, adorable. Grinning and twisted, we plunge with four arms upon ludicrous settees, over and across mountains of skirts we penetrate into each other; we do this for the sake of our miracle.

And all this we do again and again because at bottom we are never disillusioned. Our hope is immeasurable, our hope that the boundless compression of bliss will blow up everyday life. Who are we? We are the people of the big cities. We are outcasts, silhouettes between the centuries shot forth like arrows into space. We are those whose skin aches at the idea of postponement, for whom seconds of disappointment can become lifelong scorching wounds of boredom. Everything must pass so fast that the past hisses up into the air like dust clouds behind motorcars. The air must quiver about us.

I can only laugh when a synthesizer apprehenses: destruction. The moral force of destruction alone can make us happy. Proof: Political poets have always enriched the language they wrote in. They taught curse words, curse words of love unthought of in their nations before them. Whenever the political poet began to dynamite, spiritual values, indestructible and unique, were set free.

What matters is the transformation of energy. It is moral that movement should dominate; intensity that frees our life from gelatinous monadism proceeds solely from the liberation of psychic forces. Transformation of inner images into public facts, lines of force erupt into view, stage backdrops are overturned, spaces become visible, space, new abodes of thought until the next catastrophe. Our catastrophes alone give us life. The name of disturber is an honorary title for us; for us destroyer is a religious concept, inseparable for us today from creator. And therefore it is right that literature explode into politics.

And here a sentence by Robert Musil, ethical and mediterranean like fine arches of bridges. A sentence, didactic like an encyclopedist's, psychologically shrewd like a Jesuit's, vividly concrete and uttered as a rounded insight like a visionary's. He says—in his invaluable, humanitarian, and therefore unforgettably lovable volume of stories *Unions* [*Vereinigungen*]: "What matters is that we are like the process and not like the person who acts." This question had to be posed: How might a man of our understanding overthrow the evolution swindle? (We answer ourselves from kindness while trickling away into tolerated misunderstanding.)

The true artist does not write about factories, radio stations, automobiles, but of the lines of force emitted by these things and crisscrossing through space. Things exist for man. We are not believers in idylls.

EPILOGUE TO THE ACTOR*†

by Paul Kornfeld

Translated by Joseph Bernstein

I do not know whether this play [*Die Verführung*] will ever be presented on a stage. It has been written for the theatre. If it is never produced, I am prepared to accept any reason except one: namely, that its style is not good theatre. If someone were to say that it was not worthwhile offering it to the theatregoing public, I would neither agree nor disagree. But I would vigorously protest if someone asserted that it was indeed worthwhile—but not suited to the theatre.

This assumes that the director and actors will not stage it in a way that runs counter to its spirit. But as the art of acting has developed over the past few decades, this danger does lie in a definite direction. And judging from the form and spirit of most of the "modern" plays presented in these last decades, the contemporary playwright (who is also "modern") faces a double danger. Therefore I feel it necessary to address the following words to the actor. Perhaps there are here and there actors who, as they read this tragedy, will retrospectively correct the images inspired in them, or even form images out of what had previously remained mere words.

Let not the actor in this play behave as though the thoughts and words he has to express have only arisen in him at the very moment in which he recites them. If he has to die on the stage, let him not pay a visit to the hospital beforehand in order to learn how to die; or go into a bar to see how people act when they are drunk. Let him dare to stretch his

* Epilogue appended to the play *The Seduction*, 1913.
† Copyright 1949 by Toby Cole and Helen Krich Chinoy

arms out wide and with a sense of soaring speak as he has never spoken in life; let him not be an imitator or seek his models in a world alien to the actor. In short, let him not be ashamed of the fact that he is acting. Let him not deny the theatre or try to feign reality. On the one hand, he can never fully succeed in the attempt; on the other hand, such a counterfeit presentation of reality can only be given in the theatre if the dramatic art has fallen to such a low estate as to be a more or less successful imitation of physical reality and everyday life—whether steeped in emotions, moral precepts, or aphorisms.

If the actor builds his characters from his experience of the emotion or fate he has to portray and with gestures adequate to this experience, and not from his recollections of the human beings he has seen filled with these emotions or victims or this fate; in fact, if he completely banishes these recollections from his memory, he will see that his expression of a feeling which is not genuine and which has really been artificially stimulated is purer, clearer, and stronger than that of any person whose feeling is prompted by a genuine stimulus. For the expression of a human being is never crystal-clear because he himself is never crystal-clear. He is never only *one* feeling—and if he were only *one*, this *one* would always appear in a different light. If he thinks he has immersed himself in but a single experience, there are nevertheless innumerable psychic facts existing within him that falsify many aspects of his behavior. The shadow of his present environment as well as the shadow of his past falls across him. Many people are comedians to themselves; yet the actor, who merely performs, is truer in his expression than many of those who are victims of an actual fate. Concern for many things prevents the real-life person from externalizing himself completely: the memory of many things is rooted in him and the rays of a thousand events crisscross within him. So at any given moment he can only be a changing complex of behavior. But the actor is free of all that: he is no complex, he is always only *one*. He is not falsified by anything—hence only he can be crystal-clear and rectilinear. And since he is only this *one* embodiment, he can embody it completely and magnificently. By shaping the character he portrays, the actor will find his way unerringly to its essence.

Let him therefore pick out the essential attributes of reality and be nothing but a representative of thought, feeling, or fate!

The melody of a great gesture says more than the highest consummation of what is called naturalness.

Let him think of the opera, in which the dying singer still gives forth a high C and with the sweetness of his melody tells more about death than if he were to crawl and writhe. For it is more important to know that death is anguish than that it is horrible.

TWO SUPERDRAMAS*

by Yvan Goll

Translated by Walter H. Sokel

A difficult struggle has commenced for the new drama, *the superdrama*. The first drama was that of the Greeks, in which gods contested with men. A great thing it was that the gods then deemed men worthy of such a contest, something that has not since occurred. Drama meant enormous magnification of reality, a most profound, most enigmatic Pythian immersion in measureless passion, in corroding grief, and all of that colored in surreal tints.

Later followed the drama of man for man's sake. Inner conflict, psychology, problems, reason. A single reality and a single realm are to be reckoned with and, consequently, all measures are limited. All is concerned with a particular man, not *the* man. The life of the community is sorely neglected: no modern mass scene attains the power of the ancient chorus. The vast extent of the gap can be seen in the ill-begotten plays of the past century, which aimed at nothing more than being interesting, forensically pleading, or simply descriptive, imitative of life, non-creative.

Now the new dramatist feels that the final struggle is imminent: Man's struggle with all that is thinglike and beastlike around him and within him. He has penetrated into the realm of shadows, which cling to everything and lurk behind all reality. Only after their conquest will liberation be possible. The poet must learn again that there exist worlds quite different from the world of the five senses—worlds comprising the Superworld. *He* must meet this new situation head

* Preface to *The Immortals*, 1918.

on. This will by no means be a relapse into mysticism or romanticism, or into the clowning of vaudeville, although all these have one thing in common—the extrasensory.

The first task will have to be the destruction of all external form—reasonable attitudes, conventionality, morality, all the formalities of life. Man and things will be shown as naked as possible, and always through a magnifying glass for better effect.

We have forgotten entirely that the stage is nothing but a magnifying glass. Great drama had always known this. The Greeks strode on buskins, Shakespeare discoursed with the spirits of dead giants. We have forgotten entirely that the primary symbol of the theatre is the mask. The mask is rigid, unique, and impressive. It is unchangeable, inescapable; it is Fate. Every man wears his mask, wears what the ancients called his guilt. Children are afraid of it and cry. Man, complacent and sober, should learn to cry again; the stage serves that purpose. And do not the greatest works of art, a Negro god or an Egyptian king, often appear to us as masks?

In the mask lies a law, and this is the law of the drama. Non-reality becomes fact. For a moment, proof is given that the most banal can be mysterious and "divine," and that herein lies Sublime Truth. Truth is not contained in reason. It is found by the poet, not the philosopher. Life, not the intellectual abstract, is truth. Furthermore, we discover that every event, the most heart-shaking as well as the most trivial, is of eminent significance to the total life of this world. The stage must not limit itself to "real" life; it becomes "superreal" when it knows about things behind things. Pure realism was the worst error of all literature.

It is not the object of art to make life comfortable for the fat bourgeois so that he may nod his head: "Yes, yes, that's the way it is! And now let's go for a bite!" Art, insofar as it seeks to educate, to improve men, or to be in any way effective, must slay workaday man; it must frighten him as the mask frightens the child, as Euripides frightened the Athenians who staggered from the theatre. Art exists to change man back into the child he was. The simplest means to accomplish this is by the use of the grotesque—a grotesque that does not cause laughter. The dullness and stupidity of men are so enormous that only enormities can counteract them. Let the new drama be enormous.

Therefore the new drama must have recourse to all technological props which are contemporary equivalents of the ancient mask. Such props are, for instance, the phonograph, which masks the voice, the denatured masks and other accoutrements which proclaim the character in a crudely typifying manner: oversized ears, white eyes, stilts. These physiological exaggerations, which we, shapers of the new drama, do not consider exaggerations, have their equivalents in the inner hyperboles of the plot: Let the situation stand on its head; that a sentence be more effective, let it be produced as when one stares steadily at a chess board until the black squares appear white and the white squares black: when we approach the truth, concepts overlap.

We want theatre. We seek the most fantastic truth. We search for the Superdrama.

MAN IN THE TUNNEL*

by Georg Kaiser

Translated by Walter H. Sokel

Writing a drama means: thinking a thought through to its conclusion. (He who has no thoughts left takes up his past plays and assists their theatrical executions: genesis of the "sublime master.") Idea without embodiment in figure remains nonsense: Plato wrote the most exciting scenes and thus unfolded his intellectual structure. All other philosophers' tomes with each page further remove themselves from the title (and even the title is fuzzy).

One ought to submit to the formidable labor—provided one is inclined to bother with thought at all—of formulating his drama. What I am unable to deliver in compressed dialogue to my fellow man evaporates into sheer stupidity. Man speaks in order to think—and thinks in order to speak. The best mouths have, since aboriginal times, impressed themselves upon the human species—so listen! You can't brandish your whipping canes only on the ground floor in order to enlighten the top floor. Through its playwright-thinkers, mankind has set itself gigantic tasks; if they complicate your lives now— the result will triumph in your grandchildren: the individual thinks through form and forms through thought. What does his drama mean to the dramatist ultimately? He is through with it. Lengthy preoccupation with one idea is excessive torment. Ten new ideas have sprung up meanwhile. Yet the dramatist heroically continues his grip on the line until he has managed to grope his way to the final curtain. Then his idea has been thought through to its conclusion.

* From *Das Kunstblatt*, Vol. VI, 1922.

At once he sets out for new territory—he has to utilize the limited term allotted to brain and blood in this world. (At this juncture the image of the pseudo-dramatist emerges: of him who returns to his works. He talks of them, he points to them with the subtlety of a lantern swinger, he basks in conspicuous boxes before performances; he stuffs his bag of lard with past laurels, sizzling with fame at night under his snoring broadside.)

He who has understood the multiplicity of unthought ideas barely has time for love. (This sounds depressing—but in a moment I shall launch the most marvelous summer rose into my sky.) But no one head has been weighted with an intolerable quantity of reflectiveness. The totality of man shows an excellent balance.

Only this single extreme display of acumen is demanded: to stop when you see the end. He who drags on past fruitfulness forfeits his life. Life is what matters. It is the purpose of existence. The experience that fulfills it. All roads lead to it—but all roads must be tried. One of the roads leads through the intellect. In order for it to be travelled to its destination, it demands the most exacting training: the ability to think. Constructing the drama is always the means —never the end. (He who confuses the two is the "sublime master"—see above. I will not name negative names here, so as to avoid filling the next few pages with the index of literary history—but solely the positive Rimbaud, laughing as an Egyptian businessman at his Parisian fame as a poet.)*
To wish to pin a superior person down to merely a single one of his faculties is a crime—he who accepts such mutilation is ridiculous. Continuing to remain an author almost amounts to a question of morality.

The purpose of being is the attainment of record achievements. Record achievements in all areas. The man of record achievements is the dominant type of this age, which will begin tomorrow and never end. The Hindu inactive-panactive man is being outdated in our zones: the panactive

---

* Kaiser, as usual, is not quite accurate (he despised historical accuracy as mindless irrelevance). Rimbaud traded in Ethiopia, not Egypt.

man vibrates here at a speed that makes motion invisible.

Drama is a transition—but also the immediate springboard onto completeness. Man, after this schooling, is excellently equipped for establishing himself in this world. He hates stupidity—but he no longer exploits it. (Only an idiot wishes to cheat—in intellectual as well as in business matters. There is a lot of cheating—cf. histories of literature.)

It is the duty of every creator: to turn away from each of his works and go into the desert; when he reappears, he must bring a great deal with him—to build himself a villa with garage in the shade of his sycamores: that won't do. That would mean pushing shamelessness a little too far and constitute infamous competition for badly situated prostitutes. Everything is in transition: abiding in transitions (tunnels) —good for him who has a properly toughened nose—and woe, too, to him!

PART II

THE PLAYS

MURDERER THE WOMEN'S HOPE

1907

by Oskar Kokoschka

Translated by Michael Hamburger

PERSONS

MAN

WOMAN

CHORUS: MEN *and* WOMEN

Night sky. Tower with large red iron grille as door; torches the only light; black ground, rising to the tower in such a way that all the figures appear in relief.

THE MAN *in blue armor, white face, kerchief covering a wound, with a crowd of men—savage in appearance, gray-and-red kerchiefs, white-black-and-brown clothes, signs on their clothes, bare legs, long-handled torches, bells, din —creeping up with handles of torches extended and lights; wearily, reluctantly try to hold back the adventurer, pull his horse to the ground; he walks on, they open up the circle around him, crying out in a slow crescendo.*

MEN. We were the flaming wheel around him,
We were the flaming wheel around you, assailant of locked fortresses!

Hesitantly follow him again in chain formation; he, with the torch bearer in front of him, heads the procession.

MEN. Lead us, pale one!

While they are about to pull his horse to the ground, women with their leader ascend steps on the left.

WOMAN, *red clothes, loose yellow hair, tall.*

WOMAN, *loud*. With my breath I fan the yellow disc of the sun, my eye collects the jubilation of the men, their stammering lust prowls around me like a beast.

FEMALE ATTENDANTS *separate themselves from her, only now catch sight of the stranger.*

FIRST FEMALE ATTENDANT. His breath attaches itself to the virgin!

FIRST MAN *to the others*. Our master is like the moon that that rises in the East.

SECOND GIRL, *quiet, her face averted*. When will she be enfolded joyfully?

Listening, alert, the CHORUS *walks round the whole stage, dispersed in groups;* THE MAN *and the* WOMAN *meet in front of the gate.*

(*Pause.*)

WOMAN *observes him spellbound, then to herself*. Who is the stranger that has looked on me?

GIRLS *press to the fore.*

FIRST GIRL *recognizes him, cries out*. His sister died of love.

SECOND GIRL. O the singing of Time, flowers never seen.

THE MAN, *astonished; his procession halts*. Am I real? What did the shadows say?

Raising his face to her.

Did you look at me, did I look at you?

WOMAN, *filled with fear and longing*. Who is the pallid man? Hold him back.

FIRST GIRL, *with a piercing scream, runs back*. Do you let him in? It is he who strangles my little sister praying in the temple.

FIRST MAN *to the girl*. We saw him stride through the fire, his feet unharmed.

SECOND MAN. He tortured animals to death, killed neighing mares by the pressure of his thighs.

THIRD MAN. Birds that ran before us he made blind, stifled red fishes in the sand.

THE MAN *angry, heated.* Who is she that like an animal proudly grazes amidst her kin?

FIRST MAN. She divines what none has understood.

SECOND MAN. She perceives what none has seen or heard.

THIRD MAN. They say shy birds approach her and let themselves be seized.

GIRLS *in time with the men.*

FIRST GIRL. Lady, let us flee. Extinguish the flares of the leader.

SECOND GIRL. Mistress, escape!

THIRD GIRL. He shall not be our guest or breathe our air. Let him not lodge with us, he frightens me.

MEN, *hesitant, walk on,* WOMEN *crowd together anxiously. The* WOMAN *goes up to* THE MAN, *prowling, cautious.*

FIRST GIRL. He has no luck.

FIRST MAN. She has no shame.

WOMAN. Why do you bind me, man, with your gaze? Ravening light, you confound my flame! Devouring life overpowers me. O take away my terrible hope—and may torment overpower you.

THE MAN, *enraged.* My men, now brand her with my sign, hot iron into her red flesh.

MEN *carry out his order. First the* CHORUS, *with their lights, struggle with her, then the* OLD MAN *with the iron; he rips open her dress and brands her.*

WOMAN, *crying out in terrible pain.* Beat back those men, the devouring corpses.

She leaps at him with a knife and strikes a wound in his side. THE MAN *falls.*

MEN. Free this man possessed, strike down the devil. Alas for us innocents, bury the conqueror. We do not know him.

THE MAN, *in convulsions, singing with a bleeding, visible wound.* Senseless craving from horror to horror, unappeasable rotation in the void. Birth pangs without birth, hurtling down of the sun, quaking of space. The end of those who praised me. Oh, your unmerciful word.

MEN. We do not know him; spare us. Come, you singing girls,
let us celebrate our nuptials on his bed of affliction.

GIRLS. He frightens us; you we loved even before you came.

*Three masked men on the wall lower a coffin on ropes;
the wounded man, hardly stirring now, is placed inside
the tower.* WOMEN *retire with the* MEN. *The* OLD MAN *rises
and locks the door, all is dark, a torch, quiet, blue light
above in the cage.*

WOMAN, *moaning and revengeful.* He cannot live, nor die;
how white he is!

*She creeps round the cage like a panther. She crawls up
to the cage inquisitively, grips the bars lasciviously, in-
scribes a large white cross on the tower, cries out.*
Open the gate; I must be with him.
Shakes the bars in despair.

MEN *and* WOMEN, *enjoying themselves in the shadows, confused.* We have lost the key—we shall find it—have you got
it?—haven't you seen it?—we are not guilty of your plight,
we do not know you—

*They go back again. A cock crows, a pale light rises in the
background.*

WOMAN *slides her arm through the bars and prods his wound,
hissing maliciously, like an adder.* Pale one, do you re-
coil? Do you know fear? Are you only asleep? Are you
awake? Can you hear me?

THE MAN, *inside, breathing heavily, raises his head with diffi-
culty; later, moves one hand; then slowly rises, singing
higher and higher, soaring.*
Wind that wanders, time repeating time, solitude, repose
and hunger confuse me.
Worlds that circle past, no air, it grows long as evening.

WOMAN, *incipient fear.* So much light is flowing from the
gap, so much strength from the pale as a corpse he's turned.

*Once more creeps up the steps, her body trembling, tri-
umphant once more and crying out with a high voice.*

THE MAN *has slowly risen, leans against the grille, slowly
grows.*

WOMAN *weakening, furious.* A wild beast I tame in this cage; is it with hunger your song barks?

THE MAN. Am I the real one, you the dead ensnared? Why are you turning pale?

Crowing of cocks.

WOMAN, *trembling.* Do you insult me, corpse?

THE MAN, *powerfully.* Stars and moon! Woman! In dream or awake, I saw a singing creature brightly shine. Breathing, dark things become clear to me. Who nourishes me?

WOMAN *covers him entirely with her body; separated by the grille, to which she clings high up in the air like a monkey.*

THE MAN. Who suckles me with blood? I devour your melting flesh.

WOMAN. I will not let you live, you vampire, piecemeal you feed on me, weaken me, woe to you, I shall kill you—you fetter me—you I caught and caged—and you are holding me—let go of me. Your love imprisons me—grips me as with iron chains—throttles me—let go—help! I lost the key that kept you prisoner.

Lets go the grille, writhes on the steps like a dying animal, her thighs and muscles convulsed.

THE MAN *stands upright now, pulls open the gate, touches the woman—who rears up stiffly, dead white—with his fingers. She feels that her end is near, highest tension, released in a slowly diminishing scream; she collapses and, as she falls, tears away the torch from the hands of the rising leader. The torch goes out and covers everything in a shower of sparks. He stands on the highest step; men and women who attempt to flee from him run into his way, screaming.*

CHORUS. The devil! Tame him, save yourselves, save yourselves if you can—all is lost!

He walks straight towards them. Kills them like mosquitoes and leaves red behind. From very far away, crowing of cocks.

THE BEGGAR*

A DRAMATIC MISSION

FIVE ACTS

by Reinhard Sorge

Translated by
Walter H. and Jacqueline Sokel

In far-flung circles you've plowed your flights
Through darkness and chaotic dreams, gigantic,
Through torments' regions, caves of space, gigantic—
Restless at dawn and restless in your nights. . . .

When your wild screams hoist you in a gyre
Of father's curse, and every mother's pain;
Eternal procreation shows it's not in vain—:
Salvation mounts defiant from the mire. . . .

Then with your wings you'll move that bolted gate
Whose jawlike hinges crushed so many brains;
˙You love the longing leading to these pains,
You clutch it, reeling downward to your fate.

* Written 1911; published 1912.

The Human Beings:

THE POET	THE GIRL
THE FATHER	THE OLDER FRIEND
THE MOTHER	THE PATRON OF THE ARTS
THE SISTER	THE THREE CRITICS

Groups:

THE NEWSPAPER READERS, THE PROSTITUTES, THE FLIERS

Incidental Persons:

THE NURSE, THE WAITER

Mute Persons:

THE ATTENDANT, WAITER, PATRONS OF THE CAFÉ

Projections of the Poet:

THE THREE FIGURES OF THE DIALOGUE,
THE FIGURE OF THE POET, THE FIGURE OF THE GIRL

THE FIRST ACT

Before a curtain.

THE POET *and the* OLDER FRIEND *facing each other. The stage behind the curtain is illuminated. From behind the curtain, greatly muffled voices.*

THE POET. The joy and memory of the applause still linger in your eyes. . .

THE OLDER FRIEND. Yes, it was a great success. There were seven curtain calls for him. Even after the third act people applauded wildly.

THE POET. After such an experience you can hardly be in the mood for my things. . .

THE FRIEND. Don't talk like that! You know, we couldn't make the appointment for any other time; I must leave town tonight again, and your patron—I'm already beginning to call him that—incidentally, he too was in the theater tonight. . .

THE POET. Did you speak to him?

THE FRIEND. I called on him this afternoon. He seems to be really impressed with your writing; at least, he had nothing but praise. I think everything will turn out all right. Of course, you mustn't mention the demands you talked about the other day; today I tried to drop a hint, but he immediately refused.

THE POET. You mentioned it, and he said no?

THE FRIEND. Of course he refused. I only did it to convince you it was impossible. I've talked to you about it often enough; —and you do understand, don't you?

THE POET. Certainly, I understand your advice.

THE FRIEND. At last! Just imagine! A theater of your own! And at your age! Despair brought you to that, but despair is precisely what should make you humble; in your situation one must be grateful for every penny.

THE POET. Certainly, the situation is desperate.

THE FRIEND. If he merely paid for the printing of your last plays, you would be helped; you'd have a small income, you could live. You can't expect performances soon anyway; your plays are too strange and *avant-garde* for that. It would be better yet if he were to give you a permanent income, then once and for all you would be free of money worries and could develop undisturbed.

THE POET. It would be very kind of him. . .

THE FRIEND. I see you've become reasonable and have profited from my advice.

THE POET. When will you stop wanting to give me advice?

THE FRIEND. Now, my dear fellow, that sounds stubborn again. But I hope I'll be able to advise you for the rest of my life, and that you'll benefit from it; after all, I'll always be more than twenty years your senior.

THE POET. You are right there.

THE FRIEND. Well, how are things at home?

THE POET. There gloom advances every day.
On every nook the sun spews distress.
Our father's dreadful illness terrifies us.

THE FRIEND. What do the doctors say?

THE POET. They talk of my father's sound constitution, and that no one can know how long it will last. Death could come any moment, but it might also be delayed for very long. Their talk does not mean a thing; but such uncertainty, I suppose, is characteristic of this disease. . .

THE FRIEND. As far as I know, yes, that's the case. — And your mother?

THE POET.   She languishes.
Mainly she anxiously stares at the door and hearkens for my father's steps.
When they come dragging, then she forces for the madman a smile upon her lips,
So helpless and touching, that tears well up in my eyes.
She weeps so much and speaks of dying. Poverty fills her cup.

THE FRIEND. It's dreadful. —No, you can't develop in such surroundings.

Brief silence.

Come, now; we want to meet him in the foyer. The time has come. — Your hands are shaking. Be calm, all will turn out well for you.

THE POET, *while both exit slowly to the right.* My hands are shaking. . . ?! You see, it does mean something to me, after all!

Now the curtain parts in the middle and the interior of a café is seen. The café rises toward the back, steps at center back. At the right, in the foreground and center stage: Tables of the usual kind, many customers, waiters running back and forth. At the left: A free space, newspapers on the wall, clothes trees in front, in the center a long leather sofa, which is curved at the ends. On the sofa sit the NEWSPAPER READERS, *closely huddled together. At the moment the* FIRST READER *is reading aloud, seated on a second leather bench, somewhat smaller and higher than the first; two others are seated beside him: The* SECOND *and* THIRD READERS, *who, while listening, keep their papers lowered. Likewise the listeners on the lower sofa, among whom there are some without papers. In the background, tables are laid for supper; very few of them are occupied. The back wall has a few white-curtained windows. In the right-hand background there is a kind of alcove forming an octagonal space, shut off by a curtain. Right of it, leading toward the alcove, the top of a staircase leading up from the vestibule, which is to be imagined as being to the right of the stage. Electric light. The sources of the upstage illumination are invisible. Full attention is to be focused on the group of* READERS, *the rest of the public onstage speaking in muffled tones, serving as decoration. Muffled sounds of dishes.*

THE FIRST READER. . . . and it is very possible that the Italian chargé d'affaires in Constantinople has received instructions to immediately . . .

FIRST LISTENER. Stop, please! This has been read once before! Are we supposed to croak of boredom?

SECOND LISTENER. We are finished.

THIRD LISTENER. Can't we get the latest editions yet?

FOURTH LISTENER. Well, gentlemen, let's start all over again. *Laughter.*

FIFTH LISTENER. Backwards, gentlemen! Then it sounds like new. . .

SIXTH LISTENER. Let's read the ads, they are full of obscenities!

FIRST LISTENER *yawns.* Oh . . . how boring! . . .

They sit hunched over, staring vacantly, yawning, gloomy-faced.

THIRD LISTENER. Where are the critics hiding, for God's sake?

SECOND LISTENER. If it takes this long, it means a hit.

SIXTH LISTENER. Is that so. . . So Miss Gudrun was a hit—
Yawns.

or is she "Mrs."—which is it, really?

FOURTH LISTENER. Well, we'll see. . .

SIXTH LISTENER. At best, we'll hear, am I right. . . ?

FOURTH LISTENER. All right: so, we'll hear, we'll hear. . .

ALL *in a hubbub, yawning, stretching.* Yes, we'll hear.

SECOND READER *cries out.* Here come the papers!

Two waiters with papers from the left.

VOICES *lively, to and fro.* Here! Bring them here! Give me
one! Give me one! Me! Me!

No, the *Tribune!*

Allow me—

What on earth. . . ?

Hell, give it to me! !

Put it here! Put it here!

Crap. . !

*The papers have been torn out of the hands of the waiters,
are being read greedily; those who have not obtained
any read over their neighbors' shoulders.*

SEVENTH LISTENER. Good Lord. . .

EIGHTH LISTENER *without a paper.* Read aloud! Read to us!

SIXTH LISTENER. Well, boys, what did I tell you. . ?

EIGHTH LISTENER. So, let's start, for God's sake! What's holding you up?

SECOND LISTENER. Listen: earthquake in Central America!

VOICES. Ha, ha! Well, well! How many killed?

SECOND READER. Five thousand.

THIRD LISTENER. What a filthy mess!

Commotion.

SECOND READER. Skirmish near Tripolis.

VOICES. How many killed?

SECOND READER. About two hundred dead. Three hundred
and fifty wounded.

Murmur.

SECOND READER *skimming the paper.* Crash of a French pilot.

NINTH LISTENER. Always those French . . .

FOURTH LISTENER. How many dead?

Laughter.

THIRD READER. Mass revolt in Spain . . .

FIRST READER. Mine disaster . . .

SECOND READER, *continuing to skim.* Factory fire . . . Hurricane flood . . .

FIRST READER. Train accident . . .

TENTH LISTENER. Stop! I'm freezing! Brr. . .

VOICES. Stop! !

FIFTH LISTENER. I'm freezing, too. Really.

SIXTH LISTENER. Go on! Go on!

SEVENTH LISTENER. No! No! Something constructive!

THIRD READER. Constructive. Good . . . A new German warship.

VOICES. Ah! Hear, hear!

THIRD READER. Two new English warships . . .

Commotion.

EIGHTH LISTENER. Devil take it!

SIXTH LISTENER. That's unconstructive.

VOICES. What? How come?

SIXTH LISTENER. Three warships mean three years of hunger.

VOICES. Rubbish! Bravo! Subversive! Bravo! How, subversive! ?
. . . Crazy!

SEVENTH LISTENER. Quiet, please! We want to hear more constructive things!

SECOND READER. A strong healthy boy was born!

VOICES. Bravo! Bravo! Constructive boy! Constructive boy!

THIRD READER. New successful experiments with Ehrlich-Hata? !*

---

* Ehrlich, the famous German bacteriologist, together with his Japanese assistant, Hata, discovered the chemical compound Salvarsan for the treatment of syphilis in 1910, one year before Sorge's play was written.

VOICES. Ah! Bravo! Heavenly!

Great applause, clapping of hands.

THE THREE CRITICS *enter from the left.*

VOICES. Ah! Aha! Hallo!

Loud greetings.

Report! Report!

SIXTH LISTENER, *drowning out the others.* Well? ! Well! ? Was Miss Gudrun well built? Did she have her decent climaxes, hah? Did she go down nicely at the end? !

Laughter and noise. The SECOND *and* THIRD CRITICS *take seats next to the others.*

FIRST CRITIC, *more in the foreground than the others, humming grimly, as though answering the question of the* SIXTH. "Her heart a dagger pierced!" How bitter, my dear Mr. Poet!

Kindly don't bother us with such nonsense—

The Modern Woman preening herself;

Leave her at home—may I humbly request!

SIXTH LISTENER. What are you grumbling about?

The FIRST CRITIC *sits down on the right end of the sofa, since there is no other seat available. They are gradually calming down.*

FIRST LISTENER. And now, please, a sensible report! Let's hear it!

To the FIRST CRITIC.

You start!

FIRST CRITIC. Gentlemen, an unqualified success. But all mediocrity is unequivocally successful.

Voices of accord.

The play is no good at all.

SECOND CRITIC. Now, listen—no, really, I must say—that's a completely misguided opinion! . . On the contrary, it's a very good play. Quite wonderful. But it so happens that the author is not a dissolute genius and a braggart, the way the mob usually likes them, but a serious, conscientious craftsman —

FIRST CRITIC. My dear friend, you misunderstand me. I esteem the craftsman; but this one is lacking in Heavenly Inspiration, for all he can do is transplant; take from him the time-tested theme and he will starve.

SECOND CRITIC. But his beautiful language—!

FIRST CRITIC. Beautiful crowing you can hear from any rooster.

SECOND CRITIC. My God, in such a manner you can poke fun at Goethe too!

THIRD CRITIC. Allow me to butt in! On the whole, I happen to find the play quite acceptable. It shows good taste, it's tactful, it does not offend; in short: it is the work of a gentleman. And this is precisely the point—I think—this is its fatal flaw: it lacks a certain capriciousness that seeks to conquer its own particular territory; somewhere there is a weakness in it which he can't disguise for all his blood-and-thunder violence—quite the contrary, by such means he actually reveals his weakness all the sooner;— this author has a lack deep down in his depths—a lack which condemns him.

FIRST CRITIC. Bravo! And I want to tell you what's the fundamental lack: a heart that gives itself to the point of humility; self-surrender toward the world to the point of foolishness; divine blindness that penetrates profoundly into all secrets—indeed, what's missing is the visionary—!

SECOND CRITIC *interrupts laughingly.* Well! Well! Well! Don't get maudlin over it! Heart has nothing to do with either his style or his theme.

FIRST CRITIC. That's just it! You happen to see the problem upside down! That very lack relegates him forever to the ranks of sterile hacks. Poets are lovers, lovers of the world, and endlessly addicted to their love; but he is stunted in his heart, and out of his narrowness and vanity he invents vain females.

THIRD CRITIC *without a pause answering the* FIRST. And he lacks the demonic element, that great confirmation of the self transcending the self. He's always merely his own shadow, never his better self. In the face of the Spirit he turns to chaff.

SECOND CRITIC. Ah, that's just so much—

SIXTH LISTENER. Please, don't get tragic! Spare us that! Don't become fanatical!

THIRD CRITIC. With such mediocrity as we have today! Who could work himself up to fanaticism!

SECOND CRITIC. You are quick to proclaim a *tabula rasa!* Now, really! Look, among the youngest writers we have now this dramatist of the Arthurian legends!†

FIRST CRITIC. Who needs him! King Arthur and Gudrun— our own age searches—gazes far and wide—and its soul is aflame!—
Or would you add that poet who, when he had nothing more to say, still boasted of his poverty, and who is now miracle-mongering with pantomimes, woman, and pomp and circumstance?! That's enough to drive one to distraction!

THIRD CRITIC. Calm yourself! Restrain yourself! My dear friend.

SECOND CRITIC *to the* FIRST. Oh, well, you! You don't feel right unless you're bellyaching.

SIXTH LISTENER. Gentlemen, are we still going over to the Victoria Café?

MANY VOICES. Yes, of course. Let's go. To the Victoria. Right away.

Noise and general exodus.

THIRD CRITIC *who, while exiting, advances to the front in conversation with* FIRST CRITIC. That's right. We are waiting for someone who will reinterpret our destiny for us. Such a one I shall then call a dramatist and a mighty one. Our Haupt-Mann,‡ you see, is great as a craftsman,

---

† Reference to the Neo-Romantic movement of the time, which formed a stylish and stylizing opposition to the naturalist theater, but was despised by the Expressionists.

‡ This is a pun and a gibe at Gerhart Hauptmann (1862–1946), the leading dramatist of German Naturalism and, subsequently, of

but deficient as a seer. It's really high time: once again someone must take up the search for all our sakes.

Curtain falls.

The OLDER FRIEND, *the* PATRON, *and the* POET *enter from the right and walk in front of curtain to center-stage.*

THE PATRON *to the* OLDER FRIEND, *while still walking.* May I congratulate you on the fine success of your friend. . .

THE FRIEND. Thank you. I am really very happy. . .

THE PATRON. You have every reason to be. It was a truly extraordinary success, a literary event.

Turning to the POET.

But I must extend a second congratulation to you, sir. I have now read all your writings and find in them a very rich and serious talent, a promising future, and interesting potentialities. I should like to contribute towards your further education.

THE POET. Many thanks! Unfortunately, I am afraid difficulties might arise between us.

THE PATRON. Until now, sir, you have had not the least cause for such a fear.

THE FRIEND *to the* POET. You're giving yourself useless worries. . !

THE POET. I shouldn't like to speak about all of this in such a hurry. Afterwards—I believe—better occasion will be found. . .

THE PATRON. Certainly. However, I did not want to leave you unclear about my over-all impressions. Naturally, concerning details, I have many things to tell you, also I should like to see some things changed, that's only to be expected. — Please, come, a table has been reserved.

He exits to the left.

THE FRIEND *to the* POET. What possessed you to make that

Neo-Romanticism. The pun consists in the fact that "Hauptmann" means "head man" or "captain" in German.

remark about your apprehensions and difficulties? It was uncalled for. It seems to have put him out of sorts.

THE POET. Yes, it probably was uncalled for.

THE FRIEND. Speak discreetly, one word can spoil a lot. Now come, he's waiting.

He exits to left, the POET *follows.*

The curtain separates again. Now the right half of the stage is dark and deserted. From somewhere high at the left, a floodlight falls slantwise across the left half of the stage, illuminating the PROSTITUTES, *who are seated, laughing and babbling, on the lower leather bench. They are still out of breath from a quick run and are adjusting their disordered garments. Their voices emphasize the shrill and bare impression made by the floodlight. Three* PROSTITUTES *enter briskly from the left and sit down by the others.*

THE FIRST ONE. Quick! They'll be here any minute! Who's still missing?

ONE OF THE NEW ARRIVALS. The Redhead and the tall one are still primping downstairs.

A SECOND NEWCOMER. Or they're waiting for the fellows because they'd like to smack their lips over the first kisses!

THE SECOND *to a* NEIGHBOR. How many?

THE NEIGHBOR. About a dozen!

THE SECOND. Ha, a good catch!

THE FOURTH *bending over the* FIRST. The Redhead is rich now, she only wears real stuff.

THE FIRST. Oh, you little dope! You still believe that fraud? *Three* PROSTITUTES *on the right side of the bench, who until now have been whispering, suddenly burst into loud laughter.*

THE THIRD. Yes, sure the Redhead has an Englishman, all stiff with money. And he has red eyes and the jaws of a horse!

THE FOURTH. Ha, ha! I saw him too; I think he's an American.

THE FIRST. She is stupid; if she's so well fixed, what's she going with us for?

THE .THIRD. She can never get enough.

They laugh.

ONE OF THE THREE PROSTITUTES ON THE RIGHT, *screeching.* And she simply smacked him one on his ass?! Hee-hee! *Laughter.*

A PROSTITUTE *approaches from the left.*

THE THIRD *to the one entering.* You pale tall one with the craving for death—where is the Redhead hiding herself? Has she already gone to bed with them down there?

THE TALL ONE. No, she is only painting herself. The others aren't here yet.

THE SECOND *yawns.* That red bitch'll choke on her paint some day.

THE TALL ONE. She's got the best paint, from Paris. .

THE FIRST. Hey, there she is!

The REDHEAD *approaches from the left.*

THE SECOND. Where you been hiding, painted gypsy!

THE THIRD AND THE FOURTH, *screeching.* Hi, painted gypsy!

THE REDHEAD *slaps the* SECOND. There, take this. . . That'll show you. . . there!

THE OTHERS, *laughing, all together.* Hey, she's mad. . .

THE REDHEAD, *scuffling with them.* You fresh cockroach—fresh . . .

In the heat of battle, a compact drops from the REDHEAD'S *handbag, opens, and the powder dusts out.*

THE SECOND, *convulsed with laughter.* Her powder! Ho, ho! Parisian powder! Ho, ho!

THE THREE ON THE RIGHT, *becoming attentive.* Hey, look! Her powder. . !

VOICES. Powder . . . powder . . . ha, ha!

Noise and laughter.

THE THIRD. Watch out or you'll drop your baby like that!

ONE OF THE THREE PROSTITUTES. Sit down in it; maybe that way it'll do you some good!

THE REDHEAD, *in a rage.* You whores! nyeh!

Grimacing at them. She quickly picks up the compact and cleans up what has been spilled.

THE THIRD. Sh-h-h. . . sh-h-h. . . They're coming now!

The three PROSTITUTES *burst into laughter again.*

THE FOURTH. Hush, be quiet!

All are listening intently.

THE SECOND. Ah, rubbish, it's all quiet — It's not them yet.

THE THIRD, *to the* FOURTH. Say, does my hair look all right?

THE FOURTH. Sure. How's mine?

THE SECOND, *to the* FOURTH, *while looking into a compact mirror.* Lend me your makeup! I'm all dark around my eyes.

THE FOURTH *hands it to her.* Here.

THE REDHEAD, *to the* SECOND. Gee, you're cross-eyed! No paint will help you—ha-ha! You'd be better off with a glass eye!

Steps and VOICES *at the left. Silence quickly descends.*

THE SECOND *puts out her tongue.* You horror! !

VOICES. Shh. . . shh. . .

All quiet. The PROSTITUTES, *staring to the left, grin. Their expressions and postures are all alike. The* LOVERS *(eight or nine) enter from the left. They stop short at the sight of the* PROSTITUTES. *They make their selections, bargain with each other, pointing their fingers at individual prostitutes. Their talk is rapid and the individual remarks fuse into each other.*

FIRST. There they are. Ha! Choice! Here is selection!

SECOND. Come on! Forward! Hoi—this flesh! What the devil!

SOME, *holding him back.* You, control yourself!

THIRD. I'll take the redhead!

FIRST. I the one next to her. . .

FOURTH. You won't take the redhead!

THIRD. She gave me looks. . .

VOICES. Let me at them! Not yet! Choose first! What? Choose first! ?

FIFTH. That brunette there for me. . .

SIXTH. Fine. And for me the tall one.

SEVENTH. Man, no. . . that one's too short. The other—

EIGHTH. That one looks dangerous. She's cross-eyed.

FOURTH. I get this one here.

SECOND, *furious*. What! Let me go! Do you want me to suffocate! ? You ——!

MANY VOICES. Forward! Let's go! Let's go!

They rush toward the girls. Noise, screeching, pushing, embraces, shrill laughter. Wild commotion of the group swaying back and forth in the white beam of the floodlight.

VOICES OF THE PROSTITUTES AND LOVERS, *back and forth.*

Take *me!* Not him! I'm strong as a bear!

It isn't true! He's a weakling! Me!

You know how to kiss, girl! Kiss me, girl!

What are you being coy for, why don't you let me grab you?

Keep out, you! You bald-headed fright! Get away from me, you horror!

So take the two of us! You won't die of it!

You are white as a sheet! Ho! How you scratch me with your kisses!

Crazy about her breasts?! Slap them and they'll explode!

You're driving me crazy. . . Ouch, you're biting me!

Yes, up there! Come fast, you bewitching brunette!

One couple sits down on the raised leather couch, which is roomy enough for three persons.

You want something sweet, huh? Something sweet? Fine!

Slap his filthy face! Slug him! Slug him!

Let go, buster! Want to get slapped?

I'll get sherbet. . . Any kind you want. Vanilla?

Let's go home! Into bed. Quick! Get a move on! Whee, you thieving bitch!

At the end the group postures as a monument.

The VOICES *resound rhythmically, like chanting.*

You feed me flames; I'm burned to ashes, wild one, you!

You crush like iron, you'll smother me!

I'll teach you joys that you have never known!

I'll show you nights of which you've never dreamed!
You are Hell's bottom and are black with lust!
You are like Satan and I want your thrust!

Lights out. Darkness. The noise fades. Brief silence. Then the space in front of the alcove is lit. The GIRL *and the* NURSE *have just come up the steps from the vestibule and are now standing in front of the curtain.*

THE GIRL. Here, please, Nurse! There is no one up here. Here people can't see us.

THE NURSE. Why don't you want to sit among people? You shouldn't worry so much. The doctor has told you so often enough. You should spare yourself as much as possible, and you've just seen how necessary it is. We shouldn't have gone to the theater yet. We had hardly walked ten minutes when you became dizzy! Don't torment yourself unnecessarily! Your fate can't be changed any more, and God will surely forgive you your baby.

THE GIRL. No waiter here? I'd like to sit here.

A WAITER *comes up the steps.*

THE NURSE. We'd like to have a quiet table.

THE WAITER. Certainly!

The WAITER *draws the curtain back so that the octagonal alcove becomes visible. In it are a table and chairs. Through the windows one sees the night sky. A star sparkles brightly. Clouds drift past. The alcove is lit; the source of the light is invisible.*

THE GIRL. Yes, we'd like to sit here!

As the WAITER *wants to pull the curtain shut.*

Please, let us have the view, don't close the curtains!

THE NURSE. Why not? There always is a little draft through the cracks, and you catch cold so easily. You can close them!

The WAITER *does so.*

The GIRL *and the* NURSE *sit down at the table opposite each other, in profile to the audience. Now the lights within and in front of the alcove go out, and during the subsequent scene the two figures can be seen only as shadows. The* WAITER *soon leaves, and after some time brings the order. In the moment of darkening of the alcove, the rest of the proscenium turns bright. Approximately in the center sit the* PATRON, *the* OLDER FRIEND *and the* POET, *eating. A* WAITER *comes and goes from time to time.*

THE POET, *beginning to speak almost simultaneously with the brightening of the proscenium.* On the basis of my writings, you've explained my aims so accurately that I can now speak to you with increased hope for a favorable result. Still, an aspiring young author can so easily be misunderstood and give the impression of being immature and on the wrong path——you do understand, don't you? *Brief pause.*

My friend spoke to you about my situation; you know in what kind of an environment I have to work—— And the theaters reject my plays—so much in them is novel that they shy away from risking the experiment of a performance.

THE PATRON. I agree with you. You are in an unfortunate position, since your plays only tend to become more and more peculiar and strange, and—if I may speak frankly— they actually have less and less chance of acceptance. Of course, one can't be completely sure about that.

THE POET. I am glad you anticipate the same things I do, and are therefore in a position to understand my ideas all the better. This impossibility of getting a performance is my greatest handicap. For me performance is a necessity, the one basic condition for creation. It is my duty toward my work.

THE OLDER FRIEND. Please, consider what I told you before! *Brief pause.*

THE POET. You'll realize that the mere printed publication of my plays can't mean very much to me; that would always be merely a half measure, never my final purpose—

that is performance. So I have just this one request: Help me found my own theater.

THE OLDER FRIEND. Be reasonable, please! This is absurd!

THE POET. Let me finish my say. I am speaking after careful deliberation.

THE PATRON. Yes, sir, let him finish what he has to say.

THE OLDER FRIEND. I only want the best for you. That will never be in your best interest.

THE POET. I've reflected at length about all this and examined it from all angles, considered every alternative, but I've always come back to this: I must be performed — I see my writings as the foundation and beginning of a rejuvenated drama; you yourself expressed a very similar idea a moment ago. But this new drama can become properly effective only by being performed; the only solution is a stage of my own.

THE PATRON. You are speaking of a new drama; considering the state of our modern theater, I think you're justified in some degree. And your plays seem indeed to bear within them so many seeds of future possibilities that one can understand your high opinion of yourself. On the whole, I can assure you I understand your ideas and your decision very well. If in spite of that I propose a different course, I don't do so from lack of understanding but from sound insight. I see your near future in a different light—even though I fully sympathize with your request — I see so many risks and problems in realizing it that a different solution appears necessary to me and, I believe, I have found one.

THE POET. Please, tell me! What is it?

THE PATRON. I consider this proposal sound and fruitful. I shall grant you a fixed income, sufficient to cover your expenses in the next few years so that you can live as you desire. Above all—I think—it's time for you to do some traveling. Unless you find new stimulation in your environment, you're threatened with sterility. Let ten years pass in this fashion and we shall be able to discuss the other questions. You'll have developed greatly, the risk will no longer be so great. What do you say?

THE OLDER FRIEND. Your fate is now in your own hands.

Brief pause.

THE POET. Sir, I've pondered over this possibility too, for a long time, and have rejected it. I do not need external inspiration for future creation, but I must gain experience of theatrical technique by seeing my finished works performed. I must be able to test in practice the extent of what is possible on the stage. I must test experimentally the limits of drama. My writings are still deficient in this respect. Only by mastering these matters can I mature. The external world is necessary only secondarily, and sterility will never threaten me! My mission dictates this one path; therefore, I have to decline your offer.

THE PATRON. You talk heedlessly! You overlook the real advantage of my proposal—your mental growth in undisturbed security. That is what you need. Dramatic performances would actually be harmful to you, because your whole being would be so engrossed in them, there would be no peace left for your work; and your work can flourish only in peace and quiet.

THE POET. I will be able to unite work and fulfillment. I have the call, and hence I can accomplish what I must do.

THE PATRON. Forgive me, but now you are becoming fantastic, and we want to consider only what's realistic.

Brief pause.

THE POET *abruptly bursting forth.*

I see, you'll never want to grant me this?!
I know this well, you only think fantastic nonsense
What I demand, such as my thoughts about
My calling! ? . . . How shall I begin my tale? !
Shall I relate how this began in me with visions,
Even when I was a child, and then matured
And grew in might, compelling me and driving me
Into much loneliness and tortured grief—
How it imposed upon me such laws which sundered ties

Between my loved ones and myself, condemning me
To cruelties against those nearest me, whose blood I
    share? I
My work! My work! My work alone was master!
How best to say it . . . I want to show you images
Of coming things which have in me arisen
In all splendor, visions that led me on
To where I am today, and neither love nor lust
Has hitherto been able to displace them
Or even for one instant make them dim!
You shall see what riches wait for you,
What vast good fortune.
Truly this will prove a gold mine! And no risk at all!
Just listen now: this will become
The heart of art: from all the continents,
To this source of health, people will stream
To be restored and saved, not just a tiny esoteric
Group! . . . Masses of workmen will be swept
By intimations of a higher life
In mighty waves, for there they will see
From smokestack and towering scaffold, from
The daily danger of clamoring cogs arise
Their souls, beauteous, and wholly purged
Of swarming accidents, in glorious
Sublimity, conquerors of gripping misery,
Living steel and spire soaring up
In defiant yearning, regally. . . . Starving girls,
Emaciated bodies bent, toiling for their children
Out of wedlock born, in this shall find their bread
And resolutely raise their little ones aloft,
Even though these lie already lifeless in their arms!
Cripples, whose twisted limbs betoken the teeming
Misery of this crooked age, whose bitter souls
Ooze from their poor misshapen forms,
Will then with courage and from love of straight-limbed
    life
Repress their bile and toss to Death
The fallow refuse that was their lives. But men
Shall toughen their brows in sorrow and joy,

And open their hearts to yearn and—renounce!
Let woman excel in allegiance to man!
Let his aim be: graciously to yield to her!

- -

To lofty birth let a highborn but in many ways corrupted
    age
Advance toward me;
Indeed, this age shall truly view itself
In mirrors of omnipotence and lapse in silence when
From the deep reaches of the skies
Issues the gracious vision of the anchor which holds us all
Inexorably, like rock-bound ore,
To the bottom of divinity.

During the POET's *verses the* GIRL *has risen and steps softly nearer, until she stands to the left by the entrance to the alcove. Subsequently the* NURSE *joins her. Standing on tiptoe, she looks curiously over the* GIRL's *shoulder.*

THE PATRON. Please, sir, calm yourself! — What you envision as the future is a figment of your imagination, a dream that will never come true. Therefore, I feel really justified in declining your request, first of all because in a few years' time you will think of your plans with greater maturity. Then perhaps you will have learned to realize and appreciate more seriously the limits of possibility; your ideas will have adjusted to them, and we both will have it easier.

THE POET. Your words have been unmistakable and we are finished!

The NURSE *has meanwhile returned to her table, but the* GIRL *remains rooted to the spot, hearkening, slightly bent forward. The light upstage goes out immediately after the* POET's *last word. Left downstage is dimly illuminated. In the chiaroscuro one can see the* FIVE FLIERS *seated on the lower bench. Their rigid posture makes each resemble all the others. They also are unified by their sharp and steely expressions.*

FIRST FLIER, *rhythmically.*
Of course, you speak for joyfulness,
But fetters of constraining fear hold fast my senses.

SECOND FLIER. I feel like him. My pulse beat overwhelms
My laughter with gloom and violence.

THIRD FLIER. Grief does not befit this festive hour,
Even the worst fate merits more than that. . .

FOURTH FLIER. How his eyes gazed upward radiantly at the sun
In ardent communion, joyous in holy effort. . .

FIFTH FLIER. How his courage, assured, gave strength to his handshake,
His every word betokened success. .

FIRST FLIER. His courage pushed his hands too far,
Overconfidence has shattered many—

SECOND FLIER. Too much like the sun were his eyes,
Many have burned to ashes near the sun—

THIRD FLIER. Grief does not befit this festive hour,
Even the worst fate merits more than that.

FOURTH FLIER. Still, let us wait, let us not heed vague apprehensions—

FIFTH FLIER. They often deceived us; soon we shall know.

SIXTH FLIER *enters from the left, steps in front of the others, turns his face toward them, and remains in this posture during the subsequent scene.*

FIRST FLIER. Woe. . . Your eyes bespeak the airy grave. . .

SECOND FLIER. Your brow foreshadows a desolate coffin.

SIXTH FLIER. Woe: The storms of heaven shattered the airplane.
It splintered on the rock-covered earth. . .

ALL EXCEPT THE THIRD AND SIXTH. Woe . . .

FIRST FLIER. My apprehension did not deceive me,
Rightly did fear hold me in clammy embrace!

SECOND FLIER. Rightly did engulfing waves of
Bitter sadness drown all my laughter!

SIXTH FLIER. Woe: Dead he lies with his brains spilled out,
And his hand still clutches rudder and wing.

ALL EXCEPT THE THIRD AND SIXTH. Woe . . .

FOURTH FLIER. His courage lifted him into the stormy skies—
Raging elements have no respect for courage in man!

FIFTH FLIER. Brightly his eyes greeted the sun—
The radiant star scorns the greeting of man!

ALL EXCEPT THE THIRD. Let the monotonous dirge resound,
the soul's lament,
Psalm and organ for the dead.

THIRD FLIER. Grief does not befit the festive hour,
Worst fate merits a nobler choral.

FIRST FLIER. Which god's gospel do your words proclaim?

SECOND FLIER. Which is the freedom your trumpets declare?

THIRD FLIER. From storms of destruction rises my God,
From death-dealing rays He draws living breath.

FOURTH FLIER. Your word of courage moves the boulder from
the grave
And adumbrates the verdict against death.

FIFTH FLIER. Your hope unseals hidden accords,
Yes. . . It intones eternal life.

SIXTH FLIER. Give us the gift of wisdom, give us the gift of
omnipotence!

THIRD FLIER. Where has his fervor gone out, where has his
courage been broken?
All the more fiery was it infused into us!

FIRST FLIER. Yes, you're piercing the clouds of my heart with
heavenly rays—!

SECOND FLIER. You transfigure my sorrow with inward shared
smiles!

THIRD FLIER. Think it through! Descend deep down into
yourselves!
Did he die? Or did he rise in resurrection?
Our eyes now see with sight from his soul—

FOURTH FLIER, *with gesture.* His longing lifts high our hands.

FIFTH FLIER. His death has been solder for our union:
It has welded and fused us—deepest nerve and broadest
dominion. . .

Silence.

THIRD FLIER, *softer, yet more intent—his voice comes as though from far.* Prophetic vision above and beyond the groping of language—

ALL, *as though groping.* Prophetic vision above and beyond the groping of language—

THIRD FLIER. Beyond uncertain solace—faith.

ALL, *their heads bowed.* Beyond uncertain solace—faith!

Darkening of downstage, center upstage is lit. Only the OLDER FRIEND *and the* POET *are left at the table.*

THE OLDER FRIEND. You have killed your last opportunity. Do you realize what this means? I've warned you so many times. You appeared to agree with me, but it was all pretense. I detest from the bottom of my heart such secretiveness. I can't comprehend what's happened! It will be a long time before I can forgive you for this. What's going to happen? How do you expect to get on?

THE POET. I did not like being secretive with you. I'd expressed many objections to you, but you rejected them all out of hand and you repeated your very definite opinions again and again. So I let it be. You held my wish in your hands and contemplated it like a lifeless thing, like a stone or a piece of wood. But there was organic development here, ever-changing and unfathomable, so much soul and mystery that neither you nor I could know anything absolute about it. Yet this is your way, your bitter habit: you had tagged me with a number and were looking for the formula it would fit. But I myself had not yet found my number and my law. Now, don't be angry with me!

THE FRIEND. I am upset by what's happened. This obstinacy and blindness of yours make one wonder. You are too young to afford such negativity.

Pause. He looks at his watch.

It's time now to catch my train. Goodbye. Look me up soon at home. In any case, let's not be angry.

They shake hands.

THE POET. I thank you. Farewell!

The FRIEND *exits to the right, past the alcove and down the steps.*

The POET *looks silently into space.*

Lights dim. The alcove is lit.

The GIRL *still standing rooted as before. The* NURSE *seated, sipping her cup of chocolate.*

THE NURSE. Do sit down! Your chocolate is all cold by now. Besides it's high time you were home.

The GIRL *still standing rooted as before. The* NURSE *seated, at the right.* Excuse me, Nurse!

Exits to the right.

Lights out on this part of the stage; the lower stage is lit. It is completely deserted. The POET *descends slowly downstage while speaking the subsequent monologue. Right after the first few words, the* GIRL *appears downstage at the right, remains standing there, staring at the* POET *and listening intently to his words.*

THE POET. You hurled a sky-high rock
Upon my road—
With rocks you cluttered, too, my brain, and
I can barely think.
Yet your hostile force steels all my pulses,
O Destiny!
One day I shall stretch up defiantly toward blue sun. . ,
An eagle,
I shall spread my wings
Toward the fires of the sun.
Talon and eagle! And your rock becomes a mote.

He continues to descend the steps and is about to turn right. Just then,

THE GIRL *advances toward him, blocks his way, and lifts her arm as though to stop him, saying.* I must speak to you, wondrous stranger. . .

Curtains close.

THE SECOND ACT

In front of a curtain.

The FATHER in a blue dressing gown. He hammers away with an outsized drumstick at a multicolored toy drum. Even before the curtain opens, the first drumbeats can be heard; while the stage becomes visible, the drumbeats follow each other more and more rapidly, finally merge in a furious roll.

THE FATHER, *screaming over the din.* Yippee! Yippee! Whee! Hallo! Away! Away with you, you scoundrels! Yippee! Look at them run! Away, away with you, scoundrels! Get out! Get out! Beat! Beat, my good drum, beat!

He stops himself.

Ah—now they're gone.

Looking up.

Haha, I can see you again, Mars, I can see you again. . ! And you shall have a kiss, drum, because you're so kind, and chased away those old rascals. So here it is. . .

Kisses his drum.

Shame on them, those old rascals. — Here a fire, over there a coffin lid and smoke; over here a louse, over there a toad; there a heart, there a heart with a knife stuck in it; here a bucket of tears, there a chest filled with murder—surely it's enough to drive one mad. But I have my drum now—nyaa—yes, I have my drum. The good Lord still means well by his old master builder. Up there in the attic it lay all forgotten — the old drum, when I went up to look for my old blueprints. Hahaha, the good Lord still means well by his master builder, yah, yah.

Short drumbeats.

One, two, three, and I see Mars again.

Sends up a kiss.

Good day, dear Mars, how do you do, good Mars, I have my drum now!

Abruptly changing.

What, you mean fellow. . . what! You smoky giant, don't block my view of Mars, you!

He starts drumming again.

Hallo, yippee, get out, get out, will you! You devil. . . get out of there! get out! Will you go! go! away!

Wildly drumming, he advances to the left as though driving someone out. For a short while the drumming can be heard behind the scene, then silence descends.

Now the curtain parts, and opens on a view of a living room. Downstage at the right, a settee. In front of a red curtain in the center of the back wall a table and three chairs. Left center an armchair. Upstage at the left, a door papered with the same paper as the surrounding wall. Red carpet, red wallpaper, red furniture cushions, red table cover.

The MOTHER *and the* SON *(the* POET*) seated at the table opposite each other. (In profile to the audience.)*

THE MOTHER. . . . it's the first time since your return that you deign to grant me a free hour. And you've been back for over a week. But you stay in your room all day or take walks. You don't concern yourself at all about me, I only see you at meals; for that I'm good enough. If you only knew. . . I cry over you. . .

THE SON. Dearest, let's use this free hour for talking of other things. . .

THE MOTHER. No, no, I must be able to talk about it. You, of course, don't like that! Ah, I'm dead to you—do you tell me anything at all about your inner life? It was bad enough those last few months, but now, since you met that girl, you've become completely closemouthed! You haven't told me a thing about your trip; why did you come back so soon?

THE SON. You know that I undertook the trip to gather some stimulation for my art. I came back when I got enough. . . .

THE MOTHER. And you've come back so soon? I But I think you went on that trip for quite different reasons, I'm quite certain of that. In that connection you had some bad experience and that's why you came back so soon.

THE SON. Where do you get all that information?

THE MOTHER. When you came back, I noticed that something deep inside was troubling you. And it had to be something sad, I noticed that too. After all, I know you! After all, I know what goes on inside you! Oh, I know! Perhaps you went there to sell a play of yours, and it was turned down.

THE SON. Ah, don't trouble yourself with these useless thoughts. . .

THE MOTHER. Yes, I notice it all right, it's true. I thought so . . .

Sighs.

At the left, behind the scene, slamming of a door is heard.

THE MOTHER, *startled.* Listen! that was his bedroom! What does this mean? What is he up to? Isn't he asleep? he won't be coming in here, will he?

Brief silence.

THE SON. It's all quiet.

THE MOTHER. The attendant is with him, I hope?

THE SON. Shall I go look?

THE MOTHER. Yes, go, go, but quietly! If he's asleep, don't wake him by any means. Maybe it's better you don't go? .

THE SON. I'd better go.

THE MOTHER. Yes, but very quietly, yes, it's better you go, I suppose. After all, one never knows. . But very softly, do you hear?

The SON *nods and exits through curtain. Silence.*

THE MOTHER, *inclining her head sorrowfully, folding her hands, stares straight ahead, and then she prays monotonously and mournfully.* Lord, you bring everything to its rightful ending—All my sorrow, too! O Lord, O Lord, take my hands and lead me. . .

A wild sobbing causes her head to jerk. A chair is moved

behind the scene; the MOTHER *quickly wipes away her tears and looks at the curtain.*

THE SON, *returning.* Yes, the attendant is with him.

THE MOTHER. Is Father sleeping?

THE SON. He's lying on the bed in his dressing gown and seems to be asleep.

THE MOTHER. Didn't you talk to the attendant?

THE SON, *resuming his seat.* No, I didn't go into the room at all. I only peeped in through the open door, no one heard me.

THE MOTHER. Ah, when I think that this can go on another year, or even longer, — I can't endure it.

THE SON. Did you write to Aunt once more?

THE MOTHER. She wrote again herself. I meant to show you her letter.

Searching in her dress.

Where did I put it. . ? Maybe I left it upstairs. . .

THE SON. What does she write?

THE MOTHER. She writes with no heart at all. . . No, I don't have the letter now.

THE SON. She writes heartlessly again?

THE MOTHER. She ignored everything I said. She falls back on the statement of the doctors and insists on his spending his last days, not in the institution, but at home. She accuses me of lacking in love because I wanted it the other way. But you know how I love him. . .

THE SON. One can't reach her, appeals are of no use. She gives us so much money that we are dependent on her.

THE MOTHER. If at least it were *his* heart's desire! If it could only relieve his last days. Yes, then I would take everything upon myself! But the doctor told me himself that those afflicted with his illness don't care at all. . ah, it's so difficult, I can't sleep any more from fear. . .

THE SON. She loves her brother, to be sure, but she can't sympathize with our torments here and with your great love. .

THE MOTHER, *bowing her head.* Yes, I love him utterly and I'm always with him. .

THE SON, *more softly.* Know this, I love you completely and am always near you. .

The MOTHER *looks up sorrowfully.*

THE MOTHER. I weep for both of you in my pillows at night. One eye weeps for your father, the other for you!

A door is slammed, right afterwards another one. Steps are heard approaching.

THE MOTHER *jumps up, screaming.* That's him! he's coming!

She flees into a corner of the room.

Bolt the door!

Tries to run out through the door upstage left.

Oh God, the door is locked!

THE SON. Calm yourself! Stay here! Calm yourself!

THE MOTHER, *fleeing through the room into the farthest corner.* For heaven's sake, call the attendant!

The red curtain in the background opens up, the FATHER *appears in the door frame. He is again in his blue robe.*

THE FATHER, *in the door frame.* Now I'm away
Tralala
And can dance
Trala!

He enters the room from the right, circumventing the table, without being aware of the others, who stand at the side to his right; the SON *puts his hand on his* MOTHER's *arm to calm her.*

THE FATHER. So you see, my dearest Boss,
I'm no longer at a loss.
One! two! three!
Hahaha!
Tralala!
Pretending I was a stupid mule,
I played my patron for a fool,
Now I can laugh at him—
Whoops—

Scoff at him—
Whoops—
And say I have enough of him—
Boomps.

He twirls around. Then he perceives SON *and* MOTHER.

THE FATHER. Ah, there you are! Good evening! Good evening!

THE MOTHER. Good evening, little papa. Not asleep yet?

THE FATHER. Hahaho—how do you like that—I've only pretended I was asleep! But that fellow fell into my trap and thought I was really asleep. So I've gotten rid of him in a nice way—hahah—I'm rid of him. I'm dancing with joy, you shouldn't think I'm crazy. I only dance with joy! I Yes, let's all dance, where is Hedi, let her play the piano. Hopsa . . hopsa . . tralala . . Well, how do you like that, I am even a poet! That poem was good, wasn't it? A crazy man couldn't make such poetry! Yes, poetry, that's always been my forte. You still remember, Mommy?
Oh, dearest bride with myrtle wreath,
With a goose you're putting your groom at ease. .
Hahaha. . .

Brief silence.

But sit down, sit down! What are you standing around for? Mommy, come, come here!

They all take seats around the table.

Well, my boy, you really should be in bed already—but you aren't a child any more. Time was when you had to be in bed by half-past seven on the dot. . Punctually at half-past seven! March, to bed—nothing to be done about it! I still remember—haha—five minutes before, you already cast side glances at the clock, and winked all secretly to yourself. . but you couldn't fool me, I saw it anyway. And you always begged to take your book along to bed, but that was out of the question.—Yes, you were a rascal! And do you still remember how we did the puzzles, son? We two always solved them—one, two, three, just like that, but Mommy could never solve them. . never . .

Pats her shoulder.

Yes, yes, Mommy. It's not as simple as all that. Haha.

THE SON. Sometimes you had the answer before I'd been able to finish reading the puzzle.

THE MOTHER. Yes, little papa, you really could solve them beautifully.

THE FATHER. But now, how is it now! We must discuss what we are to do. I am well again now, and we'll fire the attendant on the first. I think, Mommy, we two will first take a nice trip south, anywhere else it would still be too cold. Yes, I've figured it all out. Well, will you be surprised, little mommy!

THE MOTHER. That'll be wonderful. .

THE FATHER. It sure will be wonderful! And afterwards with new strength I'll buckle down to work. And at full steam! Haha, if you only knew. . .
> Work makes our life so sweet
> Never is a burden—

Oh yes, oh yes.

THE MOTHER. The other day you fetched your old blueprints from the attic —.

THE FATHER. Yes, that's right. . . and the drum too! Haha, have you already heard the story of my dear old drum. . ? Well, I'll tell you that another time. Mommy, you don't have to make such an anxious face right away, it's true about the drum. . . yes—well—what were we talking about. .

THE MOTHER. Of your old blueprints, little papa, and your work.

THE FATHER. Oh yes, the blueprints, I need them for something—haha! Yes, there is lots to be done, ho, if you only knew! We'll get filthy rich someday, we'll laugh at everyone. But we mustn't let anyone know.

THE SON. You have a special project lined up, haven't you?

THE FATHER. No, nothing must be divulged. Well, maybe I'll tell it to you, my boy, now you are "a colleague." How are you doing? Pretty busy, aren't you? How long will it take you to become construction boss. . Mommy, do you still remember, when I. . .

The MOTHER *nods.*

Hahaha, you still remember that. My boy, as soon as I am well, we'll go drinking together, absolutely, I want to have a real drinking spree again with the boys of the fraternity. *Ad exercitium salamandri.* .* one, two, three . . . yes, yes, I can still do it. . one doesn't forget that.

The MOTHER *has gotten up quietly and is about to exit through curtain.*

THE FATHER. Where are you going, Mommy? Oh, no, you stay here! Tonight you can stay up a little longer, for my sake, can't you? Can't you, my dear little wifey?

THE MOTHER *sits down again.* Certainly, little papa.

THE FATHER. You can sleep late tomorrow, tomorrow is Sunday. Sunday we never got out of bed before nine! My God, how long it's been now that we slept together, you and I! But just let the attendant go, it will soon be the first. Let him go, Mommy, and we'll have our wedding ceremony a second time. My dear, beautiful wifey!

Silence.

The MOTHER *regards the* FATHER *with increasing anxiety.*

THE FATHER *slowly.* Tell me— —

Silence.

THE MOTHER, *timidly.* What. . . ?

THE FATHER. Tell me, what was it I wanted to discuss with you. . . what was it—what was it —

Silence.

. . . Well, just you wait, Mommy, when I start earning again! Then I won't come home with a miserly six thousand marks, but with no less than six hundred thousand. Yes, then you'll be surprised, but you have to wait a little. It's so dreadful that I couldn't do anything at all these years. I go crazy even now when I think of it. Here, here—

Rolls up right sleeve.

---

* A drinking ritual of the student fraternities.

I bit my own flesh with rage, but it was no use, I could not make myself work. I could bite and bite as much as I pleased. . .

THE SON. But now you're planning new work again, Father.

THE FATHER. Yes, now everything is fine again. So my biting was good for something anyway. Haha, enough blood flowed out, one time a whole bowl was full! Haha, but now we can laugh and be happy! Mommy, you know, we could afford a bottle of wine to celebrate the day. And— you know what—I'll bring Hedi along too, she must join in our toast . .

He rises quickly, rubbing his hands, and hops around with joy.

Hopsa, we'll have a grand time. . .

The MOTHER *whispers with the* SON *by the curtain in the back, while the* FATHER, *humming, entirely self-absorbed, paces up and down the room. The* MOTHER *leaves the room. The* SON *comes downstage, seats himself on the settee, and looks at the* FATHER. *Silence.*

THE SON. You wanted to talk to me about your project, Father. .

THE FATHER, *stopping.* Of my project; of course! — — Well, it can't be told that easily. . .

THE SON. How long have you been working on it actually?

THE FATHER. Hmm, the first thought or the dream of it came to me already four months ago. And then I finished the plan, but at that time I hadn't come back home yet. — The blueprint itself I started only yesterday.

THE SON. You have to show me everything. What were you saying before about a dream. . ?

THE FATHER. Well—as I said—it's not so easy to explain. There is something great, miraculous, behind this work, you know —an utterly mysterious power — yes, I know it sounds crazy, but it isn't. Just listen to me. — How can I begin. . .

THE SON. You had a dream?

THE FATHER. Yes, that's it! Yes! Just imagine! One night I

saw the planet Mars in my dream, I saw it in the sky just as usual, but suddenly it grew brighter and brighter and bigger and bigger, it grew and grew, finally it became as large as this room here, and it was so near I could have touched it—so minutely visible, imagine, I could see the canals quite clearly. The Mars canals, you know?

THE SON. Yes.

THE FATHER. I saw them distinctly shimmering and flowing —they ran straight through across the whole planet, straight as a yardstick.

THE SON. Had you seen them at any time before through a telescope?

THE FATHER. Yes, but much, much smaller, not bigger than a five-mark piece, but then I saw them as large as this wall.

THE SON. How miraculous.

THE FATHER. Yes, truly miraculous! For the next night I dreamt the same, only this time I could see them building on one of the Mars canals!

THE SON. Ah . . .

THE FATHER, *growing in stature as he revels in his vision.* I saw the scaffolds and ditches—I saw everything!— and very curiously shaped — and it all hummed and whirred so in front of me that I became quite dizzy! I also saw people, very much like ourselves, except that they all had long trailing garments on and pointed hats, exactly the way I had once read it in a novel.

THE SON. Had you read it all?

THE FATHER. How could I have? . . I had read about the people there, but nothing of all the other things; in that case there would have been nothing miraculous about it at all. Hahaha! Now. . where was I . .

THE SON. With the people and the machines.

THE FATHER. Right. As I said—of course I hadn't read anything whatever about the machines and the whole construction. Otherwise there would have been nothing to this!

THE SON. How was it then on the third night?

THE FATHER. On the third night? Well, then I saw a little more of the construction site, and everything even more distinct! Then I also saw gigantic objects on the water—ships probably — I didn't understand at all how those monsters could float! I didn't comprehend anything, not the machines, not a single construction, nothing at all, I stood like a dumb ox before all those things! Gradually, however, I began to sense this and that—ah—I racked my brains trying to understand those things. They could drive one out of his mind, but I was probing into them! What times those were, my boy! I raced like a madman through the days, hardly able to wait for the night to come. I believe I must have been in a permanent state of fever from waiting. I burned. At night, when my glance fell on Mars, all red in the sky, I spoke to him. Then, in the night, I was up there. Yes, I was up there, every night for weeks, I didn't dream—it was real, what I saw— —

THE SON. I believe you, Father. And how did it go on?

Sounds behind the curtain. The MOTHER *and the* SISTER *come. The* SISTER *carries a tray with a bottle of wine and four glasses. The* MOTHER *carries a tray. They put these on the table. The* SISTER's *long blond hair streams down loose; she has a robe over her shoulders.*

The FATHER, *having thrown a rapid glance at them entering, paces back and forth, confused and completely absorbed in his visions.*

THE MOTHER, *anxiously.* Here we are, little papa. . .

The FATHER *fails to hear her.*

THE SISTER. I'd already gone to bed, little papa. That's why it took me so long. . .

THE SON, *getting up.* Come, Father, now we'll drink a toast.

Leads the FATHER *to the table.*

THE FATHER, *as above.* Well . . . well . . . well . . .

Now he stands by the table; at that moment his glance lights on the tray, he wakes from his trance, and speaks in a lively tone:

Ah! Macaroons! Hurrah, Mommy! Is this a surprise! Macaroons! My favorites!

THE MOTHER, *radiantly.* They are still quite fresh, little papa. Actually, you were not supposed to get them till tomorrow.

THE FATHER. Well, in that case I have to taste one right now—

Eats a macaroon.

Mmm, delicious!

Eats another one.

Really superb, Mommy, the way you make them. —

Continues eating.

Oh, does this taste good!

THE SON. Let's all sit down!

THE FATHER. Right, all around the table! We are short one chair. . .

THE SON *pushes a chair to the table, at an angle.* Here, take this chair, Father.

THE FATHER, *taking it.* Yes, I take the chair. Sick man that I am! — But now a toast! . . . Mommy, where do you have the corkscrew?

THE MOTHER *hands him the corkscrew.* Here.

THE FATHER. Well . . . tralala . . . this will taste out of this world!

He tries to pull the cork.

Hopla . . Well, this is a difficult business. . .

Tries again.

THE SON. Let me try, Father!

All sit around the table.

THE FATHER. All right, you try. This is damn complicated— damn complicated.

The SON *drives the screw further and pulls out the cork.*

THE FATHER. Ah, this boy is getting clever. . just look at him!

THE MOTHER. Yes, he used to be our all-thumbs.

THE FATHER. Sure enough! . . . And now let's pour.

Pours and fills the glass till it overflows and spills.

Hopla . . . this is too good. Well, let the rug too take part in the feast.

THE SISTER. Let me pour, little papa.

She takes the bottle from him and fills the other glasses.

THE FATHER. How do you like our children, Mommy —, Efficient, aren't they?

THE MOTHER. Yes, very, little papa!

THE FATHER. Wouldn't you like to make a speech, my boy? — Well? You used to love doing it. No birthday passed without one of your speeches.

THE SON. Yes, I still remember. I always made long speeches, but tonight, I think, we'll just toast quietly.

THE FATHER. No, no, that's impossible, you have to speak! Really, you have to make a speech!

The SON rises, raps on his glass.

THE FATHER. Ah. . psst. . psst. . quiet! Listen to the speaker!

THE SON. Fraternity brothers!

THE FATHER. Splendid. This will be a real fraternity carousal.

THE SON. Tonight we welcome in our midst our dear old brother restored to his old gay and happy disposition. For a long time he stayed away from our drinking bouts, and his absence kept away good cheer. Now we can delight together with him in his health, and wish him the best for his future and his great enterprise.

THE FATHER, *wiping off his tears.* Listen to him! Go on, go on, my boy!

THE SON. Fraternity brothers! I call on you in honor of our dear senior brother to whom we owe so much, who has always been and always will be an inspiration for us and an example of loyalty, earnestness, and sense of duty, in honor of our dear senior brother, I call on you for a rousing toast in our best tradition: *Ad exercitium salamandris: Estisne parati?†*

† The Son in this scene engages in a ritual of the German student fraternities—the so-called *"Salamanderreiben,"* or "stirring the Salamander," which constitutes one of the highlights of the fraterni-

THE FATHER, *with radiant face and booming voice. Sumus!*

THE SON. One, two, three—

The FATHER *rubs his glass on the table and gestures to* MOTHER *and* SISTER *to follow his example. They copy him halfheartedly.*

One, two—*bibite!*

They drink.

Three . . . *Salamander ex-est.*

THE FATHER, *embracing him, with tears in his eyes.* That was a wonderful thing you did, my boy! A wonderful thing. — And now another toast. All of us together, let's clink glasses. To the future!

They all raise their glasses; as the FATHER *is about to clink his glass with the* SON's, *he says:*

To Mars!

THE SON. Yes, to Mars!

THE FATHER, *to* MOTHER *and* SISTER. That's our secret.

MOTHER *and* SISTER *have joined timidly, smiling reluctantly, to humor his gaiety.*

THE FATHER *turns to the* SON. But I want to go on with my story — !

THE SON, *to* MOTHER *and* SISTER. Wouldn't you like to go to bed? Father and I might stay up a while yet. . .

THE FATHER. Yes, indeed, you must go to bed, — good night, Mommy. See how well-behaved I am, I'm not going with you. But just wait a while . . . a week from now. . . oh, that will be nice. . .

THE MOTHER. Yes! Good night, little papa.

THE FATHER *goes rapidly to her and kisses her.* Good night, good night, my wifey!

Kisses her more ardently.

Good night!

THE SON *touches his arm gently.* You meant to be well-behaved, didn't you, Father?

---

ties' drinking feast. The ceremonial is described here; the formal language of the fraternities' rituals is Latin.

THE FATHER, *letting* MOTHER *go.* Tonight, yes, but in a week. . .

The SISTER *extends her hand, wishing him "Good night."*

Good night, Hedi.

Throws MOTHER *a kiss as she exits.*

Good night, good night!

MOTHER *and* SISTER *leave the room.*

THE FATHER, *looking after them.* She is really getting more and more beautiful, our dear little Mommy!

He starts pacing up and down.

Just wait, just wait, my dear wifey! This week shall also pass. — One, two, three, one, two, three. . . *bibite. . .* oh, yes.

He sits down in a corner at the foot of the sofa.

THE SON. So tell me more of your plans, Father!

THE FATHER. Yes, I'll surely do that, my boy. What I've begun, I must also finish. That's the way it should be, shouldn't it?

THE SON, *in front of him.* You'd been talking about the machines and how you gradually were beginning to understand their construction, and how in general . . .

THE FATHER, *transformed; under the impact of his vision.* Yes, the machines! God, what advances compared to ours! Look here . . .

He bends down and draws shapes on the floor with his finger. His mind is obviously throbbing with these visions and frequently interrupts the flow of his speech. The SON *stands in front of him.*

. . . The great drilling machine, for instance, it hung suspended on springs like this and like this—the frame looked like this, here, like this, the two beams here diagonally, the center beams here, you see, crosswise, see—like this . . . There the upper beam divided, suspended wires connected it with the lower part, four of them disappeared here underneath the center structure. Later on I could see that center structure in cross-section; the ignition was

installed there, a complicated construction, didn't become
clear to me for a long time. Now there, below the ignition,
were enormous hooks, and underneath these was the driller.
They had some kind of induction—I'm telling you, it took
me ages to find my way! But finally I found out everything, everything!—And then there was a dredge, my God,
you could have cried for joy. . . we have absolutely nothing even remotely comparable! — This drill now had. . .
well, it's hard to describe, I have to show you the blueprints, then you'll see it clearly.

Teeth clenched; he jumps up.

Yes, my boy, wasn't it an enormous good fortune to be
privileged to see all that! ? And how I let it sink in! All of
Mars burned itself, as it were, into my brain. And my
brain was like a gigantic spider, embracing Mars, and
inserting his proboscis into it, a sharp pointed sting, and
sucking out all its secrets. . . all.

Sits down again.

Pause.

THE SON. And now you wish to . . .

THE FATHER, *ecstatic.*   . . . and now, and now—
        I wish to
Shower happiness upon this earth! You hear! I'm holding
Treasures—Miracles of Mars! Riches of the stars! World
        happiness!
I hold omnipotence in my hand! I can stamp
This whole great earth into dust! When I stamp the ground
It bursts asunder. The solid rocks rip apart
In dead center! In dead center! Ah—they are bursting even
        now!
Mountains turn and wander far afield.
Whither I command. The chasms fill
With rocks or flames or flowers.
Because I wish it so! Or with fields! And green!
I make the craters! I beat out depths,
Most dreadful depths—here! with this fist!
I call the oceans from the poles
And all the seas! the seas to me,

To make them full. . . Fertile! Fruitful! Fruitful!

He sinks back.

The SON *beds the* FATHER *upon the sofa. He rests his hand on the* FATHER's *forehead.*

The FATHER *tries to raise himself again; twitches with the effort.*

Silence.

THE FATHER. The plan! . . the plan! . . the plan!

THE SON. Now be quiet, Father, and don't talk about it any more.

THE FATHER. The plan. . . you have to see the plan!

Wards off the SON's *hand.*

Let me go—it's all right.

Half raised up.

It's all right. — You must see the plan.

He reaches into the pocket of his robe and pulls out the folded and voluminous blueprint. He quickly unfolds it, putting it on the floor. The blueprint measures approximately three-fourths the length of the sofa in both dimensions.

THE FATHER. Here it is! my work! my work! This is it!

. . . .

Yes, great! proud! glorious! blissful! marvelous!

Mars filled all my brain when I created it!

Mars rolled and glowed red-hot, and whirled thoughts round,

And raised my arms electrically,

And guided them! They carved these lines,

The cosmos carved and all the stars came to my aid!

Omnipotence created this through me! So proud. . . so

THE SON, *pacifying.* Father.

THE FATHER. Let me glorify! You shall not stop me! Glorify! Away and on!

Look here and marvel: This line here

Undercuts the Himalayas! What this signifies is but this:

Away with Himalaya! I push it

Out of my way! Here this yellow bedbug—
Sahara is its name—will soon be in full flight from me,
God only knows where to! And Himalaya, this tiny bug,
Shall likewise run from me!
I shall drown both in oceans deep, with these
Two arms, sore with cosmic strength and radiance!
They burn! you hear! they're sore! . . Here these lines,
All these black lines will soon gleam silver-white
With broad canals! They will bring lasting happiness to
    earth
Through power that is mine alone! And will be fruitful!
    fruitful!
Many white sails are sailing to and fro,
They are the white doves of my love. Forward, forward,
On and on! . . .
And harbors! ports and havens! they will stretch
Many miles, black and strong and sooty
With bellies swollen of all these blessings! Blessings!
Yes, blessings! Bread and marrow floating through air,
And derricks will link them. Oh, blessings! Broadly flung
Brother bridges will join shore to shore!
Fraternal, yes! A clanking and clattering in the air,
And seeds are blown dustlike through the sky
In giant clouds. In swelling clouds. Fragrant
Clouds! All miracles! All miracles!
He leans back.

Ah! I am weary from all that splendor! What splendor!
Creating makes one weary! I want to build myself a house
by the side of the road, and lie peacefully and view my
happiness. From my windows. Lying there, looking, I want
nothing else. . . And I want to die! I am cold. Please cover
me. . . I am so cold! My cover . . .

The SON *takes a red cover from the foot of the sofa and
spreads it over his* FATHER.

THE FATHER.   This is good . . .
Hear me. . I want to die. . . I've longed for this
All my days. . . My work is done!

Creating has been beautiful! Create further,
My son!
You will do it! Thank you! You! Now give me your hand!
Love me well and help me die. Remember . . .
Give me poison! Give poison to your poor father!
I'll thank you for it! You see, I'm shedding tears!
Yes, you'll give me poison and help me leave this life,
Which tortures me so much. . . I want my bed. . .

The SON *helps the* FATHER *raise himself up.*

THE FATHER. . . . Well . . . well
You have no inkling how I am tormented! Believe your
father!
It torments, torments, and no one knows the true extent!
One is alone. . . and black with anguish is the world
And one is mute. And turns insane! You too will suffer it,
one day!
Give me the poison! Poison me! Redeem your father!
The others too will be relieved when I am gone; —
Then you will need no more attendants! . . . Well, to bed!

The SON *leads the* FATHER *away.*

. . . .

For a short while the stage is empty. Lights are out.

The SON *re-enters through the door at upstage left, having
released the bolt outside. He pulls the curtain aside, and
in the window frame the sickle of the waxing moon appears. A star sparkles above it.*

THE YOUTH, *seating himself at the foot of the settee. His
posture: Leaning back, supporting himself on his stiffened
arms.* Night—profound—night so blue—how marvelous. —
Redemption. — Silver moon.

. . . .

Now drops the stony oppression of the day;
Cooled, I can bed myself in nearness to you,
Conversing in heavenly dialogue, silvery miracle—you!

The left half of the back wall and the adjoining half of the

*left side wall recede and the view opens on the deep blue
night sky; stars. Mars glows in striking redness.*

*Silhouetted against the sky, on the threshold of the room,
these three figures become visible: Two* WOMEN, *deeply
veiled, kneeling. Behind them, erect, likewise veiled, the*
FIGURE OF A MAN. *All have long-flowing, loose, dark garments. — The* YOUTH *raises himself, gazing.*

THE FIGURE OF THE MAN *speaks.* In the day's
Anguished toil and need,
Under death's
Brightly tinted lead,
Borne on wan
Poverty's reed—
Have you not your task forgotten?
That ironclad command,
Anchored with chains above you in the skies?
This
To ever-new signs
Choosing you,
In every pulse beat
Using you,
No martyr's woe
Refusing you,
In blackest pit not
Losing you,
With fires of stars
Fusing you—
Have you forgotten it?
Brief silence.

THE FIGURE OF THE FIRST WOMAN *speaks.*
Onto your narrow path
Your loving mother's star
Threw many a burnt-out rock
Freighted with pain and woe,
Many a sterile stone
Many a dry dead bone.
Has such disturbing confusion,
Such humdrum intrusion

Never embittered
Your glance when you gazed on
Maternal radiance
In the deep blue of night? !
Brief silence.

THE FIGURE OF THE MAN *speaks.* With reddish glow
Insane-creative,
Your father's meteor
With restless wandering,
Encircling Mars—
Did you understand
In flaming eruptions
Of tormented craters
Him, who begot you?
Brief silence.

THE FIGURE OF THE SECOND WOMAN *speaks.*
When despair was very near you
The great ominpotent Will
Brought the girl's love to your path.
When sorrow bestrides you,
Enmity chides you,
All power fights you,
Your song even spites you—
Ever constant will·her love receive you,
Her hands caressing, will relieve you.
Your frozen features she will thaw
And spread out, blooming, into smiles—
Under the gentle nearness of her gaze,
In ever-constant warmth of her embrace.
Oh, you, let the breath of her kiss,
Let her chaste embrace
Be a sacred symbol of mystic might:
Let the force of her attachment
Symbolize mystic motherhood.

THE YOUTH.
I hear your every word. You are the stars and the voices
Among which I always live. Your signs
Have been carved into me deeply, those signs

Will speak to me always. When you speak,
All becomes eternity and healing consolation. . .

CHORUS OF THE THREE.

Thundering constellations
Set us above you
As your physical stars;
Behold us, you that are body and person!
Other stars,
Many, will still rise for you,
Kindly stars,
Many, will still set for you in blood-red glow;
Hark our voices, body and person!
Hearken, hark
To us, your physical eternity—
Feel us deeply,
Us, Mothers of
Your future immortalities!

*As they disappear, the walls close again. The voice of
the* MAN *can still be heard growing fainter in the distance:*

Your father implored you. Hearken. Do well.

Lights go up gradually.

THE YOUTH *rises.*

My father asked his death from me. I sympathize
With his request. Yet this one question still arises:
Did he create a fruitful work? He must not die
If he can still create. Has perhaps his brain,
In its deluded state, given birth to
Deeply thought-out wonders? —
An expert must decide on this.

The sound of a door is heard from downstairs.

The YOUTH, *startled, listens, then goes quickly to the door
at upstage left and opens it. Quick steps are heard mounting the staircase. The door stays open. The* YOUTH *turns
and crosses the room once more. The* GIRL *enters. She shuts
the door behind her. Stepping close to him, she lays her
hands on his shoulders. The* YOUTH *kisses her on forehead
and both eyes.*

THE GIRL, *after a pause.* I'm very late, beloved. We were so busy in the office. We didn't get through till nine.

THE YOUTH. Is this job more exacting than the ones you had before?

THE GIRL. Yes, it is, but that doesn't matter. I am so happy I got it and that I can now live in the same town with you. And one has to get adjusted, you know. Four days isn't a long time.

THE YOUTH, *leading her to the settee.* Yes, we were lucky that my friend could get you the job so fast.

THE GIRL. How fast it's all happened.

She is about to sit down.

Ah, you know, let us sit down the way we did last night. Shall we? — It was so wonderful.

THE YOUTH. This way—

He moves the chair in front of the right-hand post of the door frame in the back, seats himself in the chair, while the GIRL settles on the floor, nestling her head on his knees. She does not withdraw her hand. Behind both is the night sky, moon, and stars.

THE GIRL, *after a brief silence.* Tonight you begin to tell, beloved, because I'll have so much to tell you later.

THE YOUTH. Is it something bad, my love?

THE GIRL. Please, you start.

THE YOUTH. I don't have much to tell. I did some writing this morning and took a walk at noon. . . My love, you have no idea how you've changed me! Remember, that evening in Berlin, when my last way out was blocked, and I no longer knew where I should turn, and yet was driven on by aspiration, driven on? No, I did not know then how I could go on to live my life! Then you came forward and confined the surge of my longing, and my inner drive no longer pushed me onward, but upward, my love! I was driven into gyres still unknown to me, and I'm still being driven in them, higher and higher. I wonder how it will continue. . .

Silence.

THE YOUTH, *bending down and kissing the* GIRL. And now, you tell me of yourself! Have you finally had some news about your baby?

THE GIRL. Yes, this morning I received a letter. The baby is fine.

She smiles painfully.

And is getting rounder every day, they write.

THE YOUTH, *kissing the tears away from the* GIRL's *lashes.* He's probably well taken care of in the Home.

THE GIRL. Yes, very well.

Brief silence.

And now read this letter.

Hands him a letter.

THE YOUTH, *unfolding it.* Who sent it?

THE GIRL. From my uncle, the master builder.

THE YOUTH, *skimming through the lines:* What does he suggest? . . . what? . . . You are to give your child away?

THE GIRL *nods painfully.* He wants me to offer it for adoption.

Silence.

THE YOUTH. I still don't understand it— you know—it's so dreadfully unnatural, so alien to me. . .

THE GIRL. I too couldn't understand it at first! And I never wanted to give my child away. Never! But then reason began to speak up, and I had to agree with my uncle: What am I, with my tiny salary, able to offer to the child, and how he would be benefited by being brought up in a decent family.

THE YOUTH. But suppose he comes to people who can't offer the child anything but their decency, who are not rich but with their prejudiced views and miseducation will spoil the child's youth. . .

THE GIRL. At least he will have a respectable name! That's necessary for his future! . . . And my uncle would inform himself very carefully before about the family.

THE YOUTH. What are we talking about — I We are talking as

if a human destiny could be predetermined and constructed with a little common sense. And yet we know nothing of the possibilities which might perhaps lead the child to his happiness if he remains with you, and perhaps to his misery if you give him away. What do *we* know!

THE GIRL. Yes, everything is so difficult. . .

THE YOUTH. What will you decide, darling. . . ?

THE GIRL. I have already decided. One thing alone determined my decision.

Softer. Lowering her voice.

If I give the child away, nothing will tie me any more. . . and I can love you exclusively. . . and I can serve you with my undivided self. . .

Profound silence.

THE YOUTH. My girl . . . mine . . . it is so strange . . . so much . . . it is so good . . . incomprehensibly good.

He stirs on his seat, rises, bends over backward, staring up toward the sky.

O miracle! This miracle! It rushes toward me . . . it bends . . .

Me into the Heavens . . . into the beyond . . . bends me . . . rushes—

O girl! O love! You are so good—so good

And wholly . . .

He bends down and passionately kisses the crown of her head, then sits down again on the chair, leaning forward over her, pondering.

Yet there is something warning me—

I am afraid. I fear your matricide.

Raising his head and trunk high, erect.

. . . And that the screams of strangled motherhood

Will fill you and encircle your heart,

Lay waste your being and shriek above the wasteland!

Desist! Desist! Love your child and me!

And do not kill!

THE GIRL. I bear you too much love!

THE YOUTH.

Dearest, your sacrifice intoxicates my inmost depths!
Your goodness dazzles me and gives a taste of Heaven!
For years I have been longing for such love!
It is unnamable! It is unthinkable! It remains desire only
　　and good!
Don't do it! Don't! Though I do want you to so much!
　　Don't do it!
Concern advises well! . . .

THE GIRL.　. . . Fear is past and gone. . .

THE YOUTH. It is too much. Too quick. We have to wait. .
Silence.

Until your uncle informs you of something definite, much
time may pass, and we can meanwhile think it over many
times. Try to understand me the right way, my darling girl!
The GIRL *tenses her body and gazes steadily up at the*
YOUTH. *The moon has almost set, only the tip of the sickle
peeks up in silvery gleam; more stars have appeared.*

THE GIRL *speaks.*

I cannot understand you,
I cannot well reflect,
I only can implore you,
And give to you—
All my heart
Desires to be near you
And wants merely to give you. To give to you itself.

THE YOUTH, *uttering the first verses bent down over the* GIRL,
the last ones erect, gazing to the sky.

The depths of Heaven
Shall surround us,
The beauty of stars
Shall be within us—
What do I care about understanding,
What do I care about comprehending —
Omnipotent power
Will lead me to my goal.

THE GIRL. All my heart

Shall always be with you,
I want your songs
Kept in my heart—
You can only give me, you can only bless me—
What can I give you, how fructify you —?
Faithful I shall be to you,
Faithfully depart with you into the heavenly beyond.

Curtains close.

THE THIRD ACT

Scene: Left, a garden. A partial view of a terrace jutting out from the middle of the wall for a quarter of the stage. The terrace consists of stone and has stone balustrades. All the way left, an ivy-grown segment of wall connects it with the ground, otherwise it stands freely, elevated. In front of the terrace and past it leads a path into the garden; another path from right front joins it. A young birch tree opposite the terrace; in front of it a backless bench. Upstage: A lawn divided by the path curving to the left. A hedge shuts the garden off. Blue spring sky. Morning.

The MOTHER *seated on the bench under the birch tree, her hands in her lap, her eyes closed. Silence. After a while the* SON *approaches from the left.*

THE SON. Good morning, Mother.

THE MOTHER. Is Father back again?

THE SON. No, not yet.

THE MOTHER. I sat down in the sun here, it's so nice, spring has come. The sun feels so warm on me. And on my hands.

THE SON. The sun will do you good. You look tired. I guess you haven't slept since then?

THE MOTHER. Why do you remind me of that again. . . I

want to rest quietly here and think of nothing, and you are bringing it up again.

THE SON. You are very right. Let's not talk about it any more.

THE MOTHER. No, not any more. . . You were about to tell me how he stood in front of the fire and threw the old blueprints in, singing and dancing all the while? It's true, isn't it?

THE SON. Let's not talk about it any more.

THE MOTHER. No, tell me; it did happen. . . And he ran around, horrible, with his head burning, and screaming so dreadfully? Did it really happen? Or is it all unreal?

THE SON. Mommy, rather enjoy the birch tree and spring all around you!

THE MOTHER. Yes, here is our lovely birch— — — I'm so afraid.

THE SON. Tell me: Of what are you afraid?

THE MOTHER, *anxiously frowning.* Tell me: All this has never happened, I have only dreamt it. I know for sure I dreamt about something. But many things did happen.

THE SON. Whatever happened, beloved, is past now, and what you dreamt of is also past. Don't think of either any more.

THE MOTHER. Do you see how I'm withering away. . .

THE SON. Dear Mother! Spring will make you young.

THE MOTHER. Yes, you're a darling! Well, soon it will be cool around me; soon I'll be allowed to lie in the earth. I ask God every day to take me away to Him. Then all will be well.

THE SON, *kissing her forehead.* Soon all will be well; you'll see, Mother!

THE MOTHER. Yes, you're a darling! But my fear won't leave me, and neither will my dream. And real life exists and stays. Oh, it's consuming me, but never mind!

THE SON. You know that Susanne will come to dinner today?

THE MOTHER. What a darling you are, you've still kept your kind heart! Yes, now I have to go in and see to the meal. Hedi isn't back yet, is she?

THE SON, *helping her rise.* I don't think so.

THE MOTHER. Ah. My knees are shaking again. Well! Thank you, thank you so much.

Exits right.

THE SON, *leaning on the birch tree; after a silence.*
My friend has sent me now the poison. Ripe is
The moment too. The time is overripe!
My mother's infirm age accelerates its course downward
    toward the grave;
And they have deemed my father's work—as mad.

He ponders, plucking a birch twig, absorbed in thought.

Quickly the deed arose in me. It almost
Blotted out the torment of its genesis.
My beloved too laid her smile lovingly upon the wound,
Yet under golden bridges, it bleeds on and on: this
    wound. . .
And if I delve far down, the root of this deed also
Shoots forth from out this bloody stream. Do not deceive
    yourself! Your torment was its soil!
Father, Mother, Sister offered up themselves
To it as pillars. — Am I then a soul towering
Strangely up above a single will —? — For me this is
A symbol of spring which has become a need,
And rising sun and first sight of blue.

The GIRL *and the* SISTER *enter from upstage left. Hearing their steps, the* SON *turns around.*

THE SON. Good morning, you two!

THE TWO. Good morning!

THE SISTER. We met at the garden gate.

THE GIRL. How wonderful this birch tree looks!

THE SON. Spring is everywhere.

The SISTER *throws a meaningful glance at the* BROTHER. *Silence.*

THE SISTER *to the* BROTHER. Could you still sleep last night after that?

THE BROTHER. No, and you neither?

THE SISTER. No, no. All nights recently have been disturbed.

THE BROTHER. You look so pale. You too, Susanne.

THE SISTER. It comes without one's realizing it. Is Father back again?

THE BROTHER. Not yet, I think.

THE SISTER. Has Mother asked for me?

THE BROTHER. Yes, she is in the kitchen now.

THE SISTER. I'll go to her.

THE GIRL. Just look at the birch tree in the breeze! Like blond hair. How beautiful it looks.

While the SISTER *exits to the right, she gazes up at the birch tree.*

THE YOUTH *kisses the* GIRL *on her forehead and takes her hands in his.* Good morning, my love, did you sleep badly?

THE GIRL. No, I had a good sleep, sound and deep. . . .

THE YOUTH. But you look pale and you've grown thin.

THE GIRL. I feel well, my love.

THE YOUTH *kisses her hair, sits down on the bench and draws the* GIRL *down next to him.* I well know how you suffer.

Silence.

THE GIRL. Let it be spring!

THE YOUTH. Let spring enter into you!

THE GIRL. What can I do for it? — It just comes over one; you understand. . . ?

THE YOUTH, *kissing her forehead.* This is different.

THE GIRL. No! . . .

Silence.

THE GIRL. I wonder. . . I have nursed renunciation in me and now I love it. . . I love myself in it. . . my better self. . . I wonder.

THE SISTER *rushes in from the right and seizes the* BROTHER'S *arm.* Father is home! And he wants to come here. .

THE BROTHER *rises.* He wants to come into the garden?

THE SISTER. Yes, he is coming with the attendant.

THE YOUTH. Then you two go! I wish to be alone with Father.

THE SISTER. Here he is already.

Leaves upstage with the GIRL *and they exit left.*

The FATHER *enters from the right, the* ATTENDANT *behind him. The* FATHER *carries a large folio full of drawings under his arm, the* ATTENDANT *carries the drafting instruments—compass box, rulers, etc. The* FATHER *wears a green spring suit; the suit is too big and hangs on him. The top buttons of his vest are open. His cravat has slipped over the very low coat collar.*

THE SON. Good morning, Father.

THE FATHER. *You* here! But you must go away, I want to work here. In such weather one has to work in the garden. . Yes, what weather. . . !

He leans the folio against the birch tree. To the ATTENDANT.

Just put these things on the bench there.

The ATTENDANT *obeys.*

THE SON *to the* ATTENDANT. Please, ask Madame to give you the cellar keys, and fetch us a bottle of wine and two glasses.

The ATTENDANT *nods, exits right.*

THE FATHER. Wine? So early in the morning? You're a fine fellow!

THE SON. Well, we want to drink a toast to your work.

THE FATHER. All right, we might as well drink a toast first.

He has meanwhile opened the folio and lifted out a drawing (on thin cardboard). Now he is about to nail it to the birch tree with a hammer and nail which the ATTENDANT *had previously brought.*

THE SON. What are you trying to do?

THE FATHER. None of your business, my boy.

Hammers the nail in.

I'm going to nail my blueprints up here, one next to the other—darn, I missed it—I'm going to nail my blueprints up here, one next to the other—and I want them—I want them all next to each other in a row. Because—ah, this is the first out of the way—

Takes another drawing from the folio.

Now the second above it. . .

Climbs on the bench and nails the second drawing above the first.

You remember—we don't have such a large table. . at home. And this is important—it is important for the view of the whole, one can see better. Ah. Now we'll get the bottom one. . .

Takes a third sheet and nails it beneath the first, bending while doing so.

How do you like my idea—this damn nail; don't we have some pliers here. . . ?

THE SON *hands them to him.* There.

THE FATHER. Thank you. . . Now we can really drink a toast. . . I've earned it, now, really. Didn't shut an eye these past few nights. . here, one more nail— well, I've made progress. Fine—now one more in the center—convenient, isn't it. . Fine.

The birch tree is now covered with three large cardboards; the strangest crosswork of lines is fantastically drawn on these, curves and loops, the weirdest ornaments, but having a most powerful rhythmic quality. The drawings are all in India ink.

THE FATHER, *looking at the birch.* It looks fine, splendid, doesn't it?

The ATTENDANT *enters from the right with wine and glasses.*

THE SON. Here is the wine. Thank you. You may go, I'll stay with Father.

ATTENDANT *exits to the right.*

THE FATHER, *laying out his instruments on the bench.* All right, let's drink the toast now! And then to work! There isn't so much left to do—perhaps I'll even get finished today. Ah, that would be something!

The SON *is filling the two glasses that stand on the bench.* Yes, we'll have our toast right now! Just let me unpack

first. Oh! I've run out of red India ink. Hmm—the maid
must get me some immediately.

THE SON. It's Sunday, the stores are closed.

THE FATHER. That's right, it's Sunday—uh, how maddening.
What am I to do now! I need red India ink desperately.

Pointing to the blueprint.

There. . down here, all this will be filled in with red India
ink.

THE SON. Can't you finish another area?

THE FATHER. Well, that would be possible.

Pointing again.

Here, for example—here I'd only need black and green.
But that's soon done, and without the red I can't finish
today. .

THE SON. So you'll finish tomorrow.

THE FATHER. Ah, tomorrow! tomorrow! Who knows what will
be tomorrow. I might be dead by then. Haha. . yes, really.
What am I to do. . . It's maddening.

*Softly whistling in frustration, his head bent, his hands
in his pockets, he walks past the bench, turns to the right,
and proceeds a short distance upstage. In doing so, he
catches sight of a fledgling bird on the ground, which must
have dropped out of a nest.*

THE FATHER. Ah, look, what is this down here?

Bends down.

A little birdie, sure enough! Now, look at that!

Picks it up.

Such a thing! How did he get down here! It probably fell
out of a nest. Why are you chirping so pathetically? Are
you hungry? . . Hahaha, so am I!

*Very brief pause. The FATHER is staring incessantly at the
bird, then squeezing its body.*

Does this hurt?! does this hurt?! Hahaha. . . what do
you think. .

During this, the FATHER turns his back to the SON. The SON fills both glasses, quickly pulls a paper out of his breast pocket, and pours the poison into one of the glasses. Then he searches for something to stir the liquid with, rapidly breaks a green twig off the birch and uses it to stir with.

The FATHER *turns around now, the* SON *drops the twig.*

THE FATHER, *holding the fledgling.* Ha, I've got an idea! Magnificent, really! Do you know how I'll get my red India ink? Do you know? Well, see if anybody else can match this! Watch!

Very rapidly he takes one of the compasses and drives one of the points deep into the flesh of the bird.

There. . .

The SON *automatically seizes the* FATHER'S *arm and tries to stop him.*

THE FATHER. There, there, that's the way to do it. And now the drawing pen.

Takes a drawing pen and dips it into the bird.

There. . . go ahead and chirp now!

THE SON *makes a motion to take the little bird.* Leave it alone, Father!

THE FATHER. What?! What?! What do you want?! Watch out, watch out, I'm warning you! What, I'm not to have my red India ink? Watch out! Don't be presumptuous, my boy! I won't have that, once and for all! !

THE SON, *pacifying.* Don't get excited. . .

THE FATHER, *nearly screaming.* I need this red India ink, do you understand I must have it! I have got to have it! Who cares about a bird? Who? I must have my red ink. I'd stab a human being, I'm telling you. I must have it!

THE SON. You are quite right, Father. I didn't think far enough. What does such a fledgling bird amount to? And you need your red ink. . .

THE FATHER. Now you are sensible. That's good. . . Well, I've taught you a lesson. . sure. .

Working.

You see how easily it's going, haha. . . it's going magnificently!

THE SON. Shouldn't we have our toast first?

THE FATHER. Toast, yes. . we really must have it. We must drink to my clever idea.

The SON has quickly taken his glass, the FATHER raises the poisoned drink. Suddenly the MOTHER enters from the right. When the FATHER sees her, he puts down his glass without having drunk.

THE FATHER. Look who is here? Our Mommy!

Advances toward her and leads her on.

Come along, little mommy, you too shall have a toast with us. Oh, I must show you something —

He picks up the dead bird and shows it to the MOTHER.

Here, look, that's the way to get red India ink when you've run out of it and the stores are closed. How do you like that. . ? Haha! . . . Well, don't get so scared about this. Is a dead bird such a horrible thing? No, don't be scared, I won't harm you.

Throws the bird away.

Well. . satisfied now? What? . . . And now let's have our toast. Fetch another glass, my boy, for our Mommy.

The SON quickly exits to right. During the subsequent scene, the SISTER and the GIRL appear upstage from left, picking flowers.

THE FATHER. My God, you're still looking at me so frightened. Really, I won't do anything to hurt you. And you look so pale—ah, really sick with worry. And deep shadows under your eyes. . .

The MOTHER tries to smile.

No, not this kind of smile; it is worse than tears. I know, I know: It's all my fault, your pallor and the circles under your eyes, and your wrinkles here and here. . .

The MOTHER shakes her head.

Yes! Don't shake your head! It's been caused by the nights you have cried for me. I know it! I know you, after all!

The MOTHER *smiles quite painfully, tears welling up into her eyes.*

Don't cry! Don't cry!—All will turn out well now. I am healthy, you see, and I can work again! The future lies before us blue and beautiful like this day, doesn't it, Mommy? No, don't grieve any more! Don't make yourself sick! . . Mommy, you must stay well for me, what would I be without you. . . ! Who has cared for me all this time so beautifully and fondly —? It was you. You've always been loving. When I was nasty, you forgave me right away. You have made a happy home for me and borne my children.

Tears glittering in his eyes.

THE MOTHER. My only one, what would my life be without you? You have always been my staff; I am so fragile and feeble and I need support. You have always been that. You made me a mother, you made me happy. . I can't exist without you. . .

THE FATHER, *nodding slowly.* The future will be bright! I swear to you. My illness only cemented our love! You see, that was the good it worked.

He raises a glass and, gazing at the MOTHER *with a very solemn expression, drinks half. Now the* MOTHER *takes the other glass, nods smiling, and also drinks.* GIRL *and* SISTER *continue to pick flowers upstage as before.*

THE FATHER. Oh, that's good. . .

THE MOTHER. You like the wine?

THE FATHER. Why shouldn't I like it? How well it warms! Ah! Spring is here. . . !

He puts his arm around the MOTHER.

Ah, my dear sweet little wife! Can you guess what I am thinking now?

He begins whisperingly, then ever louder and more intense. Intonation like a child's.

Once again I want to see you
In your bridal gown,
All wrapped in silk,
And stand before you, waiting.

Once more the night lamp
Shall glow in crimson hue of fairyland,
And all your splendor bring
Happy tears to my eyes—
Then, shy and trembling,
You will let fall the silk,
And humbly I shall lift your veil,
Absorbed in thoughts of joy to come. .
Then you will hold your hands
To hide your nakedness,
My power you will swell
To mighty size!
Then . . all around us . .
Many stars will blink. .
Soon it will be, this bliss—
Come! Let us drink!

He takes the glass from which the MOTHER *had drunk before and empties it. The* MOTHER *takes the other glass, but it drops from her trembling hands and crashes to the ground.*

THE FATHER. Well, Mommy, what do you think you're doing. . .

The SON *enters from right carrying a third wineglass.*

THE SON *in front of his parents, his face turned upstage.* You both have drunk?

THE FATHER. Yes, we'd already drunk one toast before. Now you must drink your own toast by yourself, my boy, that can't be helped. . .

THE SON. Here are broken pieces — ? —

THE FATHER. Mother dropped her glass. Maybe this might mean good luck, after all. Right, Mommy?

THE SON. So you didn't drink. . .

THE MOTHER. Oh yes, yes! I did drink all right, but when I tried the second time I dropped the glass.

THE SON, *unwittingly eased.* Ah—

THE FATHER. But don't stand around there now with your empty glass. Drink!

Takes the bottle.

Come, let me pour it for you!

Pours into the SON's *glass.*

And now say a toast to our health, my boy!

The SON *drinks, posture unchanged.*

THE FATHER. Well, well, don't you throw your glass down too! Your hands are shaking pretty badly. Well, that's what you get from running so fast.

The SON *places the empty glass upon the bench.*

THE MOTHER. I am tired, my limbs feel so heavy. I'll go rest a little before dinner.

Looks at her watch.

I still have some time.

The FATHER *has meanwhile turned to his work again, and readies the instruments.*

THE SON. Your limbs are heavy. . . ?

THE MOTHER. Like lead. Remember . . .

Softly.

The night—

THE FATHER. Yes, Mommy, go, go and rest! But have dinner ready on time.

THE MOTHER. Yes, for half-past one.

She exits to the left. Soon afterwards she appears on the terrace, a collapsible armchair under her arm. She sets it up.

THE SON *makes a half turn, takes a few steps forward, and up to his mother.* Are you feeling very badly. . . ?

THE MOTHER. I'm only tired. Merely tired . . . First I must have a good long rest again and sleep, you know. . .

She leans back in the chair, closing her eyes.

Just for a little while!

Silence.

THE SON *watches the* FATHER *working busily; then he looks down at the pieces of broken glass and gently touches*

*them with the tip of his foot. Wipes his forehead with his
right hand.* How is this to be understood —?

THE FATHER *has wiped his forehead twice with his hand,
now puts the instruments aside.* That's that. Now all that's
left is an insignificant little corner, and then it'll be finished.
*Steps in front of the bench, stands arms akimbo, gazing
at the blueprints.*

Here it's hanging now — my great project. . . yes, here it
is, my work.

*His eyes are gradually getting misty. He works himself
up gradually into an ever-intensifying state of rapture.*

Yes, it is finished . . . at last. . . Just look at it, my boy.
. . look at it! Ah, now there is a moment's peace in me. . .
But it won't last long. . . I know myself. . . . Soon I'll
have to go on. . . begin with another star. . . I know it.
There is no peace in this life. . . work! always work. . .
when one star is done, it's the next one's turn. . . Uh-
huh. . . just look at it, my boy, it's finished. — And you are
to give it life, do you hear? I'm entrusting it to you. . .
With haste I want to help you too . . . You shall have it
easy . . . like this . . . yes, like this! . . . My hands over
my brain . . . and I reach into my brain . . . you see
. . . deep . . . and now, here . . .

*He takes his hands from his own head and lays them on
his* SON's.

I'm pouring it into you . . . I'm leaving it to you . . .
pressing it into you . . . pressing it—does it hurt?

He presses more violently.

Does it hurt? . . . It must hurt, hahaha. . . Ah.

Drops his hands breathlessly.

Now I've become your father for a second time and you
my son. Isn't it so? Haven't I pressed my work into your
brain? ! Hahaha, that's the way it is. Now you are to complete it . . . and carry it further! . . carry further this
work! Do you hear? — What do you have your mother for,
if not for that? That's the way it is . . . that's the way
it is. . . Why did I marry. . . I did not marry. . . ha!

My work had sucked forth new blood. . . My work wished you to continue it. . . haha, it's the same with marriage! Shame on you, if you don't create. . . Produce! produce! I am your father and keep my eye on you. . . Don't think you can do what you please! . . . I command you. . . you shall develop my work still further. . . I'm laying this on you as your duty. . . I am your father and may command you. . . You must obey me. . . And here you have my kisses too. . .

Kissing his head impetuously.

I love you. . . You *are* my son . . . and have to do what I wish. . . I love you . . . and you must . . . Kisses! Kisses! ah . .

He falls back, the SON *holds him, he sinks onto the bench, drops his head to the side and leans it upon the birch, on one of the blueprints.*

He is dead.

The SISTER *and* GIRL *approach together down center stage. Each carries a bunch of loose violets.*

THE SISTER *hands her flowers to the* BROTHER. Take this for Father! . . . Is he asleep?

THE GIRL *hands her flowers.* Take this for Mother.

Both exit together to the right.

The SON *puts one bunch beside the* FATHER *on the bench where the two wineglasses rest and the* FATHER's *instruments are scattered about. He keeps the second bouquet in his hand. Suddenly he drops to his knees and presses his head impetuously into his* FATHER's *lap. —Silence.— He rises and exits left.*

Stage empty for a short time.

Then the SON *appears on the terrace where the* MOTHER *is resting; he walks on tiptoe, peering at her to see if she is asleep.*

THE MOTHER. You can come nearer, I'm not asleep.

THE SON *steps up to her.* But weren't you about to fall asleep?

THE MOTHER. Yes, I'm very tired. . . Oh, look, these beautiful violets! . . are they from the garden?

THE SON. Yes. Susanne sends them to you. And Hedi picked some for Father.

THE MOTHER, *accepting the flowers and burying her face in them.* Ah, this makes me happy! He was so sweet to me just before, it was like a shaft of joy into my heart. And he spoke so confidently about his health that I myself began to believe at last that he would get well again someday. Oh, perhaps he really will!

The SON *kneels down by the* MOTHER's *side and takes her hand.*

Ah, yes. . . take my hand, that is good. Yes . . . firmly . . . like this. . .

THE SON. Are you feeling very badly?

THE MOTHER. Just tired—and so strange—so unlike myself—so very strange I feel—my hands and my body and all—so unlike myself; — I hope I won't get sick —

THE SON. Does your head ache?

THE MOTHER. No. — All this results from these last few years—all these upsets, you know — and this constant anxiety—and then also this worry about you—and last night— —oh, for a long time already I have been wishing myself in the grave.

THE SON, *his hand on her brow.* Dear Mother, you mustn't feel this way, you know—if one wishes for death all the time, death will come at last. . .

THE MOTHER, *smiling.* If Father gets well, I don't want to die — I want to be where he is—that's what I would like —

Silence.

THE MOTHER.

He spoke so fondly. It entered deep into my soul.
He spoke so sweetly of our second wedding feast.
It was to come soon now, for he was well.
I should then step in front of him in my bridal silk again,
Just as it had been long ago, he would kneel down before
    me . . .
Oh . . .
Perhaps it will be so. Perhaps I shall be his bride once
    more,

After so many tribulations he shall be mine once more.
That would be heaven. Even more beautiful than it was.
I know life now and its share of grief,
And he knows illness and imprisonment.
This then will be like resurrection from our anguished
    woes—
Not merely youthful pleasure, but marvelous through
    knowledge.
We shall be happier in a better way than we had been.
    All will be joy sublime. . .
Oh then. . . how gladly would my breasts then nurse his
    child again!

Her head falls back.

THE SON, *kneeling and without looking up to her.*

Loved one, sacred is the sleep slept at your breasts.
Many things I hear stream past. That is your way, mothers.

He looks up.

Silence.

O Mother, how beautiful has been your death. . .

Silence.

Mother, your death belonged to you.

. . . .

The stage darkens. The SON's *voice is heard sonorously
from the darkness.*

You lived beyond, lonely, on the height,
And knew of nothing. .
The abyss gaped and darkness shrouded us,
You failed to see me. . .

But every longing which arose in me and grew,
You knew it. .
And every tear that rose in me and flowed,
You saw it. . .

Invisibly one bond did bind us:
It held and throbbed. .
A touching song without a word:
'Twas sung and sung. . .

Oft from your somber rock your grieving blood
Dripped down at me,
With gesture and with smile I often spilled
Maternal blood. .
Yet from darkest woe it still conveyed
To me its furtive gleam of love.
Now it ascends, becomes a star,
Radiant and sublime.

Curtains close.

EDITOR'S NOTE: Only the first three acts of this play, which constitute about four-fifths of the total length, are given here. The last two acts have been omitted because their inclusion would have made this selection excessively long, and also because the substance of the play is contained in the first three acts. No real development takes place in the remainder, which consists mostly of the Poet's monologues. He takes a job with a newspaper, then quickly decides to give it up, rejects his friend's request to change a passage in his play, and accepts the Girl's offer to give her first child away after she tells him she is carrying his child. There is no real end, but a hymnic invocation of the vistas of existence beckoning to them.

THE STRONGBOX

1912

A COMEDY

by Carl Sternheim

Translated by
Maurice Edwards and Valerie Reich

CAST OF CHARACTERS

HENRY KRULL, *professor*
FANNY KRULL, *his second wife*
LYDIA KRULL, *his daughter by his first marriage*
ELSPETH TRUE
ALPHONSE SILKENBAND, *photographer*
EMMA, *Krull's maid*
DETTMICHEL, *Notary*

The scene throughout is laid in Krull's middle-class living room.

ACT I

SCENE 1

SILKENBAND *enters.* Nobody up yet, Emma?

EMMA. It's just eight o'clock, Mr. Silkenband. But they're already up and about inside.

SILKENBAND. Mr. Silkenband, honey! How do they put it? Give me your sweet little lips! Had a good time last night? Quite a charmer, aren't you? Here are the photos—they came out all right, didn't they! What about this one?

He hands her a photograph.

EMMA. The spinster aunt: that's her to a "T"!

SILKENBAND. If only all my clientele were as easy to satisfy as you, you little charmer. Tonight, at the same time, if you please.

EMMA. But Master and his wife are returning from their honeymoon.

SILKENBAND. Before noon, I think. So things will calm down again by nightfall. The young couple have hardly been away one week. Along the Rhine. You're smiling, my love?

EMMA. Because you said the "young couple." Him, with his forty-seven years!

SILKENBAND. But hers add up to barely twenty.

EMMA. She's something!

SILKENBAND. Something? What do you mean?

EMMA. Haven't I been putting her odds and ends in order for four years now? What she accumulates in her chests and drawers!

SILKENBAND. Oh, she does, does she?

EMMA. Ribbons, perfume, and switches, to boot! Even when her sister, the Professor's first wife, was still alive. A basketful of sponges. Three washbasins, one on a stand. And how she kept after him, even while the first was still alive. Phooey!

SILKENBAND. Good. Now will you give the pictures to our dear Miss Auntie?

EMMA. She lived next door to him even then, just like today. Was this the proper thing for a young girl to do?

SILKENBAND. You little scandalmonger! So long until tonight, *au clair de lune.* Wear your little blue blouse.

EMMA. Does it become me?

SILKENBAND. Divinely! But more of that later. Now give the pictures to Miss True, with regards from Silkenband, Senior. *Exits.*

SCENE 2

LYDIA *enters.* Wasn't that Silkenband? I had a heavenly dream. I was about to take a swim, and there was a man standing upright in a lake, singing in the sunshine.

EMMA. If you're thinking of such things already at seventeen, you could dress better! Ah, if I had a figure like yours . . .

LYDIA. Have I a good figure?

EMMA. Your stepmother is a model of how to dress.

LYDIA. She snared my father with garments and gewgaws, and poisoned him to the core with love, as Auntie says. His glowing travel letters are an outrage to me. I despise such devices.

EMMA. All right! Good heavens! The garland must be set over the door!
Climbs up the stepladder.

LYDIA. Marriage should be a communion of souls. But one shouldn't swallow the other hide and hair the way Fanny gobbled up Father. I hate her—and Auntie. She had better beware.

EMMY. Is it all right?
A red placard with the inscription "A hearty welcome to the young bride!" becomes visible.

LYDIA. "Hearty" should be lower. She's returning, only to
sit on a keg of dynamite.

EMMA *climbs down.* You'll be seeing things around here. Was
that a bomb Auntie dragged up last night—that thing
wrapped in a black cloth? It weighed a quarter of a ton
and felt like a chest or a strongbox.

LYDIA. Rather than worry herself to death, she oughtn't wait
even a day with it. The mine might blow up.

EMMA. My God!

LYDIA. Think what Auntie had to give up for him: Mother
let her have free run of the house. Had Mummy dreamt
what it would come to. . .

She bursts into tears.

Auntie never stopped warning her about Fanny; even on
her deathbed she gave Mother no peace and started talking
about what she really wanted for Father, should it be the
Lord's will to summon her away.

EMMA. And?

LYDIA. Mother smiled.

EMMA. How terrible! Bitterly?

LYDIA. Lovingly. Death's mildness hovered over her. Then I
solemnly pledged to battle shoulder to shoulder with Auntie
for my good mother—against Fanny.

EMMA, *showing her the photos.* And what do you think of
these pictures?

LYDIA. What an artist! He's really divinely inspired. Did I
ever tell you—the man in the lake looked exactly like
Silkenband?

EMMA. As you stood naked—and him, too?

LYDIA. Naturally I didn't look in his direction.

EMMA. The clock is striking one! I guess we'd better let
Auntie in on your dreams.

LYDIA. You'd give me away?

Suddenly:

The carriage!

She runs to the window.

EMMA, *after her*. There it is, for sure!

    And runs out.

LYDIA, *toward the left*. Auntie, they're coming!

SCENE 3

ELSPETH TRUE'S *voice, from her room*. Should I plant myself as maiden of honor at the entrance? Is it not fit that they meet me on my own threshold?

LYDIA. And here are Mr. Silkenband's photos.

SCENE 4

    KRULL *and* FANNY *enter*.

KRULL. Oh, my darlings! Dearest daughter!

LYDIA *runs and throws her arms around him*. Daddy!

KRULL. And Auntie?

LYDIA, *embracing* FANNY. Fanny!

EMMA, *approaching* KRULL. Professor!

KRULL. Good Emma! And Aunt Elspeth?

EMMA. In her room, Professor.

KRULL, *in* ELSPETH TRUE'S *door*. Auntie, Auntie dear!

    Disappears into her room.

    Beloved Aunt Elspeth!

    KRULL *and* ELSPETH *enter*.

ELSPETH. You didn't shave.

KRULL. Of course not! Straight from the train into your arms! Doesn't Fanny look enchanting? A little moss rose in bloom!

    Toward FANNY: My doll!

ELSPETH, *stiffly*. Good day, Fanny.

FANNY, *stiffly*. Good day, Aunt Elspeth.

    They embrace.

KRULL. But now the coffee from the stove, Emma! Around the table, all of you.

To FANNY:

See how we honor the little lady: "A hearty welcome!" Bravo! Divine!

All sit down.

KRULL. Children, all's right with God's world on a beautiful spring morning! Gliding down German rivers into the valley, proud castles salute us below. Germania greets you, and the Lorelei, too, until on the brazen horse in Coblenz—

FANNY. In Coblenz we had ourselves photographed on postcards.

KRULL. Ah, Coblenz! Children, Coblenz! We were in seventh heaven. A delicious Walporzheimer wine sent bliss coursing through our veins. A hundred moods enveloped us. Nothing, there's nothing in God's world more resplendent than a morning on the Rhine.

EMMA *brings the coffee.*

KRULL, *reading the inscription on the cake.* "Peace and Blessing upon the Lovers." How refined!

To FANNY:

My sweet doll!

ELSPETH. In a word: you had a good time, you were satisfied.

KRULL. If I could but give you half an idea.

ELSPETH. We get it all.

LYDIA. Mr. Silkenband didn't find the photograph from Coblenz in very good taste.

KRULL. A child of caprice must be taken in a comparable spirit. For us it will always conjure up heavenly memories.

LYDIA. But Auntie had her picture taken.

ELSPETH. Hush!

KRULL. Have you actually overcome your old aversion?

ELSPETH. Just a proof. Not the real thing yet.

LYDIA. But a perfect work of art.

FANNY. Let's see your picture.

LYDIA. Do bring it. Father won't believe his eyes.

ELSPETH *goes into her room.*

KRULL, *to* LYDIA. And what do you think of your new little Mummy? Isn't she beautiful, wrapped in glory? Adorable doll!

ELSPETH *returns and hands the picture to* KRULL.

KRULL. Aha!

He hands it, in turn, to FANNY, *who breaks out in a fit of laughter.*

ELSPETH. What is it?

FANNY. Schiller's Lady Macbeth all over!

ELSPETH, *snatching the picture out of her hands.* This is really—

FANNY. Like Blücher at Caub—leg on the stool.

ELSPETH. —tasteless.

LYDIA. Mr. Silkenband is a divinely inspired artist. He called your Coblenz snapshot *kitsch,* shoddy trash—a disgrace to the profession.

KRULL. A caprice, to be taken in a comparable spirit.

FANNY, *to* ELSPETH. Besides, you look sixty in the picture, five years too many!

KRULL. For goodness' sake, hear me out! Let me tell you about Ehrenbreitstein. On top of hilly vineyards stretching down to the Rhine . . .

ELSPETH. All these extravaganzas—Lorelei and Walporzheimer. This trip must have eaten up a lot.

KRULL. By Jove! Does this one fling at pleasure have to be soured with ill-tempered calculations? I even had to borrow two hundred marks from our friends, the Susmichels, in Andernach.

ELSPETH. Awful! How'll you pay them back?

FANNY. Don't worry.

ELSPETH. At the end of March, your bank account showed a balance of 276 marks in favor of the bank.

KRULL. Damn it, how's that possible?

ELSPETH. Trifles for you: the same old story!

KRULL. That would mean 476 marks in the red.

FANNY. Henry bought me another genuine lace kerchief in Cologne.

To LYDIA:

I brought a light-blue parasol for you.

LYDIA. Where is it?

FANNY. In the trunk. On top. Here's the key.

LYDIA. A million thanks, dear Fanny. I have so many important things to tell you.

FANNY *and* LYDIA *go off quickly to* FANNY's *room.*

FANNY, *in the doorway.* And for you, Aunt—

ELSPETH. No presents for me on borrowed money.

FANNY. That's what I call character!

She follows LYDIA *quickly.*

KRULL. A delightful wench, a ray of sunshine! A living doll!

ELSPETH. The twelve hundred marks you borrowed from me must also be paid back. To clean up our affairs at last.

KRULL. Aunt Elspeth, what a wet blanket on our moving in!

ELSPETH. In a word, Lady Macbeth.

KRULL. Banter.

ELSPETH. Malice! I know my little niece down to the roots of her hair.

KRULL *laughs.* Roots of her hair!

ELSPETH. Don't laugh! She and I are both women. Don't make fun. Every greeting from your trip was vile.

KRULL. How often we thought kindly of you. Which reminds me how Fanny toasted you with the seasoned wine at Susmichel's . . . The goblets tingled with the tone of genuine emotion.

ELSPETH. The Rhine has had an unfavorable effect on your penchant for the cliché. No protestations, no arguments. You owe me money, you grow more obligated to me. I demand respect.

KRULL. Every member of the household will grant you that.

ELSPETH. You want to come into my money.

KRULL. If you love us. We're next of kin.

ELSPETH. That always calls for action.

KRULL. Affection and gratitude guaranteed.

ELSPETH. Greatest courtesy and more. Are you willing? Look me in the eye. You didn't bat an eyelash.

KRULL, *laughing convulsively.* You can look into my heart as into a mirror.

The bright laughter of women is heard from the adjacent room.

Listen: how heartily they laugh!

ELSPETH *leaves the room without a word.*

KRULL, *taking the photograph from the table.* Excellent. The real Elspeth.

He sighs.

Ah, yes . . .

SCENE 5

FANNY *enters.* Did she toss around figures?

KRULL. What do I care about such frippery? It'll turn out all right. But be nice to her. Not with feigned love. Simply on this basis: we want to inherit.

FANNY. We shall, in any case. For one thing, there's no other relative, however distant. But then there's her notorious sense of family . . .

KRULL. She means well.

FANNY. With you, perhaps. But enough of her. Her role here is finished, once and for all. On that we are agreed.

KRULL. Completely.

FANNY. I took Sidonie's place at your side on that condition.

KRULL. Certainly. She gets the attention due her—and that's all, *basta.*

FANNY. I must have lost my locket.

KRULL. The gold one with my picture?

FANNY. I felt it in my bosom on the train this morning.
She unbuttons.

KRULL. That would be—

FANNY. Can you reach it?

KRULL, *feeling his way.* I have it!
He pulls it out.
Sweet little wife, sweet . . .

FANNY. Henry.

KRULL. The world, ah the world is beautiful! To sink—
They embrace.
After a moment.
How much could she have?

FANNY. Fifty, sixty thousand at least.

KRULL. Sixty thousand. I thought so, too!
Kisses her.
Sweetie pie!

FANNY. Dearest!

SCENE 6

EMMA *enters.* The coffee dishes . . .
FANNY *returns quickly to her room.*

KRULL. Otherwise nothing of importance, Emma, while we
were away?

EMMA. One day like the next. What could happen? At most—
the strongbox, maybe . . .

KRULL. What? What's that?

EMMA. Which Miss True dragged up.

KRULL. The strongbox?

EMMA. Wrapped in black cloth. Weighed a quarter of a
ton, and felt like it.

KRULL, *jumping up.* What kind of a strongbox, in God's name?

EMMA. Just a heavy chest.

KRULL. Pull yourself together, girl. Think back carefully, slowly, for God's sake. Give yourself time. When? Dragged up—wrapped in black cloth—a quarter of a ton—where from —in here—all by herself—with whom—in the evening—in the morning? And then—where was it put? But you clean the room. What is it—just a heavy chest—what became of it?

EMMA. I never saw it again.

KRULL. Disappeared, then?

EMMA. As if by magic.

KRULL. It's hidden!

EMMA, *whining.* And the mine would explode, or the bomb, she said to Lydia.

KRULL. Would explode?

EMMA, *crying.* That's what she said.

KRULL. An iron strongbox?

EMMA. I think so.

KRULL, *whistling through his teeth.* Ha! Enough! Away!

EMMA *leaves.*

KRULL *springs over to aunt's door.* Which means: to arms! Attention!

Looks through the keyhole.

Which means—good Lord, what went on here in my absence? For all that—in spite of wedding and fuss and bother—one heart and one soul. Well, then, what kind of influences, what shifts, what rebellion? What did she do— what decisions did she have the audacity to make—what is there to write now? To whom? I must do my utmost. She's looking at something—holding it toward the light— what? The photos? Moves away from the table, comes toward—

He steps back from the door, out into the center of the room.

SCENE 7

ELSPETH. You will write Mr. Silkenband that I refuse the photographs.

KRULL. If I'm not mistaken, acceptance of proofs entails a subsequent order.

ELSPETH. They make me look like a music-hall headliner, not a lady of respectable society.

KRULL. One has only to . . .

ELSPETH. In brief: I demand your manly assistance in settling this matter.

KRULL. That is to say: no payment.

ELSPETH. Not one penny.

KRULL. Won't be easy.

ELSPETH. You don't want to?

KRULL. I see no way out, especially since, for my part, I find the photographs excellent.

ELSPETH. They're indecent. The raised knee! An insult, to put it bluntly. If you permit such an offense to my person, you must let me draw my own conclusions.

KRULL. Was it Fanny's remark you look a few years older. . . ?

ELSPETH. You can't ever recall seeing me vain.

KRULL. But I've—I can't myself—if I assure you—

ELSPETH. Haven't you tormented me enough? Wasn't it enough that the excitement you stirred up aggravated my kidney trouble beyond measure? Dr. Stössl finds salt in my urine.

KRULL. Dr. Stössl is a charlatan.

ELSPETH. He's an eminent specialist. Are you going to write that letter, after all?

KRULL. I'm sure it won't accomplish anything, and I'll only make a fool of myself.

ELSPETH. Don't give me ideas! If I didn't feel that the husband of my sole relative were a man who could make his unalterable will prevail in the right places, my intentions in regard to my estate might become irrelevant.

KRULL. Perhaps I should appeal to your sense of justice?

ELSPETH. Ha! A nobody of a photographer insults a well-to-do lady of the highest standing, and you, when asked to come to her defense, can do nothing more than—

KRULL. Should I let myself be carried away, and pay no heed to the considerations I owe my position?

ELSPETH. It's what I expect of you. In my view, something extraordinary of you. And rest assured, the report on what takes place determines the decision in regard to my Last Will and Testament.

KRULL. Last Will and Testament? Such hypochondrias, dearest Aunt.

ELSPETH. Silence! Not one superfluous word! The letter, the letter! I have set the next few days for the winding up of my earthly accounts, and have transferred my possessions here with my own hands. How to effect the best disposition of one hundred and forty thousand marks torments the soul with scruples. I expect much of you.

She goes into her room.

KRULL. One hundred and forty thousand marks! The strongbox! Lord—what a cold sweat! One hundred and forty thousand . . .

SCENE 8

FANNY *enters with a tray, a bottle and glasses on it. She says, affectedly.* Gremlins!

KRULL, *roaring.* Quiet!

FANNY *lets the tray fall.*

Curtain.

ACT II

SCENE 1

ELSPETH *emerges from her bedroom in bed jacket and cap, sneaks through the room, and listens at the door to* KRULL'S *bedroom. After a few moments, she spits out in disgust:*

ELSPETH. Phooey! How I hate that woman! Look how she tries to grab him while he's still asleep!

FANNY *opens the door abruptly, confronting* ELSPETH *in negligée, sizes her up, and slams the door shut again.*

ELSPETH. Could I but smash heaven down upon her! Just wait: her day will come, too!

Disappears in her room.

SCENE 2

LYDIA *and* SILKENBAND *enter.*

SILKENBAND. I take it as a good omen, milady, that it is you who lets me in.

LYDIA. Our maid is out early this morning, mailing a letter for Miss True.

SILKENBAND. Just think, I received a letter from your father: the photographs having aroused great displeasure in the lady who ordered them, she declines to accept them. How do you account for this most mortifying business? Your father remains absolutely correct in tone and attitude—read it yourself.

LYDIA, *reading it.* "Miss True holds that the likeness is not achieved to the extent she feels she must insist on in a perfect photographic portrait, and so, to her utmost regret, she must desist from accepting the pictures. Please accept, my dear Mr."— But Mr. Silkenband, this is terrible!

SILKENBAND. The most outrageous incident in a five-year-old, well-established practice, flooded with recognition from the highest quarters. I am beside myself; you see me blustering with rage. Am I only run-of-the-mill? Don't they read the papers in this family? This procedure is unheard of. Perhaps because I'm a tenant in the house? I pay rent and—that's all! I owe it to my honor to set a precedent here. Should anyone get wind of this, it might damage incalculably my studio's *renommé*.

LYDIA. Could I make good? Auntie's so obstinate.

SILKENBAND. And I so sensitive—to the brink of unconsciousness—in matters of honor.

LYDIA. If she's unwilling, no power on earth can get money out of her.

SILKENBAND. Money! Even if I were finally to get my fee, how could I ever make up for the story of the rejected pictures around town? This third day of April is the most catastrophic day of my life. My Waterloo! Miss True finds fault with photographs from Silkenband *ainé*. One has detractors, enemies, beasts.

LYDIA. It's really unheard of!

SILKENBAND. And the large circle of her acquaintances! *Fama!*

LYDIA. Hyperbole!

SILKENBAND. Krüger & Son will trumpet it forth around the world. You make a name for yourself through your work, and a bolt drops right down out of the clear, blue sky; but you stand unprepared to meet it.

Pause.

LYDIA. But if I were to have my pictures taken?

SILKENBAND. What?

LYDIA. Only I don't have the means. My allowance—

SILKENBAND. But Miss Lydia, Ma'am! That would be a heroine's act! It would mean disavowing your family. The idea stuns me. But don't you risk too much?

LYDIA. True, I really do. The shots would have to be taken secretly. They would try to stop me.

SILKENBAND. I shall not rest until then.

LYDIA. Quiet! They'll hear us.

SILKENBAND. When shall it be done?

LYDIA. Father is spending the last hours of his vacation on a family outing down on the village green. I will pretend I have a morning rehearsal for the Easter cantata, and try to stay behind.

SILKENBAND. What time, then?

LYDIA. Eleven.

SILKENBAND. The shots taken, I can most emphatically ensure my honor. You're my angel!

LYDIA. Go.

SILKENBAND. In view of the circumstances, better say nothing of my visit.

LYDIA. Nothing.

SILKENBAND. What day is today?

LYDIA. The third of April.

SILKENBAND. A day to remember.

He leaves, followed by LYDIA.

SCENE 3

FANNY *and* KRULL *enter.*

FANNY. I snatched the door out of her hand; the woman practically fell into my arms.

KRULL. Amazing!

FANNY. A hate-distorted face hissed and spat. Striking proof of my contention: parliamentary procedure won't do here. She or I. Trust me, Henry: our happiness is at stake. I will not put up with it like Sidonie.

KRULL. Fiddlesticks. It goes without saying, I will establish my authority unmistakably, right from the start.

FANNY. It's *you* she wants. To live off your breath, your potency to think and to act. With every gesture you're at the mercy of her greed.

KRULL. She shall not utter a sound. I'll take it all out of her hands.

FANNY. This early morning raid on our privacy—in our bed, almost!

KRULL. Some nerve!

FANNY. Have no qualms. Back her into the wall until she gasps for air. Crush her insolence once and for all. I shall keep Lydia and the maid occupied, so there'll be no witness. Whatever happens between you, she won't be able to prove a thing. But I cannot live until you've fulfilled your duty to me.

KRULL, *roaring*. It's enough to lose your mind. Just a few hours back—in Germany's most blessed regions. Now here —in a sewer of moral depravity.

FANNY. Eye and ear pressed against your bedroom door! How far will it go? Go in! Take the bull by the horns.

KRULL. You mean?

FANNY. Be my hero, as you seem to be in our nights together. I'm suffering. Liberate me—my superman, my king!

KRULL. I'll fricassee her—my sweet little doll.

FANNY. And rest assured, no one'll hear you or see you. Go ahead!

She leaves quickly.

SCENE 4

ELSPETH *enters*. I'm flying high. Can't you carry on your arguments at a greater distance?

KRULL. There can be no question of argument: Fanny and I are of one mind.

ELSPETH. Indeed?

KRULL. So?

ELSPETH. Is the matter taken care of? The letter?

KRULL. Mailed.

ELSPETH. And?

KRULL. The impression will be sensational. Let's skip it. . . .

ELSPETH. What do you mean "Let's skip it"? Before it's all straightened out! I presume you submitted him a modest, delicately couched suggestion.

KRULL. My letter is a breviary of thundering protest. Cutting in tone to the brink of insult.

ELSPETH. Did you not go too far?

KRULL. Perhaps, if he's a gentleman. *I* would box the writer's ears.

ELSPETH. But that was not my intention.

KRULL. Did he not, according to your own statement, grossly insult you? We're not lambs.

ELSPETH. Nevertheless—

KRULL. You should have thought of that before.

ELSPETH. However—

KRULL. I've fought five duels. I'm no slouch with firearms.

ELSPETH. I forbid you to duel. Do you hear me?

KRULL. I can promise nothing any more.

ELSPETH. Then I know what I have to do.

KRULL. Should I permit you to be insulted in my own rooms by this gallivanting photographer?

ELSPETH. After all, he's not responsible for his camera.

KRULL. You, set down on a photographic plate like a music-hall headliner, a coquette with raised legs.

ELSPETH. It's not as bad as all that.

KRULL, *loudly.* Shocking!

ELSPETH. Only the foot—see for yourself. . . .

She goes into her room and leaves the door open.

KRULL *very loud.* How shameless you look! Like a woman of the streets. A common wench!

SCENE 5

FANNY, *sticking her head into the room.* Well?

KRULL, *softly.* Did you hear? Shameless, woman of the streets, etc.? Almost a cadaver. Mutilated. But that's not the end of it.

FANNY. Darling!

Disappears quickly.

SCENE 6

ELSPETH *returns.*

KRULL, *ripping the picture out of her hand.* A clever blend of Valkyrie and concubine.

ELSPETH. The story must come to an end—by the fact that we're not paying. By insulting Silkenband you overstepped my instructions. Set that straight.

KRULL. The matter must take its own course. I eagerly await further developments.

ELSPETH. An end to it, unconditionally!

KRULL. Mr. Silkenband . . . !

ELSPETH. Enough!

Short pause.

ELSPETH *and* KRULL, *simultaneously.* By the way . . .

ELSPETH *and* KRULL, *together.* What?

KRULL. You were about to say something . . .

ELSPETH. You were saying "by the way." . . .

KRULL. Indeed I was. But after you.

ELSPETH. Have your say.

KRULL. I have time.

ELSPETH. It seems you simply had to say something.

KRULL. Not at all. Just bridging the gap in the conversation. I rather expected a preconceived opinion from you.

ELSPETH. What was it I wanted to say?

KRULL *laughs.* Neither of us knows now.

ELSPETH. How miserable you look.

KRULL. I went over piles of material until late in the night.

ELSPETH. Nothing else taxes you? You still love Fanny?

KRULL. I worship her. You recall that unhappy night after Sidonie's death when I thought I would die of grief, and saw no light in the gray, lonely future?

ELSPETH. And you never thought of the other while your first wife was still alive?

KRULL. What a quaint idea! Sidonie all over. . .

ELSPETH. You confessed just the opposite in a weak moment: You said Fanny's crystal-clear soul illuminated your life.

KRULL. Could I have said that?

ELSPETH. Crystal-clear. I assure you. And, from your current existence, you have nothing—I beg you, think it over— you have nothing to confide in me?

KRULL. I am perfectly content with Fanny's wifely love, with your gentle concern I know so well how to treasure, and with Lydia's admiration.

ELSPETH. Boundless hypocrite! You've already short-changed two lives. The third shall not be spared.

KRULL. Auntie dear, when one hears you . . .

ELSPETH. . . . one thinks: truth speaks with a fiery tongue. Wait here.

KRULL. What?

ELSPETH. Wait for me here.

Goes into her room.

KRULL *goes quickly to the door, right rear. He tells* FANNY. Now the deck is cleared, as you would have it. A few minutes more for the business details.

Slams the door again.

ELSPETH *enters, the strongbox in her hands.*

KRULL. What's that?

ELSPETH. Push the table between us. Here, the key. Open it.

KRULL *complies.*

One hundred and forty thousand marks in state securities, except for twelve thousand marks in electric stocks.

KRULL. State securities!

ELSPETH. Count the pieces.

KRULL. One, two, three, four . . .

ELSPETH. Bavarian bonds, which I preferred to all others because the Bavarian state maintains certain interest guarantees through her vast forests.

KRULL. Is that so? Twenty-four . . . twenty-five . . . twenty-six . . . vast timber reserves . . . thirty . . . thirty-one . . . interest guarantees . . . for coupons . . . forty . . .

ELSPETH. You'd lay down your life for Lydia?

KRULL. Lay down my life . . . fifty-one. Timber reserves . . . fifty-eight . . . fifty-nine . . . I'd lay down my life.

ELSPETH. Fanny is dazzlingly beautiful! Isn't she? Or does it only seem so?

KRULL. Seventy-five. Dazzlingly. Startlingly.

ELSPETH. Sensual?

KRULL. Eighty-three. Beg your pardon? Eighty-four. . .

ELSPETH. Sensual? More than enough—is my impression.

KRULL. Good Lord . . . ninety-two. Naturally—one isn't so young any more.

ELSPETH. Day after day, night after night, over and over again. . .

KRULL. You are so right. Spessart. Bavarian Forest!

ELSPETH. Frankenwald. Fichtelgebirge!

KRULL. Lower Alps. Ingenious idea. Would do credit to a financier!

ELSPETH. To tell the truth, you never really saw such a paper before.

KRULL. One hundred and twenty-eight. All right. Saw? Ha-ha-ha, only in the show-window of a bank. Never actually laid hands on one.

ELSPETH *hands him a paper.* Look at it!

KRULL. Properly speaking, it embraces the world.

ELSPETH. No more need for Susmichels.

KRULL. The sum total of the coupons represents the capital half over again.

ELSPETH. Self-evident. Of course, Fanny—goes overboard, draws from the stock.

KRULL. Perhaps. Plus the twelve electric stocks.

ELSPETH. There's something of the beast of prey in her.

KRULL. Called dividends, in this case.

ELSPETH. These twelve thousand marks reflect my lust for speculation.

KRULL. But one hundred and twenty-eight thousand are good as gold.

ELSPETH. Add thirteen hundred marks you owe me. Let's make a list of the certificate numbers. May I call upon you for this at your convenience?

KRULL. Didn't I just demonstrate complete readiness with Silkenband?

ELSPETH. You're settling it my way, then?

KRULL. Smoothly. I'll ask him for a final talk.

ELSPETH *closes the strongbox and gets up.*

But, in any case, do come with us to the village green. We want to spend my last leisure hours under God's blue heaven. Fanny is most anxious that you come.

ELSPETH, *close to him.* Once again, Henry, I urgently implore you: there's a lot more to life than a pretty wife. You've only begun to taste it.

KRULL, *in a low voice.* Indeed! Rest assured: I've already begun to show her her place.

ELSPETH. An organism is quickly run down.

KRULL. Besides, one is no Louis Quinze.

ELSPETH *smiles.* A sensible idea, those four-per-cent Bavarians, isn't it?

KRULL, *holding out his hands to her.* I congratulate you from the bottom of my heart: Bavaria is fabulous!

ELSPETH. For a long time now, I've wanted to speak with

you about such amusing things, but for the past year no one but this woman has existed for you.

KRULL. Things can change, you know.

He giggles.

ELSPETH. Then—heh-heh!—I shall get ready.

She goes toward her room.

KRULL, *next to her.* Now the gray dress with the silver shawl will be aired in the sun.

ELSPETH *slaps his cheek.* As you wish.

Goes into her room.

SCENE 7

KRULL *opens the door, right rear.*

FANNY *enters, ready for a walk.* Were you laughing?

KRULL. Queer duck. She was unspeakably comic in her remorse.

FANNY. It's harder to see through such a woman than you think. Perhaps she only made believe.

KRULL. Enough. She knows I'm dead serious when it comes to what I want. She promised heaven and earth, and she's even returning Silkenband's photos because of your crushing critique. Now that it's all straightened out, surely you won't object to her accompanying us into the woods. . .

FANNY. Of course, I'd rather—

KRULL. After all, one makes concessions for one hundred and forty thousand marks.

FANNY. One hundred and forty? I thought it was barely sixty.

KRULL. Yes, my little Fanny, that makes a tremendous difference. You probably can't conceive the real significance of such a sum—neither in itself, nor what it means in bearing interest. By the way, were you aware that interest guarantees offered by the Bavarian state are backed by her huge timber reserves?

SCENE 8

LYDIA *enters.* But I can't go with you; there's a rehearsal from eleven to twelve.

ELSPETH *enters, ready for the outing.* You oughtn't to dawdle away your time with this singsong business.

LYDIA. But it's for the Easter cantata. . . .

FANNY. It makes her happy.

ELSPETH. Henry?

KRULL. Professor Bachmann asked me once to let her do it. I am beholden to him. But first— Where's Emma?

ELSPETH. She's out on an important errand for me.

KRULL, *to* LYDIA. Catch her here before you leave, and have her go immediately to Mr. Silkenband. I want to see him.

ELSPETH. And have him take the pictures back, and that's that!

KRULL. That's that! Let him set the time!

FANNY, ELSPETH, *and* KRULL *leave.*

SCENE 9

LYDIA. The clock struck eleven. Where is he? I'm trembling.

SILKENBAND *enters after a moment.* The company marches off —down the stairs. Did something important break?

LYDIA. Father wants to talk with you.

SILKENBAND. Have they reconsidered?

LYDIA. I fear not.

SILKENBAND. So they will get to know me. I'll give him something to think about.

LYDIA. Actually, it was my stepmother who rejected the picture. Claimed Auntie looked like Lady Macbeth in it.

SILKENBAND. Actually, a superior version of a fishwife. That she looked like a lady speaks for my talent for arrangement, for conjuring up effects out of nothing. Instead of being grateful— But more of that later. Now let's make use of these few short minutes left before they surprise us. I have the camera ready. Or have you changed your mind?

LYDIA. No.

SILKENBAND *goes out the door, reappears with camera, tripod, and equipment.* I did not dare ask you into my studio. Of course, there we'd have everything more conveniently at hand. You look like a vision in the bright sun. . . . Full light, *plein air.* The camera eagerly opens its lens to devour you. Miss Krull, the moment I met you in the foyer a couple of months ago, the certainty flashed upon me that here, without question, pulsed a pronounced individuality —a thinking, up-to-date human being. May I ask you to assume a position near the desk? The back leaning slightly. Even with half a dozen figures in this town emanating such charm, there's nothing in the world so sensitive to them as a photographic plate. Except my heart, perhaps. Hands clasped: a symbol, so to speak, of maidenly feeling. May I take a look?

Runs to the camera, ducks his head under the black cloth.

Excellent! The left leg a little forward, perhaps. More expressionistic.

He runs to her, kneels down and arranges.

A little more. Just a little.

Deep sigh.

Ah, Miss Lydia! The artist who, like one of us, depends upon a model . . .

LYDIA. Ah, yes. . . !

SILKENBAND. What would Phidias have amounted to if the most beautiful women of Greece hadn't offered him their beautiful bodies without shame. Or Michelangelo?—a little more, yet. A certain inconspicuous fullness in your build, an unusually rare *pli. Fausse maigre,* says the Frenchman. Correggio's figures were like that. Hold it a moment.

He runs back under the black cloth again.

Out of this world!

To her again:

Chest somewhat out; no, rather, stomach in.

He puts her in that position and runs to camera.

Perfect beyond belief. And now, please: one, two, three,
four. Many thanks! Immediately, once again, if you please.
But now let's take a profile, sitting, more *clair obscur*. Legs
crossed nonchalantly.

LYDIA. If only I'd dressed better. But I couldn't change without arousing suspicion.

SILKENBAND. My photographs will recreate the magic charm
of your round, lush youth. The dress is immaterial. If only
I could come close to recapturing for the viewer of my
works the quality of your high F-sharp.

LYDIA. What a magnificent voice *you* have! Even when we're
standing far apart, I find it often drowns out all the others
in the hall. Then the conductor always says: "That was
Silkenband!"

SILKENBAND. I can reach low D without any trouble. The
head turned somewhat to the right; hands casually in the
lap this time. High society. Your F-sharp, Miss Lydia, floats
like a solitary beacon over the choir, stirring every heart.
You even hit high G once.

LYDIA. In the *Missa Solemnis*, because I was very moved.

She sings the passage.

SILKENBAND. It fills me with bliss! What a slender, giving
hand. See how hungrily the camera lies in wait for you.

*He steps back to the camera, sticks his head under the
cloth, and says:*

Overwhelming! I can't help it.

Runs precipitously to LYDIA *and kisses her.*

LYDIA *stands up.* Mr. Silkenband!

SILKENBAND, *stepping back quickly.* Remain seated, please!
My existence is at stake.

Under the cloth again:

Blame it on the focusing screen. Ah, if you could see how heavenly it paints you! I can hardly contain myself.

LYDIA. Mr. Silkenband!

SILKENBAND, *straddle-legged under the cloth.* Your image flows into the lens, Lydia, straight into the chambers of my heart. Separated from the universe by this cloth, I am nourished unto madness by your passionate charm. Your eye in mine. Lydia, ah. . . !

He pushes the plateholder* into the camera, lifts the ball, and squeezes it.

One, two, three, I love you! Thanks! No turning away; no offense, please. Didn't expect such impetuosity from a bass, did you? Professing love is the tenor's holy privilege. While the bass stands in the background, rolls a mournful eye, and is always resigned or playing the patsy. At best he may sing a drinking song:

"Card games, fun, and throwing dice
And a child's breast round and nice. . . ."

Accompanied by a few comic leaps. Thus.

He demonstrates.

No other outbursts are expected from him.

LYDIA. How funny you can be. I thought you favored the sublime.

SILKENBAND. I do. But also the droll. Besides, the droll can be sublime at one and the same time. We're finished. I'm saved. Exalted beyond all odds and expectations, through you.

He sets the camera aside.

You enable the free artist to respond nobly to the bourgeois *canaille,* you help him break through restraints.

LYDIA. Ah, the arts!

SILKENBAND. Lydia, yours is a passionate heart. A source of flame. Soon even you will no longer be able to tolerate

---

* Interestingly enough, the German equivalent for this, *"die Kassette,"* is also the title of this play, *The Strongbox.*

the vestiges of bourgeois habits: you will break free and powerfully forge yourself a rich individuality.

LYDIA. Do you really consider me an individuality?

SILKENBAND. Ha! Can there be any doubt about it?

> "I should like to tear off my clothes,
> stand, wrapped in ice, on the white heath,
> and whirl away into eternity —
> what wise men might call madness."

LYDIA. Whirl away? How heavenly! I feel exactly the same way!

SILKENBAND. Nirvana, Lydia!

LYDIA. Alphonse!

They embrace.

SILKENBAND. But don't let anyone know about it. Deep secrecy shall hover quietly over our union. Rancor and envy would bespatter it with venom and split us apart. Have I made any headway. . . ?

LYDIA. Then, oh God. . . !

SILKENBAND. You loved no one before me?

LYDIA. As I will love none after you. You are the light, the truth, and the life.

SILKENBAND. Divine woman!

Kisses her again.

How can we see each other clandestinely again?

LYDIA. If only I knew. Auntie doesn't let me out of her sight, and Fanny, too, is always nearby. And one doesn't know what it'll be like tomorrow. The devil's unleashed between the two of them.

SILKENBAND. A chic little lady—your stepmother!

LYDIA. Vain, silly, egotistical. I side with Auntie against her.

SILKENBAND. Cupid helps, and will give us the means. How old is this Fanny?

LYDIA. Twenty-eight. But looks much older. Are you happy?

SILKENBAND. To the fingertips. But you have a really remarkable *pli.*

LYDIA. My figure is superb.

SILKENBAND. A walk in the woods toward Spiegelsberge tomorrow after the rehearsal?

LYDIA. If Auntie doesn't fetch me. I hope the strongbox will keep her occupied.

SILKENBAND. What strongbox?

LYDIA. Important things. Concern the whole family.

SILKENBAND. A money box?

LYDIA. Yes . . . Another time . . .

SILKENBAND. Certainly. More about it later. Aha, I see . . . I look a little bit ahead. . . . Aha, I see . . .

LYDIA. Go now; otherwise they'll find us. And Father? When will you speak with him?

SILKENBAND. I'll meet him about three. It's no detriment to my honor to be considerate toward the older man. Give me your sweet little mouth again, my pet.

LYDIA. Your pet?

They embrace.

SILKENBAND. Charming little puss.

LYDIA. Sweetheart!

SILKENBAND, *waving in the exit:* Nirvana!

He leaves.

LYDIA, *following him with her glances.* How handsome he is! On the white heath—standing naked. . . .

She goes into her room.

SCENE 10

ELSPETH, FANNY, *and* KRULL *enter.*

FANNY. And I demand you let this person know in my presence, once and for all.

ELSPETH. You put up with that?

FANNY. Lydia is not to be deprived of her youth by this dragon, this cannibal. I won't have it!

ELSPETH. You put up with. . . ?

FANNY. You are my protector before God. It's your duty to throw it in her face.

ELSPETH *shrieks.* You leave me at the mercy of this hysterical goose. . . ?

FANNY. Hysterical goose! Do you hear? Your wife!

ELSPETH. Show her! Show her!

KRULL, *loudly.* For God's sake, stop it! Damn it all—this can't go on! Who the devil's master in this house anyway? ! !

He approaches ELSPETH *threateningly.*

So, once and for all . . .

SCENE 11

EMMA *enters, and says to* ELSPETH. Compliments of Mr. Dettmichel, the notary. He will be here on the dot.

ELSPETH. All right.

EMMA *goes out.*

FANNY. With no holds barred, straight in the face, right into the brain, so that she never forgets it. Or I leave the house on the spot!

KRULL *cries out again, staggers, and is about to fall.*

FANNY, *next to him, supporting him.* What's the matter?

ELSPETH, *doing likewise.* What's wrong?

FANNY *pushes* ELSPETH *away.* ELSPETH *raises her umbrella against* FANNY.

FANNY. He's *my* husband!

ELSPETH *hisses.* Ah—just wait!

Quickly off into her room.

FANNY. What's wrong, Henry, my darling?

KRULL, *moaning.* To bed, to bed!

FANNY. Collect yourself for a few seconds. Come!

First she leads the staggering man toward the door, right rear, then calls into it:

Emma, quick, get Doctor Stössl!
Then into the bedroom.

SCENE 12

EMMA, *her head in the doorway.* LYDIA *comes.*
EMMA. Father is sick. I'm off to the doctor.
Disappears.
LYDIA *slowly, toward* KRULL's *door.* If only I knew who Nirvana is. . . .

Curtain.

ACT III

SCENE 1

KRULL *steps quickly out of* ELSPETH's *room.*
KRULL. At last! You had it well hidden, but I smelled it out better. My hawklike prying glances cannot be overpraised. They discovered the narrow projecting edge of white paper, and lifted it up—the draft of your last will! Now I have in black and white before my very eyes what heretofore I could only conjure up in my imagination: "I bequeath a movable fortune of one hundred and forty thousand marks to my niece Fanny Krull under the trusteeship of her husband, Henry Krull, with the explicit instructions that the capital be held in securities sufficiently safe for investment of trust moneys, under the supervision of Notary Public Dettmichel, for the children of the above-named Henry Krull, as residuary legatees. . . ." Here the draft breaks off. Well, that's enough. God, look into my heart. Let's see—at four per cent, four times fourteen—fifty-six hundred marks. Just think, after twenty-one years' service, I'll have an income of fifty-two hundred marks for giving up thirty hours a

week to young rascals still wet behind the ears and exuding
unpleasant exhalations. I could go out of my mind at the
thought that here a sum falls into my lap giving me more
than that in interest alone, and without lifting a finger.
Fifty-six hundred marks at four per cent. Which should
put one in a position to invest fifty thousand marks at four
and a half per cent. Dettmichel, Esq., will listen to reason.
Where's the list of securities? Immaterial: I know approximately. Principally Bavarian state securities! Because of
interest guarantees in vast timber reserves. A smart
spinster. Who else would have hit upon Bavaria? Who in
the world would know such things? I studied in Würzburg
and Erlangen, yet when it comes to interest guarantees in
timber reserves—well, in a way, Bavaria has been building
up her forests to offer me guarantees for my money. What
a mountain of work behind that; what a long line of efficient souls served this goal. You can go as high as a forest
ranger in such a career. Many a night these men sat by
the lamp racking their brains over the problem of render-
ing accounts. Do I not see before me an army of worried
faces anxiously awaiting the audit of their books? What
a feeling of importance the moneyed man must have to
be truly master right down to his last drop of blood. It gives
him something to do during the long winter evenings;
and let me assure you right now, dear Auntie, I will be a
true property owner for my family. I shall minutely scruti-
nize each security as to its value and quality. I shall study,
compare, and decide. Unfathomed perspectives open up—
the nature of which, I think, stem from Rothschild. Look
up again, *Faust, Part II*, the scene with the Emperor. The
Jewish question. How rich is the man of means—my God,
how rich! I must immerse myself in statistics, in the ups
and downs of the market. Currency standard! Price quota-
tions should be more closely investigated—and all my
schoolmaster penury will fall by the wayside. Dear little
Aunt, in such moments I should like to give you much
affection, and no one will dare laugh. But now, quickly
—the paper back in its place.

He goes into the aunt's room, the door of which he had
left open, and returns at once. A knock at the door.
KRULL *opens it.*

SCENE 2

SILKENBAND *enters.*

KRULL. Had not an indisposition intervened, my dear sir, I
should have liked to talk with you yesterday at the time you
so kindly set.

SILKENBAND. The sooner a painful misunderstanding is cleared
up, the better.

KRULL. My opinion, too. To put it briefly, the pictures do
not please Miss True.

SILKENBAND. Far from submitting myself to the judgment
of the lady insofar as matters of art are concerned . . .

KRULL. Of course, far be it from her to contest artistic
qualities.

SILKENBAND. My studio has been honored with five gold and
silver medals. I was Reutlinger's master-student in Paris.
That should suffice.

KRULL. Perfectly.

SILKENBAND. What compromise do you suggest?

KRULL. Compromise—hmn. Let us shift the case from the
business to the social sphere. I would say: My esteemed
Mr. Silkenband, here are your pictures. We found your
approach extraordinarily interesting . . .

SILKENBAND. Rejected!

KRULL. Let me be quite frank with you. Our family situation
forces us to yield to the often eccentric wishes of Miss
True. My wife is the one and only heir.

SILKENBAND. And your daughter next in line?

KRULL. Yes. I don't know if you can identify with such a
situation?

SILKENBAND. To some extent. A comparable legacy awaits
me in Würzburg.

KRULL. Würzburg? Are you Bavarian?

SILKENBAND. Born there.

KRULL. Which brings to mind my university days. If this be so, I must look you over again. And here, please—read. *He points out books on his desk.*

SILKENBAND, *reading.* Buchert: *Bavarian Administrative Law.* Sutner: *Bavarian Municipal By-Laws, Hunting Rights in the Bavarian Kingdom, State Cattle Insurance in Bavaria.* . . . Well, I never!

KRULL. And were you aware that Bavaria's giant forests constitute certain interest guarantees for her securities?

SILKENBAND. No.

KRULL. That is why I prefer Bavarian loans to all other German securities.

SILKENBAND. Easily apparent! If one assumes that war devastates railroads and lowers employment—revolution!

KRULL. *Voilà!* You said it! Interest guarantees in timber reserves. They're always good!

SILKENBAND. Well-founded considerations.

KRULL. It all came home to me again, especially of late, since Miss True's . . . significant legacy . . . also . . .

SILKENBAND. May one congratulate you?

KRULL. My wife, later my daughter, will be the sole heirs.

SILKENBAND. *Intimo ex animo.*

KRULL. Latin! Graduate?

SILKENBAND. Sixth-form certificate.

KRULL. Bravo!

SILKENBAND. In a word, that is why you have to tolerate Miss True's absurdities. Your own judgment doesn't echo hers.

KRULL. By no means. I find your little portraits masterpieces.

SILKENBAND. My honor is restored. We agree. An end to this business once and for all.

KRULL. Let's shake on it; and I'm obliged to you for the future.

SILKENBAND. Pleased to establish a relationship on this footing.

KRULL. Let me fetch your property.

Goes off into ELSPETH'S *room.*

SCENE 3

FANNY *enters.*

FANNY. Mr. Silkenband! Ah, now I can thank you once again for your amiable help. But for you, I would have tripped over my shoelaces and tumbled down the stairs.

SILKENBAND. I'm grateful to fate for letting me help; I see more than mere chance in that.

KRULL *enters.* Here are your photos.

SILKENBAND. You were my Evil Fairy.

FANNY. Don't misunderstand me; I found the pictures refined and in grand style.

KRULL. Very significant.

He goes to the desk and works on the books.

SILKENBAND. But—

He laughs.

Let's bury that! In return, may I give vent to my fondest wish: Allow me, most gracious lady, to take your picture and thereby cancel out the insult done me.

FANNY. Out of gratitude for the unruly shoelace. However, Silkenband, *aîné,* is too expensive for me.

SILKENBAND. It would be my pleasure to do it—what more effective advertisement for my show-window than the beauteous Mrs. Fanny Krull? My lens burns to catch forever the significant contour of your head, the ravishing bend of your neck, the *clair obscur* expressionism of your figure. We poor artists depend to such a high degree upon the model! Where would Phidias be . . .

FANNY. Well, I don't quite know.

KRULL. Which means almost twenty thousand hectares of timberland. Colossal!

FANNY. Henry, Mr. Silkenband wants to take pictures of me

—free. The beautiful Mrs. Krull as advertisement in his show-window.

KRULL. Good. Which makes, calculating by the hectare . . .

SILKENBAND. The husband is agreed.

FANNY, *to* KRULL: Henry, did you hear what I said?

KRULL. Naturally, my dove. Yes and Amen.

FANNY. They say Mr. Silkenband is a skirt-chaser, a Don Juan.

SILKENBAND. I hope you jest, milady.

FANNY. Henry!

KRULL. Listen, she's back!

FANNY. Who?

KRULL. Quiet! Was I mistaken?

Goes to the right rear door and opens it.

SILKENBAND. Have I reason to hope, most fair lady?

FANNY. My husband will regret his consent.

SILKENBAND. Your spouse has assured me the willingness of his services.

FANNY. He is particular as to my person.

SILKENBAND. I entreat you.

FANNY. My conscience advises no.

SILKENBAND. And your heart warns you?

FANNY. What audacity. Go.

SILKENBAND. Without satisfaction, for now. It cannot, it must not be "no." Most gracious lady.

He bows and leaves. As he passes KRULL, *he says, with a slight bow:*

Good day.

KRULL. G'day, sir.

SILKENBAND *goes out.*

It was rather difficult to bully him into agreeing to take back his pictures. Not an easy fellow. What tricks such a simpleton goes into over a trifle!

FANNY. He's a Don Juan. No woman is safe with him.

KRULL. Agreed! On the other hand, he hasn't the slightest

conception of economic matters. Photographers and druggists are an abomination to me.

FANNY. Yet, a pretty handsome fellow.

KRULL. A picture of a man! Enough. And now for the great surprise: *we get it!* We're the heirs. I found the will, the draft. We have it in black and white: about six thousand marks' interest.

FANNY. I never for a moment doubted it. Not only are we next-in-line, we're also the sole heirs.

KRULL. Yet *factum* is more solid than prospect, hope, or conjecture. Let me embrace you.

FANNY. At last you find time for a kiss?

KRULL *kisses her fleetingly.*

FANNY. Of course, with us, she'll last a hundred years.

KRULL. Blessed with kidney trouble and worn-out bronchial tubes. But to be serious.

FANNY. I know what you're going to say.

KRULL. After all, she tosses a fortune into our laps. It's only just and fair that she have a substantial equivalent in return.

FANNY. I'd rather renounce this whole inheritance business. How many years of submissive waiting . . .

KRULL, *excited.* There you are! Only a woman would utter such sinful babble. It's monstrous, disgusting. Because it's so irrational.

FANNY, *frightened.* Henry.

KRULL. Oh, you! You never think of anything but yourself. You renounce, you don't want to. Mind you, there's a child whose future I can't secure on thin air, even if you fail to consider me. What in the world do you have in the way of subsidies and resources to fall back on? How dare you renounce so perfunctorily a substantial inheritance exceeding by far all expectations? Rothschild & Co., a plague on them, don't hesitate to step over anyone—we know that. Caesar-like instincts are denied our kind. We must overreach and adapt: that is the way of the world. I like him who rumbles against it. What a wealth of flattery and humiliation have I invested on this valiant frigate! And am I less than you? Have I less pride?

FANNY. We can manage with your income. Your pension will cover Lydia and me.

KRULL. So I should slave away that Madame may bolster her pride. Fantastic!

FANNY. You know me from childhood on, and should realize my opinion was never for sale. Not even to father, who wanted to crush my defiance.

KRULL. He didn't thrash you often enough!

FANNY. Henry!

KRULL. I'm boiling over. My early youth was spent in the most straitened circumstances, uncared for; my adolescence on scholarships and free board. All my life I've flattered and knuckled under. But of all people who have begrudged me a bite, the old maid has demanded the least in return.

FANNY. And why?

KRULL. Why?

FANNY. Because I'm with you—and was with you while Sidonie was still alive. Because I took over Sidonie's place. She would have devoured you long ago but for fear of my claws.

KRULL. She respects my manly convictions.

FANNY. Ha!

KRULL. She never forced anything upon me when I knew what I wanted—not to mention honor and reputation.

FANNY. If she hadn't sensed that I was ready to fight for life and death at your side, she would have annihilated you.

KRULL. You mean to say that I can't stand my ground as a man? That I'm tossed between you like a quivering shred of meat over which you two wrestle? Have you both lost all reason? Why don't you leave me alone? The measure of my feeling bestowed on you and her is left to my own judgment.

FANNY. I love you.

KRULL. What in the last analysis does this hundred-times repeated, empty twaddle mean? You've dug your fangs into
my flesh to satisfy your lust—and what do you do for me,
what?

FANNY. I protect you from her.

KRULL. And she claims she protects me from you. Don't fool
yourself. I myself am the beginning and the end—not you
or her. Come a jot too close and I'll smash the both of you.

FANNY. The strongbox. . .

KRULL. Ho, ho, ho! The strongbox! Each of you carries her
own on lifted palms, and shows it to me from morning till
night with the alluring call, "Come, little one, come, heh-
heh-heh. I've lost my medallion deep down my bosom."
Ha, ha, ha, ha. And I serve myself from there. But no
hole is so deep I'd get lost penetrating the bottom.

FANNY. She overpowers you, degrades and unmans you.

KRULL. What a grotesque imagination! Little woman . . .

FANNY, *beside herself.* Stop it! I hate you and her.

KRULL. Good. Then for the last time: peace, consideration,
and quiet.

FANNY. Legacy-hunter!

KRULL. You wish to despise me for that!

FANNY. Boundlessly. And teach her, too!

KRULL. Will she despise me for that? No. Both alternatives
leave me cold.

FANNY. Monster!

She storms out and slams the door behind her.

KRULL. Women! Either let them realize that I see through
their little tricks and bedevilments which they perform for
my enjoyment, or let them rest in hell. Willfulness, maybe,
and pranks staged on their own behalf, might not be so
bad. The strongbox—splendid requisite. Simply to continue
to care for it stimulates my imagination, makes me still
more covetous.

At his desk, turning pages in a book.

After so kaleidoscopic a rigmarole, a passage from a law-book is like manna from heaven: "Forest management must make it their highest principle to focus on permanent yield of the state woodlands." Is that not as smooth as Kant for a basis, as grandiose and vital a presence as Goethe? Should one not kiss the lawgiver's feet? Permanent yield: the highest principle. Future secure as God himself. And what majestic feeling of responsibility! You give us your money; we take care of your interests forever. Delicious! It melts the tongue. Here, ladies, are my roots. On such spirits, I lean—not to be pulled down by ropes, even if all of you pull together. Or: "It is the task of forest management to achieve highest possible production within the framework of existing rights." To chop down. Within the framework of existing rights. Attention, First Commissioner of Woods and Forests. You want to chop down pines over there, but that neighbor is entitled to the protection guaranteed his fields. Is it recorded in the registry of landed property? Commissioner, it is. *Absto.* Bravo! I have the honor . . . Halloo, halloo . . . hullabaloo. . . .

SCENE 4

ELSPETH *enters.* You're in a good mood. Illness fully subdued?

KRULL. Illness, pooh! My organism runs on steel rails. I'm unruly as an animal in the woods. Hoo-hoo-hoo!

He bounds over to her.

ELSPETH. What new tricks are you up to?

KRULL. Trained in freedom, I swing from branch to branch, hissing *Boreas* out of crevasses in the earth.

ELSPETH. You're so refreshed, it would seem you've reconsidered my advice re Fanny.

KRULL. A little, perhaps.

ELSPETH. All joking aside. Silkenband?

KRULL. Done away with.

ELSPETH. Waives payment?

KRULL. Absolutely. A picture of a man, by the way. A Don

Juan and skirt-chaser of the first rank, it goes without saying.

ELSPETH. Your wife was on the steps with him yesterday. She is careless. Do you recall that time when, still a young girl, she stayed out all night because you had offended her? And took refuge with your friend Bilse?

KRULL. But Bilse, chaste as Joseph, planted a lily by the virgin and covered his loins with aspen leaves.

ELSPETH. You're not in your right mind. How can your assurance that Silkenband renounces all claims have any validity under such circumstances?

She goes into her room, leaving the door open.

KRULL. It certainly has! It was devilishly difficult to bully him into this agreement. A contentious chap. You'd never believe how rude I had to get, even threatening at the end. Photographers and druggists are an abomination to me. *Vix me retineo.*

ELSPETH'S VOICE. But where are the pictures?

KRULL. What?

ELSPETH, *in the door.* The pictures from my desk—they're gone! Ask Emma.

KRULL. But—

ELSPETH. They were in the middle drawer. No one else enters my room.

KRULL. But the pictures are—

ELSPETH. What?

KRULL. With Silkenband.

ELSPETH. You mean?

KRULL. Of course.

ELSPETH. But that's theft. Right out of my desk. Burglary!

KRULL. But my dear aunt. . .

ELSPETH. Who had the nerve to touch my things?

KRULL. It's understandable that Silkenband must—

ELSPETH. Silkenband? Rummaging about in my bureaus? So it was him!

KRULL. Not him. I said—

ELSPETH. But you spoke as —

KRULL. I meant, he was ready to—

ELSPETH. To steal the pictures out of a locked drawer?

KRULL. To take them back without payment. The key was in the keyhole. And after my explanation, it was only natural that I deliver him his property.

ELSPETH. You? You yourself dared touch upon my most private affairs, and rummaged about in secret drawers? Ah, now I know. Now I get the picture. You can't leave the key in the keyhole any more, not even with your nearest kin. For a long time I've had the feeling you were spying on everything I do, that you went through my dirty wash. At last I have the proof in hand.

KRULL. Watch out: you'll drive a saint mad.

ELSPETH. Who gave the order to hand over the pictures?

KRULL. Damn it, you didn't want to pay for them.

ELSPETH *laughs*. Did you ever hear such nonsense? Naturally, no payment. But what should the fellow do with this useless trash? It would take no genius to wheedle the proofs from him.

KRULL. Why should you want pictures that make you look like a slut or a *cocotte?*

ELSPETH. You coined those words. And used in connection with me, they're sheer rudeness.

KRULL. You said "woman of the streets."

ELSPETH. In a word: I feel sorry for you. It's unheard of how you overstepped your authority, deceived my trust, and wronged me grossly. As to your motives—I can't stand the whole business any longer.

KRULL. Neither can I. Not any longer!

They stand close to each other.

ELSPETH. How dare you?

KRULL. So it's my freedom you're after? You tear out my tongue and rip the gall from my intestines. Your meanness is green.

ELSPETH. That shall—

KRULL *with lifted arms.* You press a conglomeration of poisons into your victim, and open wide your nostrils and eyes as the croaking cadaver spews his liquid manure over you. *He grabs her by the shoulders.*

ELSPETH, *hissing.* I must have my pictures this very evening!

KRULL, *shaking her back and forth.* I'll bash your brains in, you spider.

ELSPETH, *gasping.* The pictures, today—

KRULL. I'll toss you through the air, viper! I'll smash your bones!

ELSPETH. The pictures!

KRULL *gasps.* Beast!

He lets go of her. They face each other for a moment, silent, eyes wide open; then ELSPETH *runs into her room and slams the door.*

KRULL *falls into a chair, remains as if stunned; finally he shakes himself, stands up, and says:* Droll little animals. A good drubbing—that's what they need.

Goes to FANNY's *bedroom door, and calls.*

Fanny!

SCENE 5

FANNY's VOICE. I don't want to go to the theater tonight.

KRULL, *in the open door.* There's enough of a show right here in our own house. Go get the pictures back from Silkenband.

FANNY's VOICE, *breaking out in a laugh.* Me?

KRULL. The devil knows what made me return them to that character.

FANNY's VOICE, *still laughing.* Go—to Silkenband?

KRULL. Right away. Beg, bully, cajole them back from him. I won't hear another word of it, and will not breathe until I see them in your hands.

FANNY, *appearing in the doorway.* Go to Silkenband—to his place? To this—

KRULL. This Don Juan—I know. He won't drop into your lap in the foyer.

FANNY. Never!

KRULL. Have you lost your senses? She wants them back. You see me falling into despair. I can hardly summon up words any more. Out and upstairs to him!

FANNY. Not for anything in the world.

KRULL, *beside himself.* Must I drag you up there by the hair? Hang myself here in the corner before your eyes? Croak? Do you think you're playing with someone who's lost control of his senses?

FANNY. Go to him? Me? What would he think. . . ?

KRULL, *shouting out.* Heaven, Earth, Hell! Let him think himself into unconsciousness. But return the pictures he must! The pictures!

He has pushed her toward the outside door.

FANNY. He'll make me—

KRULL. "Me," always "me"—while I perish in madness! Out! Up to him!

FANNY. Henry!

KRULL, *with raised fist, not giving in.* Forward, march!

FANNY *in the already opened door.*

Do your utmost. And back as soon as possible!

FANNY *has disappeared through the door, which slams shut after her.*

Bitches! They need a good drubbing!

He rushes to ELSPETH's *door and knocks.*

Open. Open up!

As no answer ensues, he says to himself.

The habitual affectations.

Aloud.

Auntie, something important!

SCENE 6

ELSPETH *opens the door.* You have the cheek?

KRULL. The pictures, and what is more important: Silkenband promised them for this very evening. What in the world was that ridiculous fuss we just went through? Were we out of our minds?

ELSPETH. Not *you,* certainly!

KRULL. Does such a thing have to happen between people who like and need each other? Don't fool yourself into believing that, Auntie! Why do you wish to play the thorny comedy all through to its dénouement in a locked-up room, perhaps without supper? I extend my hand over the abyss. We'll both profit thereby.

ELSPETH. Have you come to your senses?

KRULL. No, to perfect insight. All cheap deviltry blown away. You see through me, and I'm no longer ashamed of the thoughts I just had. Isn't it possible to live together on this basis?

ELSPETH. All consequences really taken into consideration?

KRULL. Most solemn promise self-guaranteed, since there'd be no escaping your pitiless stand.

ELSPETH. I want to enjoy my wealth.

KRULL. No determined spirit would renounce that. It is not, I concede, baseness of sentiment but intelligence, adjustment to the laws of the world.

ELSPETH. I'm the one who counts in this house.

KRULL. One hundred and forty thousand marks are etched into my brain and weigh down the scales of decision from now on.

ELSPETH. I not only say: a lot of money. We know what that means. A dress costs eighty marks, a horse eight hundred, a small house about eight thousand.

KRULL. If you want to buy an important book: twenty marks —and then you don't have them.

ELSPETH. To see a performance, take a trip—for all these, always only a few hundred were lacking in life.

KRULL. *Basta!* Not another word. With me, it's facts that count.

ELSPETH. That is to say—in future you shall take the strong-box and hold it in custody.

KRULL. You mean it?

ELSPETH *goes into her room, returns with the strongbox and hands it to him.* But with this word of advice: hide it from your wife. The good soul might take umbrage over it, for reflection is alien to her.

KRULL. I'll hide it from everyone, naturally, and from her especially. Besides, since the money stems from her family, she'd feel it added weight to her voice, and her vanity knows no bounds. The owner's confidence is bestowed on me, not her. Ha, ha! A well-wrought piece, a superb strongbox! Even embossed.

ELSPETH. And here's the key, which you are to return to me. Could you draw up a list of the numbers of the securities for me, preferably right now?

KRULL. With the sincerest pleasure, indeed. I'll lock myself in the bedroom. Should Fanny come, you detain her.

ELSPETH. Isn't she said to have a divinely beautiful bosom?

KRULL *occupied with the strongbox.* How it snaps! A royal locksmith! Plain to see. So: numbers, total of coupons, the whole thing in some detail. With pleasure.

He goes into his bedroom. The key is heard turning as he locks himself in.

ELSPETH *looks at her watch.* Perfect timing.

The bell rings. ELSPETH *goes out to open the door.*

SCENE 7

ELSPETH *and* NOTARY DETTMICHEL *enter.*

ELSPETH. Good day, my dear Notary. Won't you be seated? My uncertain health . . .

DETTMICHEL. Tut-tut!

ELSPETH. Alas—attack after attack—makes it seem advisable to look death in the eye.

DETTMICHEL. Now, now!

ELSPETH. Let's get right down to business. I shall dictate to you.

DETTMICHEL. You don't wish to abstain from the plan you advised me of even in the final hour?

ELSPETH. No.

DETTMICHEL. Nor wait at least until—

ELSPETH. No.

DETTMICHEL. Oh-oh!

ELSPETH. I, Elspeth True . . .

DETTMICHEL *writes.* True . . .

ELSPETH. . . . leave behind a movable fortune of one hundred and forty thousand marks which, bypassing my niece Fanny Krull, née Remmele, I leave in the care of Reverend Pastor Stramm of St. Margaret's here, for the benefit of our All-Redeeming Church.

DETTMICHEL. But, but!

ELSPETH. I pledge to replace this provisional arrangement by a testamentary deed between the Reverend Pastor and myself immediately upon his return from his current vacation.

DETTMICHEL. Really?

ELSPETH. Indeed. Relatives, my dear Notary, are something so disgusting during one's lifetime that dealings with them must be terminated once and for all by death.

DETTMICHEL. Oh dear!

ELSPETH. I've had no inner ties with people in the course of my life. The death of my parents cut the last thread that linked me to human society. Signed: Elspeth True, the fifth of April.

DETTMICHEL. Witnessed by me: Dettmichel, Notary; Sealed!

Curtain.

ACT IV

SCENE 1

LYDIA *at the open balcony door, looking out.* The bold fellow! Should anyone see him, I'd die of shame.

SILKENBAND *appearing outside on the balcony.* A genuine rope helped me up to within a yard of you. Then, one leap, little puss, and . . . How cold the wind blows. . . !

LYDIA. My hero!

SILKENBAND. "The moon shines bright. In such a night as this,
  When the sweet wind did gently kiss the trees
  Troilus methinks mounted the Troyan walls."

Now you must answer:
  "In such a night
  Did Jessica steal from the wealthy Jew."

And then I again:
  "In such a night
  Did young Silkenband swear he loved her well."

Kiss!

He kisses her.

LYDIA. Is that Schiller?

SILKENBAND. Listen, now. I hear a man's footsteps.

LYDIA. Quiet!

They listen.

SILKENBAND. No one's coming. Somebody left. "In such a night"—are not all good, amorous spirits round us awake? Romeo and Juliet—where there is also a balcony. How warm you are!

LYDIA. I just jumped out of bed. To you!

SILKENBAND. Sweet girl.

LYDIA. My heart was in my throat. Auntie sleeps next door. When I crossed the threshold, it squeaked.

SILKENBAND. My window bolt squeaked upstairs.

LYDIA. We must flee into seclusion—away from everyone.

SILKENBAND. Later. In the off season. I have too much to do now. Of course, I don't care much about that, but the first years, particularly, you can't lay off.

LYDIA. Away to a lonely island.

SILKENBAND. How soft and round you are!

LYDIA. An Aeolian lyre hanging in the trees. I heard one once in a park with peacocks and ponds. Alphonse, it was indescribable.

SILKENBAND. You Dresden doll. Just my type. Instead of the island, let's go to Paris where you get swallowed up among a million people, and can disappear from humanity, into a hotel, on the boulevards, *clair obscur, à travers les Champs-Elysées.* . . .

LYDIA. Ah, Paris! The boulevards! Heavens! Are you as happy as I am?

SILKENBAND. Ravishingly! Enough to go out of my mind, sweetie! You emanate such warmth, it kindles a wonderful flame within me.

LYDIA. Say something poetic like before.

SILKENBAND. Shall we sing?

LYDIA. So that all the world comes running.

SILKENBAND. Trill a little scale. Your soprano excites me.

LYDIA. They'd all hear me.

SILKENBAND. An F-sharp. A kingdom for an F-sharp.

LYDIA, *her arms around his neck.* Sweetheart, madman!

SILKENBAND. Open your lovely little mouth, chirp, whisper gently, but let me hear you! Oh, your arched tongue, your oval lips; let it come forth.

LYDIA *softly sings a few notes.*

SILKENBAND. How that inflames me! What expressivity!

He embraces her.

LYDIA, *passionately.* Beloved!

SILKENBAND. Doll face!

They hear steps, and SILKENBAND *pulls* LYDIA *out onto the balcony.*

SCENE 2

KRULL *enters, looks around on all sides, sneaks through the room to his desk, which he opens, and pulls out the strongbox.* Not the best place. Better behind the secretary during the day. I won't find real peace of mind until the house is empty a few days and I'm able to make a safe hole in the wall. For days now I've felt her eyes on me. She wants to read my secrets from my forehead. But you'd rather rip out my innards. Only in bed, at night, are you mine, do I possess you in peace.

Goes with the strongbox into his bedroom.

SCENE 3

ELSPETH *comes out of her room immediately thereafter. Scuttles over to the desk and opens it.* He's wandering about with it again, he's wandering. . . . Now to get some sleep.

Rubbing her hands, she goes back to her room.

SCENE 4

SILKENBAND. Does everyone in this house sleepwalk at night?

LYDIA. You saw the strongbox?

SILKENBAND. He mumbled something over it, and pressed it against his body. What's it all about? What's inside?

LYDIA. Auntie's entire fortune, which he administers. It's supposed to be much larger than we anticipated.

SILKENBAND. Right. He talked about Bavarian securities.

LYDIA. She's piled up a fortune.

SILKENBAND. The old mole! So, all of you—you're all rich
then?

LYDIA. In your love.

SILKENBAND. And I in yours.

Embrace.

LYDIA. I must go back to bed. Father will return! Farewell,
my hero! What did you say the first time you left me?

SILKENBAND. Sweetie pie!

LYDIA. Make it a foreign word, because I'm an individuality.

SILKENBAND. Individual what?

LYDIA. Oh, I've forgotten. Farewell! How'll you get back?

SILKENBAND. Up the rope again.

LYDIA. Quiet!

They step back onto the balcony.

SCENE 5

FANNY *enters in nightgown, goes over to* KRULL's *door, and
peeps through the keyhole.* Light! Sitting up again, staring
at the monster that now takes my place in his bed. Throttled by a woman stronger than I. I could have measured
my strength against any other woman, but not against this
one. She has a firmer grip on him than the greatest beauty.

Sits down on a chair next to the door.

He doesn't see me. Not even my boldest, most seductive
pose can strike a spark in him. Gone. All is lost. But at
thirty, one isn't dead. What am I to do with myself, with
my life?

She looks through the keyhole again.

He seems to have turned gray. Weren't you younger a
few weeks ago when you passionately desired me and
ravishingly took me? Or was that another man? Was I—
was he bewitched? What should I do? I bear no grudge
against you—I'm just starved.

She goes back into her room.

SCENE 6

SILKENBAND. Quick, back into your cubbyhole! Really, there's
some commotion here today.

LYDIA. Now I have it: Nirvana!

SILKENBAND. I'm frozen through and through.

LYDIA. Didn't I warm you?

SILKENBAND. In the beginning. Go now! Danger ahead. And
do your best to find out more about the strongbox.

They kiss and LYDIA *slips into her room.*

A divine, truly sublime woman, this Fanny.

FANNY *comes back.* What if I were to try for the last time
and beg for my rights and my lawful place down on my
knees?

At the keyhole.

No! This man is no lover.

SILKENBAND, *stepping up to her brusquely.*

FANNY *emits a hushed scream.*

Hush! Quiet, not another word. Don't lie again to my face
about your love for this strange saint. No more of that.
God let me in on your secret, Fanny. Don't ask questions.
Not a sound . . .

FANNY. How did you come?

SILKENBAND. Down a rope to the window, and then flung
myself over the balcony. I love you. I burn, overflowing
with happiness, my senses aroused.

FANNY. The strongbox . . . You know?

SILKENBAND. Everything!

FANNY. He deceives me with that thing!* My love is nipped
in the bud.

SILKENBAND. Worse. A colossus of clay. A madman!

---

* Also "with *her*" in the original, since *"ihr"* stands for both persons and things. Fanny refers here to the strongbox, of course.

FANNY. My young heart choked. I must live!

SILKENBAND. Beloved, someone's coming. I'm lost. Hide me.
Both off quickly into FANNY's *room.*

KRULL *appears, lantern in hand. He steps up to* FANNY's *door.*
She's awake. No security inside. No peace. She might come
to the keyhole and spy on me. I'd better sit here at my
desk. If she comes, I can easily make up something.

*He places the strongbox on the desk, opens it, and lights
the lantern.*

We had the key copied by a master locksmith. Opens it
without a sound. Amazing to see rolls of gold specie transformed into sheets of paper that yield interest, for which
business the state maintains an army of bureaucrats.
Why doesn't the State itself, as entrepreneur, apply
this manpower to real work, pay for it from the proceeds
of the sale, and pocket the surplus? Why does it allow any
foreigner who wants these papers to take shares the same
as its own nationals? And thereby destroy—since they're
all closely tied to their business and their fortunes—the
very concept of a state? Millions of these papers are afloat
in France, but millions of French and English† bonds
are invested with us. Are not Germans affected by a Rus-
sian-English‡ war? Do they not fear for the Czar's§ mili-
tary victory, regardless of whom he fights? What counter-
mining of patriotic feeling by state government! What
schizophrenia in its well-to-do citizenry! Further: won't
the man in the street who has already turned his back on
political unity, but who might still be able to build up
within himself a feeling of great composure, be completely
shattered and destroyed by the host of anonymous societies
to whom he entrusted the remainder of his property? With

† In another edition: "French and Russian"
‡ "   "   "   : "English war"
§ "   "   "   : "King's"

each share of a joint stock company, do I not become further tied to it? Isn't my economic interest fully scattered in all directions? What, in the long run, is my business? For all that, to be responsible to my family, I must now be posted with the most minute and correct information on rubber, artificial fats, and a thousand other items. If I could—if it were possible—I would be politician, soapmaker, machine-builder, electrical engineer, margarine expert, all at one and the same time, naturally along with my real profession of teacher, physician, lawyer, and so on. Giddy I remain: I look back dazzled to the origin of my fortune. Sleepless nights do not orientate me in the least as to its real value. However, I grow strong, filled with exalted feeling. With the halo of prestige that property lends, I stretch out my claws into the world, toward the people, and make them dance in all humility before the chimera! I allow the St. Vitus' dances of the hapless and avaricious, the festive roar of the ignorant and hungry around me, lull the ever-present anxiety I feel for the uncertainty of my property. Your strategy, my good aunt, is admirable. For, whether Bavarian or whether electric shares, I am the essence of your treasure, and the question is: do my capers amuse you sufficiently at four per cent? Still, I swear by the strength of all my soul: I did not realize that in vain; I do not remain idle, but follow you; and my sole pride shall be: where you only moderately enjoy your property, I shall rejoice boundlessly over mine. A past of thirty years' artificial humility has spawned in me an undiminished lust to exploit people. What's that noise?

He goes back to FANNY's *door.*

Are you restless, poor soul? Do you feel lonely and abandoned?

Leaning against the door, with outstretched arms.

Were your nature more alien to me, or your ways more significant; were you more essential to my world-image— I would want, above all, to greedily devour your peculiarities and imbibe your vapors and emanations. But the second time around, mind you! You're too ridiculously familiar to me. Yet I see other, other . . .

He locks up the strongbox, and then, turning toward the aunt's door, says.

Good night, timid little capitalist. I demand twenty—no, fifty per cent dividends! Let my people stand on their heads. Prostitution! Ha, ha, ha, ha! !

He goes into his room.

SCENE 8

Immediately afterward, FANNY *sticks her head out the door. Then* SILKENBAND *appears;* FANNY *disappears.* SILKENBAND *runs to the balcony, tries to pull himself up on the rope, and falls down noisily.*

KRULL *appears again and finds him.* Aha! Sir, what is this? For whom are you looking?

SILKENBAND. I come to request your daughter's hand. Don't be surprised. To justify my claim for the extraordinary on so exalted an occasion, I had to come this way.

KRULL, *sizing him up carefully.* You reek romance all over. *Slowly, after a pause.*

In life, one can capitalize a great deal on the imagination of others. Bravo! It might be arranged. Approach, young man!

Curtain.

ACT V

SCENE 1

All seated around the table.

SILKENBAND. From Paris to Genoa via the French Riviera— which made a staggering impression on Lydia.

LYDIA. Darling, I had my migraine in Genoa.

SILKENBAND. And Florence! Florence at last . . .

LYDIA. Tell them how the druggist gave me a quarter gram of calomel instead of a tenth of a gram, and how it almost made me—

SILKENBAND. More about that later. Briefly, for men of culture —they say: see Florence and die. *La fiorenza*, Botticelli, Raphael, and, above all, Michelangelo, *il divino*. I received, I dare say, decisive artistic inspiration. But more about that later.

LYDIA. I sampled too much Falerner.

SILKENBAND. Chianti, my dove.

LYDIA. With my constitution—you can imagine the consequences.

KRULL. With all this chianti and calomel—the trip must have cost a fortune.

SILKENBAND. It did indeed. But more about that later. I received, I must say, decisive artistic inspiration.

KRULL. Aha!

ELSPETH. Did you thoroughly photograph the regions you traversed?

SILKENBAND. Few photos were taken. My profession became repulsive to me in that free artistic atmosphere. I longed for something higher.

ELSPETH. Oh, is that so?

KRULL. Aha!

SILKENBAND. Here's what I've brought.

He spreads a few photographs on the table.

Meanwhile, FANNY *and* LYDIA *have got up and gone over to the other side of the room.*

FANNY, *in an undertone.* How was it otherwise with you?

LYDIA. He's brutal.

FANNY. He deceives you?

LYDIA. Yes. And I'm with child.

FANNY. Have you proof of his deception?

LYDIA. He tells me himself. He claims he needs it for artistic inspiration, now that he wants to become a painter.

SILKENBAND. All in all, the trip was—

KRULL. Artistically decisive for you. You said that three times.

FANNY. With what kind of women?

LYDIA. With all kinds. On top of that, my migraine.

FANNY. Come in!

They go into FANNY's *room.*

KRULL. My dear boy, you've knocked about a great deal at our expense. We expected longer letters from you; and hoped the whims of your fancy would let us enjoy from afar the two countries you were seeing.

ELSPETH. Indeed.

KRULL. We didn't get much.

SILKENBAND. I was extraordinarily preoccupied with myself and my inner experiences.

KRULL. Your romantic disposition raises hopes for pleasant surprises. But so far our yield has been meager. Let's hope you have a big surprise in store for us today.

SILKENBAND. What do you mean by that?

KRULL. That artistic inspiration you mentioned so often— that inner emotional shock—may well have crystallized into a kind of decision which better reveals the core of a human being than letters from abroad. You hold us in suspense.

SILKENBAND. You confuse me.

KRULL. Why?

SILKENBAND. After all, if there is revolt and development within me, that remains my private affair.

KRULL. We're of a different opinion.

SILKENBAND. Yes, but—

KRULL. It was the range of your imagination that impressed me the night you fell onto my balcony. When I spoke to Miss True about you, this factor tipped the scales in your favor.

ELSPETH. Precisely.

KRULL. And it secured you a favorable place in the world
picture we create for ourselves. You mustn't suddenly let
us down now.

SILKENBAND. Damn it, that's an attack on my liberty.

ELSPETH. Hee-hee-hee!

KRULL. Haw-haw-haw!

ELSPETH. Once again, dear Henry, we're so much of the
same opinion in this matter that it suffices if one of us
comes to an understanding with Mr. Silkenband.

KRULL. Right.

ELSPETH *rises.* Until later, then, Henry.

KRULL *kisses her on the forehead.* Have a nice evening, dearest Aunt.

ELSPETH *goes into her room.*

Now to the point! We find your life with its piquant
impromptus so attractive that we intend to keep you in
mind. You are smart and agile. Come to decisions we can
enjoy.

SILKENBAND. But I wasn't born to give you pleasure.

KRULL. One must be older than you to discern the core of a
relationship between man and man. Let's keep to what's
visible. In short: you rebel?

SILKENBAND. Lifted above daily demands, I discovered the
deep-seated need of my life.

KRULL. Not bad. And then?

SILKENBAND. I'm simply fed up with slavery—I want to be a
painter.

KRULL. Excellent. A bewildering constellation—complication
of your destiny. You have no idea, young man, how I have
raised this situation, in itself ridiculously insignificant, to
the highest significance.

SILKENBAND. To Hell with this cunning sophistry. I want only
your opinion.

KRULL. How divinely put, my son!

SILKENBAND. Drop it! Well, then?

KRULL. Most violent opposition on my part.

SILKENBAND. What?

KRULL, *amused.* But that's self-evident. Not only for reasons you can grasp: because I'm a father, and your business supports my daughter. . . .

SILKENBAND. Sir, that is. . . ?

KRULL. You're marvelous. Be honest: not once did your worm's-eye view lead you to expect consent.

SILKENBAND. Not unconditionally. However, your manner . . .

KRULL, *laughing.* Rejection is rejection.

SILKENBAND. I don't give a damn.

KRULL *puts on his overcoat and hat.*

SILKENBAND, *close to him.* Listen, I don't give a damn what you think, do you understand?

KRULL. Yes! Only thus is development possible. I'm curious for more. Good evening.

He leaves.

SILKENBAND *hits the table.* Beastly, unheard of.

SCENE 2

FANNY *enters.*

SILKENBAND. What's the matter? ! World history doesn't know the abyss of rudeness. I've fallen into a den of robbers. I'm in chains, bruised by fetters. Give me air!

FANNY. Did I say too much?

SILKENBAND. Lord God in Heaven—what's to be done now?

FANNY. A clean slate with united forces. Didn't you forget me within three weeks? Didn't you deceive me?

SILKENBAND. I remained chaste as Joseph.

FANNY. Your wife is pregnant.

SILKENBAND. Just imagine.

FANNY. What about the blonde chambermaid in the Hotel Artois?

SILKENBAND. Invented along with many another because of Lydia—so as not to leave her with any illusions, right from the beginning.

FANNY. Words and oaths do not convince me. What will?

SILKENBAND. Nature.

About to embrace her.

FANNY. Careful! We can be seen here.

SILKENBAND. I'm burning. Conviction should flow from my blood into yours.

FANNY. Sweet male passion to which I succumb for my earthly existence. Boundless desire awaits you when everybody's asleep.

SILKENBAND. I'm coming. But first I must square accounts with him.

FANNY. Our position in the house is at stake once and for all. We are backed up against the wall. Throttled. Show your iron will!

SILKENBAND. This professor is a megalomaniac rascal.

FANNY. The strongbox went to his head.

SILKENBAND. Let it be filled with the riches of Croesus—I'll go on loving his wife anyway. The fool, the horned idiot. He doesn't mock me; I mock him. And will be a painter in spite of him. Should remarkable talents be stunted by such boors? I burst like ripe fruit before the masterpieces of the Renaissance. Tremendous potentials for works of art emerge from the bottom of the pit.

FANNY. And I'm your muse, your model!

SILKENBAND. I'll show these philistines a lion's claw. Gigantic problems and complexes slumber within me. No arguments. Simply a few incontestable truths tossed in his face.

FANNY. Tonight—when he comes back from the tavern.

SILKENBAND. At the door. I'll take Lydia up and return pronto.

FANNY. And the victor will find me awake, blissfully aroused by him. Do you remember what I look like?

SILKENBAND. The freckle on a certain spot? Drives me out of my mind. Heavenly lips!

FANNY. A punch in the nose for him!

SILKENBAND. I'll let him have it.

SCENE 3

LYDIA *enters, yawning.* Are we going up, darling?

FANNY. You were overcome by fatigue and fell asleep in there.

LYDIA. My migraine will return again. How happy I am to be back in my own house! And it's so peaceful when Alphonse comes home late. Two bedrooms in a hotel were too expensive for us. And what a surprise to find Emma, who knows me and the house, in our service. How sweet of Alphonse!

SILKENBAND. Be careful. Look after yourself.

LYDIA *to* FANNY. I give him a lot of trouble. I never thought I was so frail.

FANNY. Alphonse must take a stand against Aunt True. She'll use father to help curtail his liberty.

LYDIA. Oh, this Aunt! Mother always warned us about her. You can count on me unconditionally in the battle against her. I stand shoulder to shoulder with both of you.

SILKENBAND. Bravo!

LYDIA. If only my migraine would pass.

FANNY. Maybe marriage doesn't agree with you.

LYDIA. The doctor in Paris didn't think quite that. Only, one should keep within bounds. Good night.

Leaves with SILKENBAND.

FANNY. I hope Henry returns in time.

SCENE 4

ELSPETH *enters.* I learned by chance that you can get almond eggs on Horse Street for ninety-five pfennig.

FANNY. Let's keep on getting them from Rohlfing's for one mark ten. They're better.

ELSPETH. Don't you find their coffee weaker now?

FANNY. No. Anything else?

ELSPETH. Had we nothing else to discuss? Twenty-five years ago, Fanny . . .

FANNY. That's pretty far back. The past has little value.

ELSPETH. How very true. Only what's still in store for us . . .

FANNY. . . . matters.

ELSPETH. Correct. Eggs, coffee, just like before . . .

FANNY. No change, as long as it's feasible.

ELSPETH. You can find a rotten egg in every lot.

FANNY. Of course! In that case, just take another one. Good night.

She leaves.

ELSPETH. What is the new generation coming to?

Goes into her room.

SCENE 5

After a moment, KRULL *and* SILKENBAND *appear.*

KRULL. When I unlocked the gate, I was prepared to see you suddenly pop up out of the cellar.

SILKENBAND. Please, expect less from the vehemence of gesture than from the penetrating force of inner conviction.

KRULL. After spotting me, you took three or four steps at a time and cornered me in the half-open door.

SILKENBAND. In short—we resume our arguments where we left off.

KRULL. You don't give a damn for my opinion?

SILKENBAND. Not in the least.

KRULL. Capital! Settled. Good night.

SILKENBAND. I must insist that you discontinue this conde-
scending classroom tone with me.

He moves toward KRULL. KRULL *retreats.*

I demand that you respect my views, or else a thousand
devils will upset the applecart. I warn you right from the
start, I'm a brutal, hot-tempered man.

KRULL, *standing behind the table.* Got a revolver on you?

SILKENBAND. Even without a weapon I'll make my intentions
clear to the last dot. As I've already informed you: I'm
going to be a painter.

KRULL. When I was twenty, I wrote defiant plays. *Mucius
Scaevola* still lies in my desk. Do you want to hear it?

SILKENBAND. Well, I'm not twenty years old. And this isn't
based on nonsense I scribbled at twenty, but on revelations
emanating from the works of the divine Michelangelo.
From the entire cinquecento.

KRULL. Seicento. For fifteen hundred so and so, we say
seicento.

SILKENBAND. Which doesn't alter the picture one iota. Suddenly my eyes opened up to what I really am. What do
you say to that?

*He has propped a small painting up against the back of a
chair.*

KRULL. Asparagus!

SILKENBAND. Step back a bit. Left eye closed, head askew.
He maneuvers him into this position.

And now?

KRULL. Asparagus.

SILKENBAND. Huh?

KRULL. It's still asparagus. But now I open my left eye again,
and see better with both.

SILKENBAND. What?

KRULL. Why only asparagus? I thought you'd offer me a cruci-fixion, or Plato's *Banquet*, at least.

SILKENBAND. We don't paint literature any more. We keep strictly to Nature. Expressionism.

KRULL. Well, if it must be Nature, my dear man, I'd know something better to pick. Where did you get asparagus in September?

SILKENBAND. I painted it from memory.

KRULL. Really? So it wasn't edible to begin with, this painted asparagus? In that case, you could paint lunch and dinner.

SILKENBAND. I'll soon be in a position to support my family even if I give up photography.

KRULL. Until then, not a pfennig from me.

SILKENBAND. Sir! Would you commit a deadly sin by stifling a divinely endowed talent? Didn't you derive enough genu-ine learning from the chaos of your quaint erudition to realize the thorny paths famous artists have to tread? Shall another one suffer this time because of you? Sir, I swear on the— You completely throw me. I don't know myself any more.

He threatens him.

KRULL, *retreating.* Not a pfennig!

SILKENBAND, *after him.* Money!

KRULL, *retreating.* Not one peseta!

SILKENBAND, *after him, shouting.* An allowance!

KRULL, *jumping over the desk.* Not a sou!

ELSPETH *and* FANNY *open their doors and watch the antagonists.*

SILKENBAND, *chasing the fleeing* KRULL. I'll make pulp of him yet!

He seizes a book and throws it at KRULL. *All of a sudden he runs toward the chair on which the painting is propped and falls, dragging the chair and the painting down to the floor with him.*

KRULL, *standing at some distance.* Magnificent!

ELSPETH *and* FANNY *have disappeared.*

SILKENBAND, *yelling.* My knee!

KRULL. Ha!

SILKENBAND. I'm hurt, wounded. Help me up.

KRULL. Do it yourself.

SILKENBAND. Can't be done.

KRULL. You're fooling?

SILKENBAND. Hell, no!

KRULL. But if you're up to something . . .

SILKENBAND. Don't make any conditions with me.

KRULL. You mean, the war's over?

SILKENBAND. I swear, I'm weak as a child.

KRULL *approaches and bends over him.* Evidently a broken kneecap.

SILKENBAND. That'd be some joke!

KRULL. You jump clumsily. You should lift your feet higher.

SILKENBAND. That idiotic painting was in the way.

KRULL. Could be a compound fracture of the thigh.

SILKENBAND. I can stretch the leg.

KRULL. Really?

SILKENBAND. Also bend it. It doesn't seem to be so bad as all that.

KRULL. I thought it was an epileptic fit, at first. Do you have a tendency?

SILKENBAND. No.

KRULL. You were foaming at the mouth.

SILKENBAND. With rage.

KRULL. Still, at the climax of the effect, it could—

SILKENBAND. Never. You must have a tendency for it. Here, let me sit for a moment. It'll pass.

KRULL *guides the limping man to a chair.* Let's be quiet. It's late. The women are asleep.

He sits down at the desk, away from SILKENBAND, *and pulls out the strongbox.*

SILKENBAND. Halloo!

KRULL. I beg your pardon?

SILKENBAND. So that's the famous strongbox.

KRULL. Right. Well, this is it.

SILKENBAND. I'll have to make cold compresses. We've heard all kinds of things about it. It's supposed to contain more than one thought in one's boldest dreams.

KRULL. Well, well. What, in the final analysis, can match a dream?

SILKENBAND. Still. . .

KRULL. Yes, let's say: still.

SILKENBAND. The kneecap works again.

KRULL, *with strongbox in hand, steps close up to him.* Peculiar intaglio on the lid.

SILKENBAND. That's a much stronger box than the black cardboard boxes I handle. Symbol of bourgeois prosperity.

KRULL. Bourgeois prosperity. Had you any idea, Silkenband, how delightful that can be?

SILKENBAND. And how! When you come from a poor background . . .

KRULL. You, too?

SILKENBAND. Father made barely enough to feed five hungry mouths.

KRULL. And when he got sick, we had no idea where the next mouthful was coming from. But this strongbox is . . .

SILKENBAND. . . . warm as an oven. It's cold as the dickens outside, but here we sit in clover.

KRULL. You and your artistic instincts!

SILKENBAND. Mind you, even artists can earn good money.

KRULL. Your studio brings in about five thousand marks a year?

SILKENBAND. Over six thousand.

KRULL. My hat's off to you!

SILKENBAND. Still, there's a whale of a difference between hard-earned money and annuities.

KRULL. Words cannot express that, my friend.

SILKENBAND. *You* have, I'm a have-not.

KRULL. Only Bavarian government bonds, because of interest guarantees in timber reserves.

SILKENBAND. That's what you must thoroughly explain to me. It keeps haunting me at night. Brings my fatherland back to me. Who would have thought this of Bavaria!

KRULL. How is it such things excite you!

SILKENBAND. Amazing! Standing in front of a bank window, you understand. I wasn't twelve years old yet; eyes like teacups, I tell you. Boy, said my mother, gold is nothing. It's securities that count. And there I read: "Imperial Loan, Railway Priority." A shiver ran down my back, like facing wild animals in cages. I was downright shaken.

KRULL. Open up!

SILKENBAND *opens the strongbox.* Good God . . . dear father-in-law . . . really . . .

KRULL. Now, my boy?

SILKENBAND. Yes, say— Oh, my God . . . you . . .

KRULL. Eyes filled with tears!

SILKENBAND. My wretched youth . . . father's grief . . . the bailiff . . . How my mother suffered.

KRULL. Ho, my little boy, ho!

SILKENBAND. How the mind broadens and assumes world shape.

KRULL. Ho! Ho! Ho!

SILKENBAND. It's enough to leap with joy and bark with pleasure!

KRULL. Huh?! Huh?!

SILKENBAND, *half crying.* Right you are! A thousand times over! A thousand times. *Basta!*

KRULL *takes the strongbox from him and goes toward his bedroom.*

With your permission. I'd like to take the liberty of keeping you company while you retire. You clarify, you deepen my insight into these things; I have watched with admiration how you've immersed yourself in this matter.

KRULL. I have, I may safely say, gone far toward reaching the essential. Yet many a gulf still lies between me and my goal.

SILKENBAND. Enlightened by your kindness, I might be of some service, perhaps.

KRULL, *at the door.* If you please!

SILKENBAND. After you, of course, after you! How could I. . . ?

He follows KRULL *into the bedroom. The door closes behind them. The following words of* KRULL *can be distinguished:*

. . . through reforestation . . . ameliorization . . . world trade.

Meanwhile FANNY *opens her door, closes it, then opens and closes it again. Finally,* SILKENBAND *emerges. In the doorway, he takes* KRULL's *outstretched hand, with a deep bow.*

KRULL. Leave that to our further discretion. The decisions will be made known forthwith.

SILKENBAND. In the meantime, my most humble thanks. And, once again— no offense meant! *Basta?*

KRULL. *Basta! Sunt pueri pueri.* Boys will be boys.

He closes the door.

SILKENBAND, *alone on stage.* Pupillary security. Unlimited possibilities. Good Lord!

With vague gestures, he leaves the room, as if in a trance. Immediately after, FANNY *peeps out from her door and shuts it again.*

Curtain.

JOB

A DRAMA

1917

by Oskar Kokoschka

Translated by
Walter H. and Jacqueline Sokel

CHARACTERS

JOB	EROS
ANIMA, *his wife*	CHAMBERMAID
MR. RUBBERMAN	YOUNG LADIES
ADAM, *the gardener*	GENTLEMEN
	PARROT

Motto: A pain for a rib

When Adam slept on the green lawn,
God had pity, the sun stood at zenith
And He from boredom was about to sleep.
Awaken'd by a kick in his ribs, Adam cried: "Hi,"
And found himself wedded to Eve:
"My God, if only He had left my rib in peace."

FIRST ACT

JOB, *in nightcap and dressing gown, knocks at the door of his wife's room.*

CHAMBERMAID *sticks her head cautiously out the other door, hiding something behind her back.* I've been knocking and now I'm asking, sir, if you could not take something off my back. Madam has given it to me with two kicks on my backside; it's garnished with plumage and talons, tongue and beak. Her Ladyship herself went out already this morning with the young gentleman, he's handsome as a picture. This feathered thing here she has left you, sir, for your amusement.

She launches a PARROT *from a basket. The* PARROT *flies upon* JOB's *shoulder.*

CHAMBERMAID *exits trilling.* 'Tis the balmy summer night—
Vanished and sighing from a deep crevasse.
It lubricates tongues, it puts the salt in tears—
The blond lock of hair weaves and spins its web behind
the flickering flame—
Ensnares the heroes versed in dangers. . . .

JOB. But I thought she had just been here?

Pointing to the door.

She bartered her virginity for a soul—slipped from one man to the next. And leaves the skull when it's picked clean.

Points to his forehead.

Here where she nested she has quickly, even in her flight, deposited an egg, from which she leaps restored, like a phoenix. — I wish no sun to rise, no skies to loom with castles before which sphinxes converse! . . .

PARROT *flies with one flap onto* JOB's *head while* JOB *is pacing up and down.*

Woe to the youth whom she seeks to spiritualize, until he starts talking with my tongue.

Falls into a chair.

Once long ago, from the Creator's head leaped forth the Mother of Creation, secretly hiding in her womb his world.

PARROT *tears at his hair.*

Ai, Ai, my head! In a jiffy gone—where? Ai, *horror vacui! Sings.*

How love has twisted me since in this empty house a gentle woman's voice has called to me to search for her— has vexed me into a labyrinth. From it an echo teases, and a breeze of air makes me run helter-skelter everywhere. "As ye sow, ye are like to reap." Because in a moment's breath she metamorphoses by some back door into a creature that—is I myself!

ANIMA *singing behind the door.*

JOB *does not hear her, plays with the bird, entices it on his finger.* What is man's favorite—amusement?

PARROT, *imitating the female voice.* Anima—your soul, your wife—for such was meant.

JOB. My soul! Her naughtiness or flight, or whatever I call it, leaves me things to think about that . . . but . . . What name can man call his? Eh?

PARROT. Oh and Amen—Man's woe she is and— Oh, man's Ah!

PARROT *again leaps onto* JOB's *head, and scratches him trustingly.*

JOB. That treacherous woman has gone to my head—talks after my lips, looks out of my eyes, turns my insides out. Turns my outside in!

Shakes the impudent guest who is pecking at his ears.

In short, I'm like a pumpkinhead that must with a mystic halo putrefy in a ditch.

The bird spreads out on JOB's *head and puffs itself up.*

Hope or treachery, you are getting too heavy! Leave me my mind so that I can bear you. I comprehend you! Help! *Softer.*

Isn't that she talking? How. . . ?

ANIMA *echoes.* I can't relieve you—United are we! Eternally —One.

JOB. But tell me for once—in Heaven's name and Hell's—
who you are!

ANIMA *echoes.* Anima I am—your wife! Your soul I am.

JOB. Gone is—"I am"—and what remains—I?
Shaking frantically once more at the doorknob.
I had a wife, she was my world!
With tears.
The edge of the globe I thought I was grasping, then the
ground vanished from under my feet and dominion hangs
in the air like—a pig's bladder! *Horror vacui!*
More composedly.
Even if it remained only a plan, yet it was my world!
Dizzy, stumbles.

ANIMA, *gently, behind the door.* He who does not take care,
who errs in judgment, may lose his head!

JOB, *crossly.* Head or world! I see no difference! My own
words are torn from my mouth! I wish I could believe I
am learning them for the first time! As a sponge absorbs
vinegar, renders it up again without retaining . . .
*Outraged, JOB turns from the door after his efforts to gain
admission have remained futile.*

ANIMA, *softly.* Such a one surely was not to be host to me,
he who gave vinegar while desiring wine.

SECOND ACT

JOB *flees to be alone into the bathroom where men's and
women's wash is hung on lines to dry. Pulls himself up to
the small window. Storm with lightning flashes outside.
Wants to throw himself out, but notices something in the
street.* Elements! Heavens, pour out yourselves! Flood,
inundate my troubled heart! A dog . . . Come here! A
faithful dog—the last solace to him in whom humankind
inspires hate.

THE POODLE *runs through the hall, opens the door, jumps up on* JOB *wagging his tail.* Wow, wow, wow. A dog has a keen nose. I am a psychoanalyst! How . . . How . . . How. The Male sniffs Female's clothes!

MR. RUBBERMAN *wriggles out of the dog skin.* Forgive this foolish masquerade— I am the poodle's core!* So you have become a misanthrope.

Points to the hall.

This good maid would not turn a dog away when it rains cats and dogs! Hats off to a man in whom sensation twists through heart and kidneys. Whenever it should slacken — off with his head! To be sure, research has found that after the decapitation of poor sinners, the heart continues beating for a while, still full of feeling. But whether it felt pure joy has not been proved. For all our winding, every clock must someday cease to run! As I in another context already had occasion to remark—I am a psychoanalyst and can serve usefully with good advice. Defense attorney for the cause of life I've not become, because that could only kill the client. If he trusts in me then I have claims on him! That's only fair, agreed? An exchange of views may not be a trade-in of insights but rather a sellout of foresights.

From the window RUBBERMAN *sees returning the lady of the house, who then busies herself in the room next door. Curiously, he sniffs at the keyhole. Upon hearing her movements in the adjoining room,* JOB *turns away disgruntled and constrained.*

MR. RUBBERMAN. A beautiful woman! She's undressing! Pulling off . . . she pulls me on!

To JOB, *who with a great effort forces himself not to glance toward the ominous door.*

Besides, in case her difficult hour, requiring extraordinary endeavor even in dressing and addressing herself to . . .

---

* This is a reference to Goethe's *Faust,* Part I. Mephistopheles appears to Faust first in the shape of a poodle. Upon the poodle's transformation into human shape, Faust exclaims: "So that was the poodle's core!"

Looking into the keyhole with great effort, nearly crawling into it.

I am observing a woman who, in short, turns a man's head!

JOB, *reluctant, apart.* And you a doctor, friend of the weak, do not prevent this act of violence?

MR. RUBBERMAN. The personal joy of research alone prompts me. I am no doctor.

Into the door.

Experiment interests me. . . .

Joyfully.

Eureka! I have got it! . . . Her method! . . . It's discovered! Eroditis, jealousy! The seed which a bacillus incubates, erotococcus, lumbago—the witches' dart! The one discovery my colleagues left for me! This happens in cases like yours where the patient, weakened by long suffering, no longer is immune.

ANIMA, *from the next room.* Science makes the man who cannot fit its rules easily lose his head. It separates his head from him who, twisted by ideas, confused by God's or love's power, reflective for a while, forgets the little self and turns his back on it.

JOB *sees* RUBBERMAN *cleaving to the keyhole with drooling mouth and greedy eye. The door is opening slowly;* ANIMA *steps out, stops.* JOB, *crazed by the sight, twists his neck.* JOB *is no longer able to get his head back into its customary position, clutches his ears in dread, tears out huge handfuls of hair.*

MR. RUBBERMAN *rushes to* JOB, *shocked.* Let me feel your pulse! This man will die of fright under my hands! You're suffocating! Open your collar! You are doing everything wrong! The trouble comes from your twisted view of things that won't go straight!

JOB, *roaring.* They've twisted my head! They've twisted my head!

Whimpering.

Twisted!

MR. RUBBERMAN, *fingering* JOB's *chest.* The heart is still intact! I must interrupt the double circulation

Pulling out a surgeon's saw

so that the infection won't paralyze his heart. Head off, courage! If you live headless the trouble isn't half as bad!

ANIMA. My God, if I could only help! No one pays attention to me!

JOB *dances around in circles, roars away* RUBBERMAN, *who is waving his saw about.* I no longer know where I have my head! Does this one belong to me—does that one? You are nearest me. . . . That means—I must get at your throat! I'm reaching—I catch! I'm dropping—I fetch!

JOB, *shaken.* Just one more mirage, pretending to be shape that all eyes see.

To RUBBERMAN.

Why are you gaping at me so serenely? Just wait, a serene man is no match for a—deranged one!

Wanting to tear his head off his shoulders, pummeling with his fists against his forehead.

While still projected—the world rejected! The globe is turning—and rolling away! Woman has bewitched my head—twisted it. . . . It is bedeviled and possessed!

MR. RUBBERMAN, *inviting* ANIMA *to step nearer while he studies* JOB's *head.* When a woman possesses her husband's head, she always seeks a lover for it. And since I take an interest in yours— There she comes. . . . Please introduce me!

ANIMA, *innocent, bourgeois, gentle, blond.* You bad husband! You are scolding me. Me, Anima! Your wife! Born of the breath that inspired creation—whence impatience expelled Anima, before she was fulfilled.

JOB, *with hands imploring.* Anima, my soul!

PARROT, *flying into the room, screeching.* Anima, my soul!

JOB, *reaching out for* ANIMA, *who is turning to* MR. RUBBERMAN. Eluded my head, with him! And took the soul of sleepy Adam!

RUBBERMAN, *yanking* ANIMA *to his breast.* That Bible text of the old potter? Woman was not made from—your clay!

EROS *leaps through the door, precocious.* From Papa's tears in Mama's womb arose a little boy. . . .

ANIMA, *bitter;* EROS *stumbles and rubs his leg, roaring.* The mother of grief thought it would be for her joy!

RUBBERMAN. I don't understand a word! Ha, what joy to live. . . !

From now on everyone indulges in pandemonium, screaming, rushing, the PARROT *screeches incessantly,* EROS *cries.*

JOB *pacifies the child. To* RUBBERMAN. You opportunist! What seemed to her a trampoline for leaping from lust to lust is —alas—vulgarity that procreates itself! And all her seven Heavens are one Hell! An infant's birth is his fall to earth and he weeps at the entrance gate!

RUBBERMAN, *to* JOB. He's the spitting image of you. But stop this cry baby from babbling on and on. In this house everything is hexed.

Pointing to the CHAMBERMAID *and the* PARROT.

So throw out these noisy beasts!

JOB. To Hell with them from where they came.

ANIMA, *taking* EROS *by his hands and dancing in circles with him out through the door.* Let Heaven be Heaven and Hell be Hell! I love Lord Eros. With imagination I bore him— of whom I'd dreamt even as a girl. One feature I would take from this man, another from the next. To my lover I offered lips of resignation, and to my husband mocking mournfulness. From one to the other! Like a bee fickle while garnering the pollen! Until Lord Eros is arrived!

RUBBERMAN, *clamoring after the two fugitives while the general commotion subsides.* Adored lady—stay. . . . Besides, your Eros stimulates me too! . . . Purely objectively I wish to remark that the genetic development of your mythological son urges me toward an explanation by natural causes.

THIRD ACT

JOB *has fallen asleep from grief on a bench in front of his house. In the little garden there are many small flowering trees.*

FIRST YOUNG LADY, *softly, emerges with her curly head from the bed of roses, tries to awaken* JOB *and to seize his dangling hand.* Quite as you please! My God! In the wilderness the strong eat the weak. At home it's just the other way! Consequently one often has the face of a little lamb, the phlegmatic temper of a capon and . . .

JOB, *softly, in his sleep.* . . . and you the brain of a chicken.

SECOND YOUNG LADY, *softly laughing behind a tree.* Indeed, yes, when an ardent young man visits her, she goes to roost at once. She begs his pardon—does he have his red comb?

THIRD YOUNG LADY, *who has been squatting under the bench, looking up at him, softly.* You'll never again make that one lose his equilibrium! That's him all right, *Homo anthropos!* Just feel his calves!

JOB, *tickled, kicks in his sleep, so that the* YOUNG LADY *tumbles over backward.*

THIRD YOUNG LADY. Accursed frog's perspective! I'll be limping from this for the rest of my life!

FOURTH YOUNG LADY, *tickling* JOB's *ear with a flower stem, drops an apple, hiding all the while in a bush behind him.* Adam lives on in posterity because he bowed before Eve in Paradise!

JOB, *dreaming.* When one reflects how posterity is made by such worthless dalliances, he must lose faith in a better future!

FIFTH YOUNG LADY, *reaching out from the draperies of the house door for his shock of hair, softly.* 'Tis Fortune. Grab a hold! Or else she'll pull you 'round!

SIXTH YOUNG LADY, *administering him a gentle slap on the back.* As a man of the world, let him consider now which side of himself he wishes to show!

JOB, *sleepy*. Fortune is a gypsy who leads us by the nose! She wants her behind to be the object of our attention. When she performs her striptease there, beware the horn of plenty with which she might surprise you!

SEVENTH YOUNG LADY, *mockingly, from a tree*. Oh, for floating forth to meet furtive confessions and for uniting the warring sexes with the rainbow of forgiveness!

JOB, *dreaming, overcome by nostalgia*. My feelings are descending meteors hurtling down through the night of my heart and burning themselves out in it! My word, that transcends my self like the gesture of an invisible hand, remains for you mere stage effect!

ALL YOUNG LADIES, *singing softly*. Oh, how we love effects, farces and tragedies at midnight, when they hold sleep at bay. . . .

JOB, *mumbling*. Is this no demon towering in the sky who sets her heel upon me in the mud—but yet gentle angel who cools my head?

EIGHTH YOUNG LADY. Look about you, Sunday's child! Ghosts wear no clothes. What then can flesh-and-blood have on? *She comes from the path of the now dimly illuminated garden, the sun rises, she kisses his brow.*

Good day, my friend! Life smiles upon you!

JOB *snarls at her, wipes off her kiss*. I have lumbago, the witches' dart. . . .

EIGHTH YOUNG LADY, *giving him up as hopeless*. That thought at once makes love freeze stiff. . . .

JOB, *touching himself in front and back to see if some new misfortune has not befallen him, staggers into the light the better to see.*

NINTH YOUNG LADY. Uprooted plants wither in the sun no less than in the shade.

JOB, *disgruntled*. To your health, Dame Fortune! The morning crows and not the cock, the game shoots the hunter down—a weary man curses the carnival and now shuts shop.

Goes into the house. Brings a bottle of poison, a skull, and two human bones to the window, contemplates the skull, lifts the bottle to his lips. The TENTH YOUNG LADY *reaches down from her tree for it and then drums gaily with the bones on the skull.*

JOB *throws the poison bottle after the* YOUNG LADY, *who retaliates with the skull and bones, which* JOB *wraps in paper.* Women, get going, out with you!

ALL YOUNG LADIES, *singing softly to the tune of the folk song, departing.* JOB *closes the store.* "Now I lay me down to sleep," *etc.*

Brief pause.

JOB, *behind closed window shutters.* The soul of man or magic lantern. . . . Times were when it projected God and Devil into the world; these days it casts women on the wall!

Humbly.

Oh, to laugh a little, to laugh . . . And not to run after these nurses who tease us children; from out there the witch looks in and can't be overlooked.

He smiles wanly; a silvery many-voiced choir echoes— cascading laughter, a hurricane—an inundation of laughter. JOB *jumps out the window, pulls his pants tighter, stops short. In the upper story, above* JOB, *a window lights up in rosy illumination. The* PARROT *flies down from the opened window, flutters after the fugitive, opens wide her eyes, assails him, during the subsequent scene does not permit him to leave the protective wall of the house along which* JOB *runs to and fro.*

JOB *sprouts horns which develop into antlers. Whenever he rushes past the lit window, two shadows toss garments upon them so that the antlers soon become a clothes tree. Cuffs, collar, jackets, night- and under-garments of a gentleman and a lady.* JOB *grabs the doorbell and rings the house phone in deathly terror.* For pity's sake! I'm getting frightened! Anima, help! Salvation! What are they doing to me?

ANIMA, *from the window.* Conjuring spirits—do you see the plan? It's been the custom since time began.

ADAM, *the gardener, comes from the garden.* A woman, having turned his head, now makes a fool of him.

ANIMA. Mother's wit inspired me to this! An enlightened spirit has taken me to wife today, he disenchants me and now I aid him in his task!

JOB. That devil! A true enchanter he! Who bravely with kisses and fervid oaths conjures Anima up for his use. Oh, gaping Hell! Most fugitive witch! Treaties she signs, herself to surrender; confused, she blushes on bosom and neck; she opens her heart; airs secrets and skirts; and then shares in bed, in housewifely fashion, the power of the male. . . . What is it I feel? I am not like him, my opposite, that I could settle there and start begetting just like that! . . .

ANIMA *drops like a ripe apple down from the window, scantily clothed, to land with her buttocks on* JOB's *head. He collapses under* ANIMA's *weight and dies. At the window,* MR. RUBBERMAN *is still after her virtue in an obvious way.* ANIMA, *reproachfully.* But no—dear Mr. Rubberman, what do you think?

PARROT. But no, Mr. Rubberman . . .

ADAM, *gently.* You've placed your wife too high in the heavens. Only now when she falls can you see through her and view her bottom.

ADAM *draws down a curtain which covers the house, the garden,* JOB, *and* ANIMA. *Ten gentlemen in mourning are painted on the curtain. In place of their faces they have holes through which an actor puts his head when in the following dialogue the gentleman concerned has his say.*

PARROT *explodes and drifts as pinkish cloud up through the sky.*

ADAM, *looking after it.* Once long ago in Paradise this same bird whispered a warning to me. Busy gathering apples, I failed to listen.

Sighs.

ANIMA *appears, chewing an apple.* Job, God bless him, was also eager for the apple of knowledge, alas. . . .

FIRST GENTLEMAN, *impudently.* Because the apple had its worm, Eve offered Adam his share first.

ADAM. Quiet! Keep in step, it isn't your turn yet! Each in his time. First you must stick your head through here. But don't kick around too much, or else the wall will fall on you.

In consequence of the commotion, JOB's *head rolls in front of the wall.* ANIMA, *shocked, bends over it, almost goes out of her mind.*

SECOND GENTLEMAN. Madame Sphinx got poor reward
For having brought into this world—
This enigmatic garbage-heap—the Philosophic Man—
Especially his riddle-posing head.
Madame Anima is now her other name,
She lacks imagination now to understand herself!

THIRD GENTLEMAN. Divine insanity created all.

FOURTH GENTLEMAN. The poor victim of seduction should be persuaded to take her abortion back again! Let's hope she will be pregnant once again!

MR. RUBBERMAN, *stepping forward timidly.* Modern science will help!

FIFTH GENTLEMAN. Having grown ashamed of its descent, while yet in school, it limits itself to analysing all creation, trying to see if there was need of one at all.

ADAM *drags* JOB's *body out from under the screen and neatly puts the head back on again. With an angry side glance at* RUBBERMAN. The doctor invents the disease, the patient foots the bill.

SIXTH GENTLEMAN, *to* JOB, *who lies downstage with arms outspread.* Death, who hit you with Woman right in your spine, will no longer open any hell-hole for any amount of huffing and puffing.

SEVENTH GENTLEMAN, *to* SIXTH GENTLEMAN. Even in a hell-hole a single ray refracted light into a thousand hues! Darkness falls and yields its place to this enlightened age.

EIGHTH GENTLEMAN. Too much light will never become night. Swallow this, Phoenix, and die!

ADAM, *softly, guarding* JOB, *puts a handful of earth on* JOB's *breast.* Such a multitude of flowers from a single shovelful of earth. May earth rest easy on you!

ANIMA. Is he dead?

ADAM, *calmly.* No! Only his head and heart and other things are gone.

MR. RUBBERMAN, *crying.* Mankind must be elevated genetically! Marriage reform, marriage reform! Let copulation proceed before the eyes of scientists!

NINTH GENTLEMAN. Science, unpurified by the filter spirit, oozes over life and death, besmirching both!

TENTH GENTLEMAN, *forcefully.* I believe in the genius of man! Anima—Amen!

ADAM, *gently, turning off the stage lights.* Good faith is a green eyeshade! It screens the light of truth for sickly eyes. The only good I still can do is blow out the light so that it needn't shine at all.

Exits with ANIMA.

ANIMA, *in the darkness.* Perhaps Job could never help but bear a heavy cross. I, with my own eyes, have seen here how they slandered me. Perhaps I alone slander myself— and Anima, who settled the heavy cross on Job's shoulders, is truly—Eve.

HUMANITY
1918

by Walter Hasenclever

Translated by

Walter H. and Jacqueline Sokel

CHARACTERS

ALEXANDER	THE DOCTOR
THE MURDERER	BANKER
THE HEAD	JUDGE
THE TIPPLER	PROSECUTING ATTORNEY
HELPER	CLERGYMAN
LISSI	NEWSBOY
FORTUNETELLER	CONCIERGE
THE YOUTH	A GENTLEMAN IN BLACK
THE GIRL	THE NURSE
THE OLD WAITER	BEGGAR
AGATHE	THE INNKEEPER
THE FATHER	THE GUEST
THE MOTHER	COMMISSAR

Gentlemen. Lunatics. Whores. Deaf and dumb people. Policemen. Masked men. Law court. Jurors. Workers. Porters. People.

TIME: *Today*
PLACE: *The World*

TRANSLATORS' NOTE: The title *Humanity* has been preferred to the literal *Human Beings* (*Die Menschen*) because we felt that *Humanity* conveyed the precise meaning of the author's intent. *Human Beings* would mean merely a collection of individuals, and would lack the humanitarian pathos aimed at.

FIRST ACT

Cemetery.

Sunset. A cross falls down.
ALEXANDER *rises from the grave.*
THE MURDERER *comes with sack.*
ALEXANDER *startled.*
THE MURDERER. I have killed!
Hands him the sack.
ALEXANDER *stretches out his hand.*
THE MURDERER. The head is in the sack
Goes toward the grave, climbs in.
ALEXANDER *throws dirt over him.*
A gust of wind.
The chapel becomes bright.
THE YOUTH. THE GIRL.
THE YOUTH. Who is there?
THE GIRL. A corpse
Faints.
THE YOUTH. Murderer! !
ALEXANDER. Your coat
THE YOUTH *takes the coat off his shoulders.*
ALEXANDER *covers himself.*
THE YOUTH. Who are you?
ALEXANDER. I am alive
Takes the sack over his shoulders, goes.
THE GIRL *awakens.*
THE YOUTH *embraces her.*
THE GIRL *screams.* I have deceived you!

SECOND SCENE

Hall.

Night. Laid tables. Curtain in the background. A niche at either side.

The hall becomes bright.

THE OLD WAITER. THE GUEST.

THE OLD WAITER *reads the paper.* Murder

THE GUEST, *lasciviously.* Legs?

THE OLD WAITER. The head is missing

THE GUEST. One beer!

ALEXANDER *comes with the sack through the curtain.*

THE GUEST. Sex murder?

THE OLD WAITER. Reward

THE GUEST. Check!

THE OLD WAITER. One roast beef

THE GUEST. A man?

THE OLD WAITER. Three-ninety

THE GUEST *goes.*

ALEXANDER. Humanity!

THE OLD WAITER. Alexander! !

ALEXANDER. Where am I?

THE OLD WAITER. Missing

THIRD SCENE

The niche at the right becomes bright.

A ragged man sitting at a table covered with bottles.

THE TIPPLER. I am dreaming

The hall becomes dark.

ALEXANDER *enters.*

THE TIPPLER *hands him the glass.*

ALEXANDER *drinks.*

THE TIPPLER. You are starving!

ALEXANDER *looks up.*

THE TIPPLER. Brother!

Embraces him.

THE INNKEEPER *enters.* Money!

THE TIPPLER *searches in his jacket.*

THE INNKEEPER. Six bottles

ALEXANDER. I want work

THE INNKEEPER. As a waiter!

Points to the hall, goes.

LISSI *enters.* Men!

THE TIPPLER. You are sick

LISSI. I avenge myself

Goes.

ALEXANDER *stretches out his arms.* Love! !

FOURTH SCENE

The left niche becomes bright.

Men in tailcoats standing around a table. JUDGE, BANKER, HELPER.

VOICE, *invisible.* Play!

GENTLEMEN *throwing money on the table.*

The right niche becomes dark.

ALEXANDER *enters.*

BANKER. Who is there?

HELPER. A corpse!

Roaring and laughter.

BANKER, *handing him money.* Stake!

ALEXANDER *staking.*

VOICE. Thirteen

BANKER. Bravo!

HELPER. Luck

GENTLEMEN. Let it be!

VOICE. Thirteen

BANKER. Hell

GENTLEMEN. You must!

BANKER throwing money on the table.

VOICE. Thirteen

GENTLEMEN. Mr. Chairman

BANKER. The remainder

Throwing money on the table.

VOICE. Thirteen

JUDGE. The bank

BANKER. I pass

VOICE. Thirteen

Tumult.

BANKER tears off his shirt collar.

GENTLEMEN. Ruined

BANKER. My watch

Throws his watch on the table.

HELPER. His last will!

Silence.

BANKER clenches his fists.

JUDGE rings the bell.

MASKED MEN enter.

BANKER, *screaming.* My number's up!

MASKED MEN open the trapdoor, shove him in.

JUDGE. Cleaned out

The table becomes visible.

ALEXANDER stands before the money.

GENTLEMEN, *menacing.* Hands off!

A muffled shot.

HELPER *crosses himself.*

MASKED MEN *return.*

GENTLEMEN *pile money on the table.*

JUDGE. Forward!

GENTLEMEN *in convulsion.*

VOICE. Thirteen

The table collapses.

MASKED MEN *pick up the banknotes and shove them into* ALEXANDER'S *pockets.*

ALEXANDER *goes.*

A CRY. Your Excellency

GENTLEMEN *pulling revolvers.*

A CRY. Cut wages!

JUDGE *shrugs his shoulders.*

GENTLEMEN. We'll be starving to death!

HELPER *turns out the light.*

Full moon.

Pointing to the moon. Mines

A CRY. Canals

GENTLEMEN. Securities

A CRY. Money

HELPER, *switching on the light.* The moon bank!

JUDGE. Accredited

A CRY. Sign!

GENTLEMEN *write. Papers rustle.*

HELPER. The Board of Directors

Hands the list to the JUDGE.

A CRY. Benefactor

GENTLEMEN *congratulate him.*

LISSI *enters.*

GENTLEMEN *set the table up again.*

HELPER *raises the glass.*

VOICE. Play!

GENTLEMEN *throw securities on the table.*
The left niche becomes dark.

FIFTH SCENE

The hall becomes bright.

Morning. The tables are cleared; the curtain is pulled back. Factory silhouette in the background.

THE TIPPLER, *alone.* I love the world

WORKERS *approach.*

THE TIPPLER. Comrade!

WORKERS. Wage increase

THE TIPPLER. The day will come

WORKERS. The daily news!

ALEXANDER, *as a waiter.*

WORKERS. Strike

THE TIPPLER. We are poor

ALEXANDER *brings the coffee.*

THE TIPPLER. Six bottles!

ALEXANDER *ponders, pulls out the banknotes.* For you! !

Takes off his apron, leaves.

WORKERS. A rich guy

THE TIPPLER. Hell

WORKERS. Hand them over!

THE TIPPLER *hides the bills.*

WORKERS. Let 'im have it! !

They beat him till he bleeds.

THE TIPPLER *collapses. Factory siren.*

WORKERS *go to work.*

LISSI *stumbling over him, with* GENTLEMEN.

THE OLD WAITER *picks him up.*

ALEXANDER *comes with the sack.*

THE OLD WAITER. You alive?

ALEXANDER. Who am I??

End of first act.

SECOND ACT

FIRST SCENE

Cellar.

A room above the cellar. A window and view of street in the background.

The cellar becomes bright.

THE TIPPLER *with bandaged head.* Money!

BEGGAR *reaching his arm through the window.* Bread!

HELPER *steps in.*

BEGGAR *vanishes.*

THE TIPPLER. I am bleeding

HELPER. Sign!

Holds out papers to him.

THE TIPPLER. No more private property?

HELPER. Community!

THE TIPPLER. No wars?

HELPER. Peace!

THE TIPPLER, *seizing his hand.* The future!

HELPER. Shares

THE TIPPLER. Human beings?

HELPER. Slaves

THE TIPPLER *bites his own hand.*

HELPER. No more private property!

THE TIPPLER. Community??

HELPER. No wars!

THE TIPPLER. Peace? ?

Drops his handkerchief.

HELPER *bends down, reaches for his throat.* Your handkerchief

Strangles him.

THE WHORES, *standing at the window.* Golden prince!

Giggling.

THE HELPER *lets him go.*

THE WHORES *file in.* THEA, GILDA, LENA.

HELPER *jumps out the window.*

THEA. Greetings from Madam!

GILDA, *at his jacket.* Torn

LENA. You got thread?

THEA, *in front of the mirror.* How does this hat look on me?

THE TIPPLER. I'm dying

GILDA. Cigarette!

THEA. Lilac silk

LENA. Golden prince, tell us about God!

They settle about him.

THE TIPPLER. God inherits the millions

GILDA. Stingy bastard!

THEA. He's telling stories

LENA *sews his jacket.*

THE TIPPLER. We will be forgiven

Sinks back. They cover him and leave softly.

GILDA. God inherits the millions?

THE TIPPLER, *alone.* I am waiting for death

The cellar becomes dark.

SECOND SCENE

The room becomes bright.

THE YOUTH. THE GIRL.

THE GIRL. I am afraid

　THE YOUTH *gets up.*

THE GIRL. It's approaching

　THE YOUTH *walks to the door.*

THE GIRL. Something is happening!

　THE YOUTH *opens the door.*

THE GIRL. Now

　A chair falls downstairs.

THE GIRL, *screaming.* Someone has died! !

　THE YOUTH *runs down.*

　THE GIRL *falls down.*

THE YOUTH *comes back with banknotes in his hand.* Money!

　THE GIRL *is startled.*

THE YOUTH. He is dead

THE GIRL. You're trembling

THE YOUTH *tears the window open.* Life! !

THE GIRL. You don't love me

THIRD SCENE

At the Fortuneteller's.

A sofa. A table with three chairs in front of it. On the sofa the FORTUNETELLER. *Opposite her* THE GIRL. THE YOUTH *at the left. The chair on the right is empty.*

　THE YOUTH *shuffles the cards.*

FORTUNETELLER. The young lady is pale

　THE YOUTH *cuts the cards.*

FORTUNETELLER. I too was young once
  Picks up the deck.

  THE YOUTH *pulls out four cards.*

FORTUNETELLER, *looking at them.* What covers you—a heart
  What hovers over you—a queen
  At your head—luck
  At your feet—death?
  Shuffle again!

  THE YOUTH *shuffles again.*

FORTUNETELLER, *turning over the deck, shaking her head.*
  Riches!

  Pointing at each card.

  A woman—on your road— You love her—tears—

  LISSI *enters. No one sees her. She takes the empty chair.*

FORTUNETELLER. Beware of the doctor!

  Light is withdrawn from THE GIRL *and the* FORTUNETELLER.
  THE YOUTH *and* LISSI *remain illuminated. They look at
  the cards.*

FORTUNETELLER. She comes—you don't know her—black card
  —danger—sickness

  The light on the two is dimmed.

VOICE OF THE FORTUNETELLER. Death

  THE YOUTH *and* LISSI *look at each other.*

FOURTH SCENE

Consultation Room.

*A door in the background. A cubicle at each side of the
stage.*

The left cubicle becomes bright.

THE YOUTH *enters.*

VOICE, *from outside.* The doctor is here!

THE YOUTH, *in front of a picture.* "The Wedding at Cana"
  Feeling himself.

Glandular swelling

Paces around restlessly, pulls out his watch.

Half-past six

Trembling.

I am healthy!

Suddenly clutching at his heart.

Never again to love—no children—

The consultation room becomes bright.

THE YOUTH. Danger—sickness—

THE DOCTOR *steps into the consultation room.*

THE YOUTH. Death

THE DOCTOR *opens the left cubicle.*

THE YOUTH *bares his chest.*

THE DOCTOR *takes out a prepared slide with specimen.*

THE YOUTH *stares at the wall.*

THE DOCTOR *steps over to the microscope.*

THE YOUTH. Ships! Childhood!

THE DOCTOR. Date of birth?

THE YOUTH. Castles!

THE DOCTOR. Your father healthy?

THE YOUTH, *staggering to the window.* Life! !

THE DOCTOR. Suspicious symptom

THE YOUTH. I am hoarse

THE DOCTOR, *rising.* Ten marks!

THE YOUTH. Bowel movement?

THE DOCTOR. Syphilis

THE YOUTH *faints.*

THE DOCTOR *carries him into the cubicle at the left, puts him on the sofa.*

The cubicle at the right becomes bright.

THE GIRL *enters.*

THE DOCTOR *returns to the consultation room, washes his hands, opens the cubicle at the right.*

THE GIRL *throws herself at his feet.*

THE DOCTOR. Pregnant

THE GIRL. Help

THE DOCTOR. What a beauty!

THE GIRL. Poor

THE DOCTOR. Penal code

THE GIRL, *rising.* Save me!

THE DOCTOR. A kiss

   Embraces her.

THE GIRL *falls forward.* I'm falling

   THE DOCTOR *carries her into the right-hand cubicle, turns out the light.*

   The right-hand cubicle darkens.

   THE YOUTH *wakes up on the sofa.*

   Sunset.

THE YOUTH *stretches out his arms.* Sunrise! !

   The left-hand cubicle darkens.

   THE GIRL *rushes with streaming hair out of the right-hand cubicle into the consultation room, seizes a scalpel, cuts her veins. The door opens.*

   ALEXANDER *enters with the sack.*

   THE GIRL *drops the scalpel.*

   ALEXANDER *takes her hand, sucks her blood.*

   The consultation room darkens.

   ALEXANDER *opens the left-hand cubicle.*

   Moonlight.

   THE YOUTH *lies on the floor.*

   ALEXANDER *touches him.*

   THE GIRL *approaches.*

   THE YOUTH *gets up.* A skeleton; death-skull.

   ALEXANDER *takes his hand. They exit.*

FIFTH SCENE

Opera.

First-tier box. The box curtains are drawn. The box at the right is unoccupied. ALEXANDER, THE YOUTH, THE GIRL *are seated.*

USHERETTE. Opera glasses?

NEWSBOY. Extra — Sensational burglary

THE YOUTH. I am no more

VOICE, *from below.* Intermission!

ALEXANDER. We lie in the grave

THE GIRL, *pressing her hands to her abdomen.* The child is stirring

VOICE, *from below.* A chair!

THE YOUTH. Eternity

ALEXANDER. The gates are open

Curtain call.

VOICE. The finale begins!

THE YOUTH. I see the world

Muted music.

Meadows for the last time

THE DOCTOR *enters the right-hand box. Tails, white gloves.* Ten marks!

THE YOUTH *tosses over the banknotes.* I am floating

THE DOCTOR *catches the bills.*

LISSI *steps into the box of* THE DOCTOR, *smiles, relieves him of the bills.*

TENOR SOLO. "Donna è mobile"

THE DOCTOR *draws the curtain.*

The right-hand box is dark.

THE YOUTH *rises.*

ALEXANDER. Your coat!

> *Pulls his coat from his shoulders, covers* THE YOUTH *with it.*
> THE YOUTH *tears open the box curtain. The stage is bright.*
> *Music.*

> *Trumpet.*

> *He hurls himself down. A crash of all instruments.*

THE GIRL. Where are we?

ALEXANDER. Resurrection

> *End of the second act.*

THIRD ACT

FIRST SCENE

Street.

> *In the background, a house with windows. A balcony in*
> *the center. A café beneath. Three tables outside, the center*
> *one under the balcony. To the left, a red poster proclaims*
> *the word "Murder!" At the right across the way is the*
> BEGGAR.

> HELPER *sitting at the right-hand table.*

> BEGGAR *plays "Donna è mobile" on the hurdy-gurdy.* THE
> DOCTOR *and* LISSI *step out on the balcony.*

> THE OLD WAITER *pulls up the shutters in the café.*

> ALEXANDER *appears with the sack, stops in front of the*
> *poster.*

> THE DOCTOR *steps out of the house and sits down next to*
> *the* HELPER.

HELPER. Shares are rising

> ALEXANDER *sits down at the left-hand table.*

NEWSBOY. Moonbank—a new corporation

> THE OLD WAITER *brings drinks, buys a paper.*

THE DOCTOR. Coffee!

THE OLD WAITER *goes to* ALEXANDER, *reads the paper.* The murderer

ALEXANDER *looks up.*

HELPER. Capital!

THE DOCTOR *shakes his head.*

ALEXANDER. Do you believe in God?

THE OLD WAITER. We human beings

BEGGAR *grinds the hurdy-gurdy.*

THE DEAF AND DUMB *advance toward the center table.*

THE OLD WAITER *goes over to them.*

THE DEAF AND DUMB *gesticulate.*

THE DOCTOR *exclaims.* Deaf and dumb!

THE OLD WAITER *nods, walks into the house.*

AGATHE *barefooted fourteen-year-old, approaches with a box.* Matches?

HELPER *pushes her away.*

THE DOCTOR *laughs.*

THE DEAF AND DUMB *give her money.*

ALEXANDER *takes her in his arms.*

LISSI *steps onto the balcony, waves to* THE DEAF AND DUMB. Money is money!

Disappears.

HELPER. We live on credit

ALEXANDER. What's your name?

AGATHE. Agathe

HELPER. Child labor!

AGATHE. We are starving

HELPER. Shares

THE DOCTOR *pulls out the shares.* We own!

HELPER *pulls out shares.* You buy?

THE DOCTOR *puts shares into his pocket, pulls out his watch.* Child delivery

Rises.

BEGGAR *grinds the hurdy-gurdy.*

AGATHE. My mother is dying

  THE DOCTOR *goes.*

  HELPER *follows him.*

AGATHE. Help me!

  Takes ALEXANDER *by the hand. They exit.*

  THE DEAF AND DUMB *gesticulate. Point to the poster with the word "Murder."*

SECOND SCENE

Room in an attic.

To the right, hall with staircase. Slanting ceiling. In the back a window, looking out on roofs. At the left, in the bed, THE MOTHER *dying. In the center a table; three chairs;* THE FATHER, *white-haired, seated on the middle one. A travelling-bag at the right.*

The attic becomes bright.

THE MOTHER *moans.*

THE FATHER *motionless.*

The hall becomes bright.

AGATHE *and* ALEXANDER *are coming up the stairs.*

The hall becomes dark.

ALEXANDER *enters.*

THE MOTHER. There you are!

AGATHE. She is feverish

THE MOTHER. My son! !

  ALEXANDER *steps to the bed.*

THE MOTHER *seizes his hand.* I shall travel

  AGATHE *smoothes the pillows.*

THE MOTHER. The train is leaving

  ALEXANDER *steps over to the travelling-bag.*

THE MOTHER. Pack!

  ALEXANDER *opens the bag.*

THE MOTHER. Wedding

ALEXANDER *goes to the chest, fetches rags, puts them into the bag.*

THE MOTHER. My brooch

ALEXANDER *goes to the chest, finds the brooch.*

THE MOTHER. The Bible

ALEXANDER *goes to the table, takes out the Bible.*

THE MOTHER. The money!

Pulls banknotes out of the mattress, stuffs them into her mouth.

AGATHE, *folding her hands in prayer.* Thy will be done!

ALEXANDER *shuts the bag.*

THE MOTHER. My ticket! !

AGATHE *and* ALEXANDER *sit down at the table.*

THE MOTHER *moans.*

AGATHE. Father! !

THE MOTHER *rattles.*

Silence.

The window opens.

THE FATHER. Dead

They sit motionless.

The hall becomes bright.

People come up the stairs, peep through the keyhole, whispering.

The hall becomes dark.

They come in. The room fills with shadows.

A GENTLEMAN IN BLACK. Funeral!

They move closer, crush the table. THE FATHER, AGATHE, ALEXANDER *join hands. The shapes disappear. The room becomes dark. The table is illuminated.*

THE FATHER. Who are you?

ALEXANDER. I seek myself

THE FATHER. A man! !

ALEXANDER *bows before him.*

AGATHE *smiles. The table sinks into darkness. A flight of birds over the roofs.*

THIRD SCENE

Hospital.

Reception room in the center. Operating room at the right. Delivery room left.

Operating room and reception room become bright.

THE NURSE *sits in the reception room.*

THE DOCTOR *stands in the operating room; goes to the glass cabinet, takes out a foetus, holds it against the light, puts it on the operating table.*

THE NURSE *knits.*

THE DOCTOR *opens the door.* Admissions?

THE NURSE. Three

Leafs through the folder.

In the ninth month

THE DOCTOR *shuts the door.*

The operating room becomes dark. The delivery room becomes bright.

THE WHORES *lie in three beds. The fourth bed is empty.*

THEA, *with lipstick and compact mirror.* Bunk!

GILDA. Chocolate

Eats.

LENA. Golden Prince is dead

Sniffs at a bouquet.

GILDA *takes the flowers away from her.* My flowers!

THEA, *patting her belly.* It's ringing

GILDA. Come in!

Giggling.

THE GIRL *staggers into the reception room, gropes along the wall, collapses.*

THE NURSE *drags the unconscious girl to the delivery room, puts her into the fourth bed.*

THE DOCTOR *enters the reception room.*

THE NURSE *returns.* Delivery

GILDA *stretches her arms.* To dance!

THEA. The doctor!

They hide their things.

THE DOCTOR *enters, goes to* THE GIRL, *sees blood.* What a mess!

THE GIRL *opens her eyes, sees* THE DOCTOR, *screams.* Beast! !

THE DOCTOR. The mask

THE NURSE *wheels in a cart with medical instruments.*

THE GIRL *struggling.* I don't want to! !

THE DOCTOR *holds her tight.*

THE NURSE *puts on the chloroform mask.*

THE DOCTOR. Count!

THE GIRL, *growing weaker, whimpering.* Twenty-one—twenty-two—

THE DOCTOR. Get going!

THE NURSE *puts the anesthetized* GIRL *on the stretcher.*

THE DOCTOR *goes through the reception room into the operating room.*

THE NURSE *wheels the stretcher after him. The door to the operating room closes.*

THEA *moans.*

GILDA. The forceps

LENA, *wringing her hands.* Mother! !

GILDA. God in Heaven

Creeps under the blanket.

Silence.

In the operating room an instrument falls with a crash.

THEA, *propping herself up.* A child is born! !

THE DOCTOR, *stepping with bloody hands out of the operating room, washes his hands.* Crap

FOURTH SCENE

Street.

The BEGGAR *stands opposite the poster.* THE DEAF AND DUMB *sit at the center table. The other two tables are unoccupied.*

THE DEAF AND DUMB *gesticulate. Point to the poster that proclaims "Murder."*

NEWSBOY. Extra

THE OLD WAITER *buys a sheet.*

NEWSBOY *exits.*

THE BEGGAR *grinds the hurdy-gurdy.*

A funeral procession approaches from the right. Pallbearers in black carry the table of the attic. On the table lies THE MOTHER, *in her shroud, exposed. Her hands are folded on her breast. The* CLERGYMAN *walks behind the table.* THE FATHER *follows with* AGATHE. *Finally, bringing up the rear,* ALEXANDER *with the sack.*

People come from the left.

The funeral procession collides with these people in the middle of the street. They block the way, clench their fists, wave unpaid bills. The pallbearers put down the table.

PEOPLE. Debts!

A MAN. The baker

A WOMAN. The rent

PEOPLE. Money!!

They bear down on the corpse, searching it frantically.

CLERGYMAN, *appealing to them.* Dear congregation!

PEOPLE *throw rags on the ground. The corpse lies stripped.*

A GENTLEMAN IN BLACK. No money—no funeral!

The pallbearers abandon the table.

CLERGYMAN *sighs, shakes* THE FATHER's *hand. The corpse lies deserted in the street.*

ALEXANDER *steps forward. They retreat. He tears his garments off his body, covers the corpse.*

CLERGYMAN *shakes his head, exits.*

ALEXANDER *takes the corpse into his arms.*

PEOPLE *vanish with the table.*

THE DEAF AND DUMB *get up, loosen the stones in the pavement, dig a grave with their hands.*

ALEXANDER *puts the corpse into the ground. People watch from all windows.* LISSI *steps onto the balcony.*

THE DEAF AND DUMB *close the grave.*

NEWSBOY, *returning with papers.* The track of the murderer

ALEXANDER *takes the sack over his shoulders.*

NEWSBOY. The head is in the sack!

AGATHE *kneels before* ALEXANDER, *kisses his hands.*

THE OLD WAITER *watches him closely.*

FIFTH SCENE

Cradle.

THE GIRL. Sleep, baby son, sleep my beloved.
Shut your blue eyes, assured you're loved.
All is safe and hushed like the grave.
Sleep, there is no need to be brave.
Angels from Heaven, sweet like you,
Float by your crib, smiling at you.
Now, darling, is Paradise still
Which soon, alas, time renders nil.

End of the third act.

FOURTH ACT

FIRST SCENE

Warehouse.

A bed. A candle on the night table. Wall in the background.
AGATHE *undoes her dress, loosens her tresses, takes writing paper, writes.*

VOICE. Holiday eve!

AGATHE *folds the letter, smiles, takes it along with her to bed. The candle flickers.*

AGATHE. Beloved

Noise at the door.

VOICE. Shine the shoes!

AGATHE *startled, takes up the garment and sews. She smiles, presses the letter to her lips, grows pensive, cries. The candle flickers. The garment falls to the floor.*

AGATHE *falls asleep. The wall gives way to a landscape. Starry sky. The candle blows out. Sun and moon rise.*

ALEXANDER *stands at the far end of the landscape.*

AGATHE *spreading her arms.* Come!

ALEXANDER *goes straight through the landscape to her bed.*
AGATHE *hands him the letter.*

ALEXANDER *sitting by her bed.* Don't cry!

AGATHE. Lilacs

The trees bloom.

AGATHE. Wind is blowing

ALEXANDER, *caressing her.* Butterfly!

The clock strikes.

ALEXANDER. My fate

AGATHE. I'll follow you

ALEXANDER, *smiling.* Child!

A star falls across the sunny landscape.

ALEXANDER. Everything is different

Kisses her. The landscape is vanished. The wall reappears.
ALEXANDER *is gone. The candle burns once more.*

AGATHE *wakes up.*

VOICE. Get up!

The candle flickers.

AGATHE *jumps out of bed, runs to the closet, takes out an artificial branch, presses it to her heart.* Spring!

The warehouse becomes dark.

The landscape reappears, now gray, humdrum.

ALEXANDER *wakes up on a bench, finds the sack, eyes it with curiosity.*

SECOND SCENE

Drawing room.

LISSI *lies on the sofa.* THE DOCTOR *holds her feet in his lap. The doll sits on the chair.*

LISSI *fanning herself.*

THE DOCTOR, *pale, with sunken eyes.* Beloved

LISSI. Hands off!

THE DOCTOR *fondles her.*

LISSI *kicks him.*

THE DOCTOR *pulls the morphine needle out of his pocket, gives himself an injection.*

LISSI *yawns.*

THE DOCTOR. White mice! !

HELPER *enters.*

THE DOCTOR *reaches into his mouth, pulls teeth out.*

LISSI. It's crumbling

HELPER. Third stage!

THE DOCTOR *bends over the doll, puts on his dark glasses.* Pregnant

LISSI. A coffin!

THE DOCTOR. Delivery

Takes the knife from his pocket, stabs the doll.

HELPER. Money!

Injects the needle into THE DOCTOR's *head.*

THE DOCTOR *keels over.*

LISSI *pushes him away from the sofa.*

HELPER *reaches into* THE DOCTOR's *jacket, pulls out securities.*
Gold mines!

LISSI *seats the doll on her lap.*

HELPER *drags the corpse by its hair. Hairs remain in his
hands.*

LISSI. Dead is dead!

HELPER tosses corpse out the window.

THIRD SCENE

Table and chair.

The sack lies on the table. ALEXANDER *seated on the chair.*
ALEXANDER *opens the sack.*

THE HEAD *falls out.*

ALEXANDER *shrinks back.* My head!

THE HEAD. My body

ALEXANDER. I am killed?!

THE HEAD. The murderer lives

ALEXANDER. He is forgiven

Gust of wind.

ALEXANDER. He is in the grave

THE HEAD. Atonement!

ALEXANDER. I live in his stead

A dark lantern lights up.

In the ray of its light appear THE OLD WAITER, COMMIS-
SAR, POLICEMEN.

THE OLD WAITER *points his finger at* ALEXANDER. Murderer! !
    COMMISSAR *arrests him.*

THE OLD WAITER *lifts his hat.* Reward

COMMISSAR *finds the sack.* The head is in the sack!

FOURTH SCENE

Court with jury.

Law court and JUDGE *at the left. In front of them the*
PROSECUTING ATTORNEY. *The jury in the back. At the right*
the audience: THE INNKEEPER, THE GUEST, GENTLEMEN,
WHORES, BEGGAR, NEWSBOY, CONCIERGE; AGATHE *stands be-*
fore them at the bar. In front of her, the witness stand with
THE OLD WAITER *in it. On the table in the center lies* THE
HEAD. ALEXANDER *is seated on the chair next to it.*

JUDGE, *holding the sack in his hands.* The Head is an exhibit
    LAW COURT *nods.*

JUDGE. Defendant!

    ALEXANDER *looks up.*

JUDGE. Do you plead guilty?

CRY. Murderer!

AGATHE. No! !

JUDGE. Quiet!

THE OLD WAITER, *raising his hand.* I swear

JUDGE. "So help me God"

THE OLD WAITER. Amen

JUDGE. Attorney for the prosecution!

PROSECUTING ATTORNEY *rises.* Your Honor!

    JURY *rises.*

PROSECUTING ATTORNEY. A man has been murdered

    ALEXANDER *looks at him.*

PROSECUTING ATTORNEY. An eye for an eye

    AUDIENCE *leans forward.*

PROSECUTING ATTORNEY. Death penalty!

Sits down.

JUDGE. The defendant!

ALEXANDER *is silent.*

JUDGE. The court will now recess

COURT *and* JURY *retire. The courtroom empties.* AGATHE *and* ALEXANDER *remain alone.*

ALEXANDER *turns around, catches sight of* AGATHE.

AGATHE, *smiling.* I shall follow you

ALEXANDER, *bewildered, clutches at his forehead.*

AGATHE. I love you

The courtroom fills up. COURT *and* JURY *return.*

THE GIRL *appears in the* AUDIENCE, *starved, holding her child to her breast.*

JUDGE. In the name of the king!

All rise.

CHAIRMAN OF THE JURY. Guilty!

THE GIRL, *holding her child up in the courtroom.* Starving! !

COMMISSAR *pulls her back.*

JUDGE. Condemned to death

All sit down.

ALEXANDER *rises.*

Silence.

ALEXANDER. I have been murdered

JUDGE. No wisecracks!

ALEXANDER, *taking* HEAD, *holding it up.* My own head

Roar of laughter.

CRY. Well! Well!

ALEXANDER. I am atoning

JUDGE. The court is now adjourned!

ALEXANDER. All are murderers

Tumult.

CRY. To the nuthouse with him!

End of fourth act.

FIFTH ACT

FIRST SCENE

At the Fortuneteller's.

The FORTUNETELLER *on the sofa.* THE GIRL *at the left;* LISSI *at the right. The chair opposite the* FORTUNETELLER *is dark.*
FORTUNETELLER *shuffles cards.*

LISSI *cuts.*

FORTUNETELLER *takes one half of the deck in each hand, puts both down face up.* Hatred

THE GIRL *and* LISSI *look at each other.*

FORTUNETELLER *hands the deck to* LISSI.

LISSI *pulls out a card.*

FORTUNETELLER *puts it face up.* Someone is here!

LISSI *raises her hands in terror.*

THE GIRL *pulls a knife. The* FORTUNETELLER *ceases to be illuminated.*

The chair is brightly lit.

They rush upon each other. LISSI *falls onto the knife;* THE GIRL *pushes it into her breast while* LISSI *mortally strangles her.*

The chair is darkened.

Death rattles.

SECOND SCENE

Insane Asylum.

HUMAN BEINGS *in the shape of beasts.* HELPER *in the center.*
THE LUNATICS *crawl about.*
HELPER *mounts the throne.*

VOICE, *from outside.* Number 20.

　ALEXANDER *enters.*

　HELPER *sets crown on his head.*

　ALEXANDER *falls down, crawls on all fours.*

THIRD SCENE

　Street.

　THE OLD WAITER *in front of the café.*

NEWSBOY. Execution!

　ALEXANDER *is led past.*

　THE OLD WAITER *hangs himself.*

FOURTH SCENE

　Jail.

　Night. ALEXANDER *in chains. Bars in the back. Muffled knocks.*

AGATHE *enters with a candle.* I shall save you!

　She assumes his chains.

　Silence.

　The door opens.

　ALEXANDER *exits.*

　The bars are illuminated.

　Gentlemen in tailcoats stand around a scaffold. The JUDGE, *the* PROSECUTING ATTORNEY.

　CLERGYMAN *enters.*

　AGATHE *smiles. The room becomes dark. The sky appears. Chorals are sung from spires.*

FIFTH SCENE

Cemetery.

Sunrise.

ALEXANDER *enters with the sack.*

THE MURDERER *rises from the grave.*

ALEXANDER *hands him the sack.*

THE MURDERER. The sack is empty

ALEXANDER *walks to the grave and climbs down.*

The sun rises.

THE MURDERER, *spreading out his arms.* I love! !

End of fifth act.

ALKIBIADES SAVED

A PLAY IN THREE PARTS

1920

by Georg Kaiser

Translated by Bayard Quincy Morgan

"Like an immeasurable shipwreck, when the hurricanes have ceased to roar, and the boatmen have fled, and the corpse of the shattered fleet lies unrecognizable on the sandbar, so Athens lay before us, and the orphaned columns stood before us like the naked trunks of a forest which one evening were still in leaf and in the following night went up in flames."

Hölderlin: *Hyperion*

PERSONS

SOKRATES,	FIRST EULOGIST
a maker of hermae	SECOND EULOGIST
ALKIBIADES	WRESTLING MASTER
PHRYNE	HEALTH-GIVER
XANTIPPE	CAPTAIN
HOST	FORERUNNER
PRIZE-AWARDER	FLUTE PLAYER

Elders, Guests, Boys, Fishwives, Soldiers in the Field, City Soldiers, Bearers, Serving Boys

EDITOR'S NOTE: The translator has this to say about his reasons for spelling the names as he does in this translation: "I wanted to keep the Greek . . . spelling in order to make it clear that the figures whom Kaiser presents to us are not the historic Socrates and Alcibiades, but constructs of his imagination."

PART ONE

*The wrestling school. Below the exterior wall, of marble with wide red veins through it, a bronze bench. Steps leading down. Lilacs in bloom. Stretched on the bench— face down, his gay cloak tight around him—*FIRST BOY, *crying. Along the wall—colored cloaks tight up to the chin, embracing— come* SECOND *and* THIRD BOY.

THIRD BOY. He made that up!

SECOND BOY. You don't believe it?

THIRD BOY. He had no dream of Alkibiades last night!

SECOND BOY. He was still happy.

THIRD BOY. I know: he can't have dreamt!

SECOND BOY. He was all excited when he told us!

THIRD BOY. His cloak—I was facing him— opened a crack, and I saw—that he has a tuft of hair on his chest!

SECOND BOY. Ugly!

THIRD BOY. Can he have had the dream about Alkibiades?

SECOND BOY. He made it up.

THIRD BOY. No one can dream of Alkibiades—if he isn't beautiful!

They go down the steps.

SECOND BOY, *beside the bench.* Who is it?

THIRD BOY, *moving away.* Come.

FIRST BOY *lifts his face toward the two — sits up quickly, slides to the end of the bench.* You want the bench? Stay here. I'll make room for you. There's room for you too. Sit down!

They stand irresolute.

I've lain long enough. You're not getting me up. Stay down here!

THIRD BOY. Come.

He climbs the steps.

SECOND BOY *hesitates.*

FIRST BOY. I've been crying. My eyes are red and small. But now I'm not crying any more. I'm not going to cry again. I—I'm not—

He jumps up and seizes the SECOND BOY *by both arms. With streaming tears.*

I'm not crying—I'm not crying—I'm not crying at all!

THIRD BOY, *above.* Come!

FIRST BOY. Tell me why I'm crying.

SECOND BOY. You—

FIRST BOY. You will tell me why I am lying here. Why am I alone—and all the others are together? Am I not beautiful any more? Is there on my back—down my neck—on my right or left leg—under my arm—did a fly sting me some-where? Am I not beautiful any more?

THIRD BOY. Come!

FIRST BOY. Come and sit down. Beside me. We'll sit together. By the lilac. We'll push our cloaks away. You are beautiful —I am beautiful!

THIRD BOY. The rest are coming. Come!

FIRST BOY. The bench belongs to us two. Come quickly, then they won't try to disturb us!

Along the wall come FOURTH *and* FIFTH BOY—*embracing.*

FOURTH BOY, *looking down.* Who are they?

SECOND BOY, *pushing the first one away.* I won't stay with you!

He climbs the steps.

FIFTH BOY. Who is it?

FIRST BOY. Stare at me! Shout for the wrestling school to come together. All the four hundred. And the wrestling master too. Yes, goggle down at me. I'm dirt. Think I don't know it? You do? I'll tell you when all of you are up there. Send out the call. I'll shout for you!

He sets up a prolonged, shrill cry.

Up above come SIXTH *and* SEVENTH BOY; *soon* EIGHTH *and* NINTH BOY.

FIRST BOY *stops shouting.*

SIXTH BOY. That makes him ugly!

SEVENTH BOY. Awfully ugly!

THE BOYS. Ugly!

FIRST BOY. Because my mouth drivels? Because my cheeks flatten out? Because my neck swells?

THE BOYS. Ugly!

FIRST BOY. That's not it. That doesn't bother you. That doesn't count!—But I *am* dirt because I have a sister!

SECOND BOY. You—keep still!

FIRST BOY. That's so disgusting—because my sister is the wife of Alkibiades!

FIFTH *and* SIXTH BOY. Don't say it!

FIRST BOY. That's so horrible—because my sister dragged Alkibiades before the judges. The judges are above Alkibiades, because he went to the women. My sister took Alkibiades into court!

THE BOYS *are silent.*

FIRST BOY. That's why I'm lying here. That's why I'm hiding away from everyone. That's why I want to choke on lilac fumes. I loathe myself because I'm her brother!—Don't spare me. I want to die. Choke me, why don't you?—And tell Alkibiades about my death—which didn't injure my body, for it remained whole in death. Come—and bury me among the lilacs! Come!

Above, more boys have come; they pack the entire wall.

A BOY. I won't touch you!

SECOND BOY. You touched the hem of my cloak—I won't wear it again!

A BOY. Run away from the wrestling school!

A BOY. Nobody will wrestle with you any more!

A BOY. You're her brother!

ALL. Her brother!

FIRST BOY, *heatedly.* I am her brother! I'll run ahead of you. You follow! We'll rush into court! We'll threaten everyone

with our death. We'll arrive four hundred strong. All re-
solved—all of us ready. I ahead of you—run with me: we'll
save Alkibiades!

He starts up the steps.

THIRD BOY *blocks his way at mid-stair.* Stay below!

FIRST BOY, *panting.* Run with me: we'll save Alkibiades!

THIRD BOY. Don't wrestle with me!

*With a violent shove he gets free of him, the other tum-
bles down the steps.*

Is he going to incite us? Goad us into this crime? *We* run
with *him*—! Who runs like that—and arrives:—and isn't
driveling at the mouth—with red haste spotted all over
his skin—ugly?—And if he stayed here—and didn't stir
one step from this gravel—: who is beautiful—who is beautiful!—: to save Alkibiades?

THE BOYS *are silent.*

THIRD BOY. Look yourselves over—and find no blemish—grow
four hundred into one who is beautiful above all—even he
is not beautiful enough to save Alkibiades.

SECOND BOY. No one dares save Alkibiades!

THIRD BOY. Alkibiades is beautiful above all others! No one
dares lift oneself up to him and bend him down to oneself
with help and rescue. No one can save Alkibiades whom
shame at such a crime must not burn up!

FIFTH *and* SIXTH BOY. No one dares save Alkibiades!

THIRD BOY. Alkibiades is beautiful above everyone!

ALL BOYS. No one dares save Alkibiades!

THIRD BOY. Come down, all of you—we will all hide away, because we were going to insult Alkibiades!

The BOYS *come down and fill the lower space.*

FIRST BOY. Choke me in the lilacs!

THIRD BOY. Don't lay a hand on him: they would ask—and
we'd have to say what no one must say: He wanted to
save Alkibiades!

FIRST BOY *breaks through and runs up the steps.* I'll fall dead
before Alkibiades!

The aged WRESTLING MASTER *enters, above, and stops the*
FIRST BOY.

WRESTLING MASTER, *laughing happily.* Running to meet me?
Are you the most impatient one? Been crying? Because
you're her brother? Don't bear a grudge against your sister
—Alkibiades has already forgiven her!

Talking down to the rest.

Driven into a corner? Frightened? Alkibiades bursts out
laughing! He laughed when he went before the judges,
he laughed when he saw his wife with the judges, he
laughed and with a laugh he placed himself—

Shaking the FIRST BOY.

—before your sister and laughed. At first she made a face
—then her cheeks glowed—then her flesh melted—and then
she clung to Alkibiades with her two round arms. He
laughed—and didn't see the judges any more—and the two
went away—and the judges laughed—and the curious standing like a wall laughed—and laughter is ringing out over
the whole city! You don't hear it? Are you deaf? Doesn't
it rouse you—to go to Alkibiades? Aren't you storming
his house? Aren't you filling up his courtyard? Aren't you
fighting each other to get at his hands?

He claps his hands.

THE BOYS, *with a shout.* Alkibiades!

They dash up—and are already running off.

WRESTLING MASTER *looks after them, laughing. Then to the*
FIRST BOY, *who stands still.* Why aren't you behind them
or ahead of them? Aren't you the gladdest of all?

FIRST BOY, *rushing to him and pressing his face into the man's
cloak—faintly.* I wanted to save him!

WRESTLING MASTER, *stroking his hair.* Silly—save Alkibiades!

FIRST BOY, *beside himself.* I did want to save him!

WRESTLING MASTER. Only Alkibiades can save Alkibiades—
otherwise the sky would collapse over Greece!

*Cactus field. Sloping upward. Night with moon and racing
clouds. A troop of* SOLDIERS *from the right: hoplites with*

leather pants, iron cuirasses on breast and back, and low, round helmets.

CAPTAIN. Halt!

SOLDIER. Forward!

CAPTAIN. Close up!

Stragglers enter.

SOLDIER. They're still after us!

CAPTAIN. Wait! Till the moon comes out. We've got into a cactus field!

SOLDIER. We've got to get through.

SECOND SOLDIER. The enemy's chasing us!

THIRD SOLDIER. Better run into thorns than into his daggers!

FOURTH SOLDIER. They won't leave one of us alive!

FIRST SOLDIER. Forward in front!

CAPTAIN. Here comes the moon. Step high—and watch out for cactus bushes. Those long thorns push, pierce through shoes and skin!

The troop marches.

A SOLDIER *screams—stands still.*

SOLDIER. Get going!

THE SOLDIER *groans.*

SOLDIER *beside him.* If you want to be cut to ribbons—your affair!

THE SOLDIER *bends down over his foot—whimpers.*

CAPTAIN. Anyone staying behind?

SOLDIER. He hasn't had enough fighting yet!

CAPTAIN *comes back to the groaning* SOLDIER. March ahead of me—and if you twitch, I'll wrap my sword around your knees!

THE SOLDIER *does not budge from the spot.*

CAPTAIN. You dog—we've lost ten times too many men today without you. We'll be needing you tomorrow. Are you going to walk now?

THE SOLDIER *whimpers.*

CAPTAIN. You going to sleep here? Want to get out of tomorrow's fight? Look here, anyone that's dead should sleep—but if he can miaow like you, he—

He lifts his short sword.

THE SOLDIER. Not one step—!

CAPTAIN. Get going—the others will run away from me!

THE SOLDIER. Not one foot—!

CAPTAIN. You'll be cut to pieces in a quarter of an hour if you don't run. The enemy's after us!

THE SOLDIER. Better to be cut to pieces once than—

CAPTAIN. No twaddle. Start out—and get away with us!

He kicks him.

THE SOLDIER *cries out.*

CAPTAIN. Does a little blow make you howl?

THE SOLDIER. Let me alone—

CAPTAIN. I'll get you back—and if I have to take you on my back!

THE SOLDIER *takes his sword and strikes at him.* Get away from me!

CAPTAIN. Are you mad?

THE SOLDIER *hitting about him furiously.* Run as fast as you can—I — —

CAPTAIN. You dung—die in the dung.

Follows the rest, exit. The remaining SOLDIER *squats on the ground: it is* SOKRATES. *His body is short, his back round and arched. With groans he works at his shoelace.*

SOKRATES. Through the shoe — — through the skin — — deep into the flesh — — a hole torn open and then closed by this fiery stopper! — — To march: that's to impale yourself at every step — — to die a thousand deaths for one — — and revive again and—

He tries to strip off the shoe.

With the shoe get rid of the thorn, the base of which is stuck in the sole — —

With a jerk he removes the shoe.

Snapped off! — — The tip is sticking in my foot! — — Now no pincers can get it.

He studies the sole of his foot.

As if it were ingrown in the surface of the sole — — no swelling — — just pain! !

He slumps as if fainting. After a pause.

No—can't step on it. That's worse than a battle. That goes through me like fire — — That's a whirligig whirling in my blood! — — Mercy! — — I'm not budging — — I'm not picking myself up — — not ramming the whole earth against this wedge in my flesh! ! — — —

Looking around.

I march on with you? Where is the path? Through this cactus field with a thorn in my foot? You want to torture me? Are you hangmen? Trot along with you and cut myself up with thorn after thorn until I'm a sieve? Are *you* the enemy?—: they'll come and annihilate me with a single stab! — — — — I'll sit here—: they won't capture me and lead me away — — let them kill me!

On the hill at rear a warrior appears—in armor of white enamel—weaponless: ALKIBIADES. *The moonlight makes him resplendent.*

ALKIBIADES *looks about—perceives* SOKRATES—*drifts over to him.* Greek—hoplite—: which way the retreat?

SOKRATES, *vague gesture.*

ALKIBIADES. Do you know the way?

SOKRATES, *as before.*

ALKIBIADES. Get up—guide me!

SOKRATES *shakes his head.*

ALKIBIADES. You—don't you know me? Look here!

SOKRATES *does not change his behavior.*

ALKIBIADES. I am Alkibiades.

SOKRATES. Don't bump into me!

ALKIBIADES. I was the last who fought. My weapons are broken. They're after me. They're hunting me like a wild animal.

SOKRATES. Not a step!

ALKIBIADES. I've lost my way. I can't find the others. Take me there!

SOKRATES. Let go of me!

ALKIBIADES. Fellow, I'll take your sword—and beat you until you start running!

SOKRATES. I won't run with you!

ALKIBIADES. Go ahead, you—and let's join the others!

SOKRATES. Get away—I won't go ahead!

ALKIBIADES. Then I'll drive you before me like a hunting hound!

He tries to seize SOKRATES' *sword.*

SOKRATES *lays about him furiously.* Not another step—not a foot from this spot—! Run your best — — I won't run with you! !

Hostile soldiers on the height. They recognize ALKIBIADES *and shout his name.*

Alkibiades!

ALKIBIADES *to* SOKRATES. Greek—the hounds are after me— back to the Greeks!

SOKRATES. I—won't—run!

The hostile soldiers come running up.

ALKIBIADES *to* SOKRATES. Run ahead—on the way to the Greeks!

A HOSTILE SOLDIER, *calling rearward.* Here, catch Alkibiades! —Alkibiades has no weapons!

ALKIBIADES. They're coming in numbers—run with me to the Greeks!

SOKRATES. I—won't—run!

A HOSTILE SOLDIER *to the others as they appear.* Here, catch Alkibiades! Alkibiades has no weapons!

They approach.

ALKIBIADES, *kicking* SOKRATES. Run to the Greeks with me!

SOKRATES, *laying about him blindly with the sword.* Away— from—me!

ALKIBIADES, *dodging the blows, jumps behind* SOKRATES.

A HOSTILE SOLDIER, *coming up.* Aren't you capturing Alkibiades?

A HOSTILE SOLDIER. There's a man in front of Alkibiades, defending him!

A HOSTILE SOLDIER. He won't let us get at Alkibiades!

A HOSTILE SOLDIER. It's a hoplite.

A HOSTILE SOLDIER. All of them are brave!

A HOSTILE SOLDIER. Just let him get tired, then we'll run him through!

A HOSTILE SOLDIER. Until then we can't capture Alkibiades behind him!

The blows of the conflict between the blindly raging SOKRATES *and the hostile soldiers ring out loudly. On the hill,* GREEK SOLDIERS—*a shout:*

Alkibiades!

A HOSTILE SOLDIER. Greeks!

A HOSTILE SOLDIER. More Greeks!

A HOSTILE SOLDIER. Greeks in superior strength.

A HOSTILE SOLDIER. Let's run!

A HOSTILE SOLDIER *to* SOKRATES. Dog—if you hadn't laid about you like a wild bull, we'd have captured Alkibiades by now. I spit on you!

The HOSTILE SOLDIERS *go. The* GREEK SOLDIERS *come up with jubilant shouts.*

Alkibiades!

A SOLDIER. We heard the shout the enemy shouted—Alkibiades!—and the noise of fighting that rang out across the field!

A SOLDIER. You have no weapons?

A SOLDIER. Who is fighting beside you?

A SOLDIER. Whose fighting saved you?

ALKIBIADES *looks toward* SOKRATES, *lying unconscious.* Who is this man?

A SOLDIER *steps up to him.* One of the hoplites.

A SOLDIER. I'm a hoplite—lost my troop and joined you. Let me look.

He lifts SOKRATES' *head up.*

I know him. The last man in the ranks. A half hunchback.

Standing up.

Sokrates!

Silence.

ALKIBIADES *calmly.* Lay Sokrates on the shield—carry Sokrates before me:—he saved Alkibiades!

The soldiers lift him onto the shield. The troop gets in motion. The evening sinks.

Civic temple. Glittering walls and ceiling mirrors in golden green. Red marble steps to left and right leading to narrow platform. Imposing stair-complex rising steeply to the middle wall.—On high, seated, the PRIZE-AWARDER—*on the table before him the golden wreath—and the two* EULOGISTS. *Tubas and drums from the right background.*

From the right ALKIBIADES—*in white armor—is carried to the platform in a chair of gold and ivory. The four* BEARERS, *nude and white, set down the chair—go off again at right. Tubas and drums cease.*

PRIZE-AWARDER. Eulogist of Alkibiades—as your mouth fills with the voice that will tell about Alkibiades, that will tell us who were made speechless yesterday and today by the new deed of Alkibiades—speak today in praise of Alkibiades!

FIRST EULOGIST, *advancing to the edge of the staircase.* Out of muteness yesterday and muteness tomorrow, a cataract of words and words is at once let loose: I see Alkibiades. How can I endure that sight, which kindles with a white flame that roars the tumult of fame and bellies out the color of miracle? Not language is art here—my art becomes resistance to language!—I tell of the new deed of Alkibiades —and description and praise are one!—The battle was lost. The army yielded to superior force. Evening falls on the battle plain. Pursuit and darkness confuse our retreat.

Our forces in danger of total annihilation. Defenseless, on the next morning country and city. Country with women, elders, and children—city with elders, children, and women exposed to the lust of victors, horrible as victors are. Ruin swelled under the black sky, where the army melted away across the plain and the enemy rushed in among the stragglers!—Would the retreat never stop?—would it be driven farther in a flight which races faster with every fleeing step?—will all those be slain who march away out of defeat?—Where is collectedness to oppose pursuit? —where is Alkibiades? — — Alkibiades:—torch thrust into the earth marking the goal!—Alkibiades:—in white outshining the night!—Alkibiades arises in the desolate field! ! — — Alkibiades becomes the cry from cry to cry—hurried is the rush to Alkibiades—around Alkibiades the stream of flight gathers and is dammed up—troop after troop turns about—again a grim brow confronts the foe, who is startled—gives up his advantage—quails: —until Alkibiades leads the full army in firm formation out of the dangerous plain into safe territory. Greece is saved from destruction! ! —I have told what took place in the field under heavy darkness with a moon behind storm clouds. Does praise invent anything that exceeds this new deed of Alkibiades? Will a new praise pile up the long list of Alkibiades' glories, which already press against the tower of this ceiling with the mounting monuments of his praise? — — No one dares praise Alkibiades—only Alkibiades praises Alkibiades, as the deeds of Alkibiades are the deeds of Alkibiades only!

He steps back.

PRIZE-AWARDER *motions to the left. Shrill trumpets and cymbals from the left background. From the left* SOKRATES *—in brown field uniform—is carried on the shield up to the platform. The four* BEARERS*—hoplites—set down the shield on a low stand—retire again to the left. Trumpets and cymbals silent.*

PRIZE-AWARDER. Eulogizer of Sokrates—now there is stillness

for you among all those who are crowded in below the stair-
ways in the vast space of the house!

SECOND EULOGIST *stepping forward—animatedly.* In the background—men and boys—look up:—lightning darts and
strikes your eyes, which blink dazzled by the whiteness of
Alkibiades. The air grows dark—the gaze strays without dis-
tinguishing — — what is beside Alkibiades? Can shadow
become shape and step forth out of flowing gray and be
distinct beside Alkibiades? How mighty is power that
places another close to Alkibiades? How will he not be
shattered by the stab of the beam that surges from
Alkibiades? What catches up the flame and throws it back
with tremendous brilliance? Where is deed above deed
that glorified Alkibiades here—and picks it up and lays it
under foot and stands upon it higher than Alkibiades piles
it? What is the deed which lifts itself above the deed of
Alkibiades when he thrust Greece back from the abyss
that yawned? Greece did not fall—Greece endures: only
by Alkibiades could this deed be done. Alkibiades—upright
in the field—forbids foe to pursue! Weaponless he storms
across the field—after him the pack—how shall he defend
himself? His course already slackens, weary—close is the
yowling troop that captures—broad expanse empty of
armies — — how will Alkibiades save Alkibiades who saves
Greece? Does a new sword shoot out like a spark from a
star in between his fingers, and smite? — — A humpbacked
cowering is squatting somewhere in the plain—humps up
before Alkibiades—slashes circles which cut any intruder
—fights tenaciously until Greeks from here—Greeks from
there—run up—sinks down unconscious—and leaves the
saved Alkibiades among Greeks, to save Greece!—Only
Alkibiades saved could save Greece—his lauded deed arises
out of a deed which can stand before it. No longer is
Alkibiades' name like a wind that storms we know not
from where: a fuller roaring sends it out, and it thunders:
Sokrates! ! — — Sokrates rescued Alkibiades—like a husk that
protects—this deed enfolds the shimmering Alkibiades.
What shouts the fame of Sokrates louder than the fame
of Alkibiades, which now has its nest below that other?

— — Praise rolls toward Alkibiades:—Alkibiades has saved Greece!—From the praise of Alkibiades praise swells toward Sokrates: Sokrates has saved Alkibiades! !

He steps back.

PRIZE-AWARDER *rises—turns toward* ALKIBIADES. Incited by praise, such as the eulogist poured out over the height and depth of the house, thanks become loud that are meant for you—Alkibiades!

ALKIBIADES *stands.*

PRIZE-AWARDER. Tokens and tokens are a cord of great length that strings praise after praise which summoned you to the final step of the exalting steps. This is a token such that reward is bestowed upon you on the middle step. Today the gift does not demand your lofty ascent—thanks are a sound which comes to you as Greece utters it—in that what is owing to you is—Alkibiades.

Tubas and drums loud. Then silence.

ALKIBIADES *back in his chair.*

PRIZE-AWARDER, *turning toward* SOKRATES. Worthless is speech that would void debt to you—Sokrates!

SOKRATES *does not move on the shield.*

PRIZE-AWARDER. Sound bursts against lips—taciturn, the word halts and the attempt is denied. In poverty Greece should stand before you and dismiss you from mid-stairway, since she does not possess what is of equal value. Speech is mute—hands become active, giving you the only prize which glorifies Greece, since she bestows it with a rarity beyond rarity: the golden wreath!

He raises the golden wreath.

From the middle step, to which the four bore you, mount alone over the last stairway of supreme steepness, which only he overcomes for whom the best prize is proper. Set your foot on tread and tread above tread, until all the steps bring you to the crown of the golden wreath! !

SOKRATES *arches his body in a monstrous convulsion—ends the motion. Calmly.* I give — — the golden wreath — — to Alkibiades.

ALKIBIADES *bends forward—clutching his chair—staring.*
Long silence.

PRIZE-AWARDER, *composing himself.* Sokrates has saved Alkibiades — — Alkibiades has saved Greece — — : Sokrates now superimposes the rescue of Greece upon his deed which saved Alkibiades! ! — — Sokrates declines the golden wreath — — Sokrates wishes to crown Alkibiades! !

ALKIBIADES *rises at last from his chair—and begins with enormous effort to overcome the resistance of each step. Tubas, trumpets, drums, cymbals tumultuous.*

PART TWO

Attic room—gray whitewash, bare. Two doors at rear. At right a small window in slanting wall. SOKRATES *sitting before the left wall—supporting one leg, bent at the knee, on a footstool—making a herma, for which he takes the clay from a tub.* XANTIPPE *enters through the right rear door—kitchen behind it—and places herself under the window, which her face does not reach. Goes out again.* SOKRATES *goes on working, bending forward.*

XANTIPPE *returns with a footstool—places it beneath the window and steps on it. Now she opens the window and thrusts her head out.* SOKRATES *bends low over the tub.*

XANTIPPE, *stepping down.* Roofs out there—no end of roofs and roofs—those are walls around the mind!

SOKRATES *silent.*

XANTIPPE. That's a street—and a street through streets—they cross and angle—it makes your head swim!

SOKRATES *silent.*

XANTIPPE. This is a stone box—it rattles and creaks upstairs, downstairs—screeches and whispers through every wall — — it drives you to jump through the window so as to stop seeing and hearing!

SOKRATES *silent.*

XANTIPPE. Why did we move inside the city wall?

SOKRATES *silent.*

XANTIPPE. Give me one valid reason. A man would have to think up a thousand reasons to justify himself! — — There was a house. For whom? For us!—There was a garden patch. For everyone? With a fence, for us!—There was fresh air—sun, wind, rain—our share, whatever our share was. That belonged to us from morning till midnight, every leaf and stem and tree—and woe to anyone who came in uninvited. I'd have helped him over the pickets!

SOKRATES. — — I needed quiet.

XANTIPPE. That wasn't deserted enough for you—and here you settle down in an anthill? !

SOKRATES. The rush was coming.

XANTIPPE. On your account? !

SOKRATES. I saved Alkibiades.

XANTIPPE. That's war stuff. Now we're at peace. Nobody wants to talk about that lost campaign!

SOKRATES. I declined the wreath of honor.

XANTIPPE. Will that make a sensation?

SOKRATES. Not overnight.

XANTIPPE. And the consequences?

SOKRATES. Intruders—gapers—twaddlers.

XANTIPPE. Does that frighten you?

SOKRATES. Am I to work with them crowding around my tub —bumping into my elbows? An artist can only work in solitude.

XANTIPPE. — — ? — — You, an — — ? ! — — I won't repeat the word! — — You're a maker of hermae by the dozen — — hermae that people put in gateways. — —

SOKRATES. You're defaming the sacred things of the city.

XANTIPPE. *Those* hermae stand in the public places—they are sacred to me—: that's not what *you* make! The one who is offending here is the man who compares his cheap goods with the sacred ones!

SOKRATES. My skill can be developed.

XANTIPPE. In an attic room lighted by a cellar window?!
SOKRATES *silent.*

XANTIPPE. You saved Alkibiades—you rejected the prize of honor—: that's a start. That sort of thing can be developed. But now I've guessed—you want them to come and be astonished: that is Sokrates, there he sits and makes hermae. Hermae by Sokrates—that's going to be all the rage. Art, nonsense! — — Your fists formed it. That's sufficient—you'll have more orders than you can fill. Now life's going to begin. I'll take hold with both hands!

SOKRATES. Wife!

XANTIPPE. We're going to pack up here—that's done in three shakes. I'll laugh, set free!—There are your roofs, streets, stone boxes—farewell!—Out there blossoms the air—garden patch grows green—neighbors greet you over the fence—let's go!!

SOKRATES. Wife!!

XANTIPPE. I'll shout till the whole house gathers — — I'll stir up the quarter — — I'll scream for help: — — here is Sokrates — — who wants to murder me!!!

SOKRATES. — — I must stay—where we are, wife.

XANTIPPE. Am I to choke to death in these walls?!

SOKRATES. What crushes me is — — space.

XANTIPPE *taken aback—eyes him.* Husband—!

SOKRATES. I have fled to this attic — — and must conceal myself.

XANTIPPE. What have you done?

SOKRATES. I — — saved Alkibiades and gave the golden wreath to Alkibiades.

XANTIPPE. Are you afraid—of your own heroic deed?

SOKRATES. It doesn't exist. I didn't want to save Alkibiades —and I didn't want to give Alkibiades the golden wreath.

XANTIPPE. You saved Alkibiades—

SOKRATES. I—I with my humpback—the last in line—: must they not place me above Alkibiades, who shimmers

white in body and armor? Who am I—I who even gave
the wreath to Alkibiades—and set myself above reward
and thanks that are due to him? — — Who am I? — — A
badly wounded man who drove a thorn into his foot in
the cactus field and could not go along in the retreat! — —
who laid about him because a man wanted to stir him
up to be in his guide! — — who was indifferent to anyone
who came, whether friend or foe — — : only wanting to
go on sitting, so that no footstep should drive the thorn
deeper into his foot! — — who could not climb the steps
in the civic temple, because the thorn was like fire in his
flesh — — — — just as it is a terrible fire now, if I don't
support my foot—over this stool, which lets it dangle a
hand's-breadth above the floor.

XANTIPPE, *beside him.* You didn't pull the thorn out?

SOKRATES. The base of it broke off.

XANTIPPE. I'll get a doctor.

SOKRATES. He would bring it to light—and more would be
revealed: — — the monstrous swindle, which would make
Alkibiades ridiculous for all time!

XANTIPPE. A thorn you ran into your foot—

SOKRATES. On the level street? The cactus field extends over
the plain on which we retreated. That is notorious—and
now a cactus thorn is stuck in my foot. One can't walk ten
steps like this—and I stayed behind—and saved Alkibiades
—and gave away the golden wreath under the perpendic-
ular stairs. The doctor will quickly make me well — — but
he'll make Alkibiades sick to the end of his spine!

XANTIPPE. What in the world will you do?

SOKRATES. Save Alkibiades! ! ! !

XANTIPPE. You are suffering!

SOKRATES. Beyond words, wife! ! — — It splits me from the
bottom up — — sparks shoot across my eyes — — when I
step on my foot! ! I am terrified of every step — — as of
being executed with ax and noose — — but that only kills
once. — — I die a thousand times — — in every hour — —
and cannot die! ! ! !

XANTIPPE, *stepping back.* At the door—somebody!

SOKRATES. Not for me!

XANTIPPE. For you!

SOKRATES. I'm not alive!

The door at left rear is shaken—jerked open: ALKIBIADES, *in gray cloak and cap, on the threshold.* SOKRATES *works with concentration.* XANTIPPE *looks inquiringly at* ALKI-BIADES.

ALKIBIADES, *closing the door—smiling with embarrassment.* That's a trip up here—and in the dim light you bump into unforeseen obstacles. I could hardly find the door.

XANTIPPE. Who — — ?

ALKIBIADES. Your wife, Sokrates?

SOKRATES *does not look up.*

XANTIPPE. We have no acquaintances here.

ALKIBIADES. I beg you, Sokrates, ask your wife to leave the room.

SOKRATES, *without looking at her.* Customer, wife.

XANTIPPE *takes the footstool with her—goes out slowly at right rear.*

ALKIBIADES. Is it going to be a matter of course to you that I run through the reeking slums and climb up to your dizzy attic?

SOKRATES *turns his face toward him.*

ALKIBIADES. Don't you know me?

SOKRATES. No.

ALKIBIADES. A Greek—who doesn't distinguish Alkibiades—in any disguise?!

Suddenly he sweeps off his cap and opens his cloak: glorious nudity beneath it.

SOKRATES, *casually.* You are Alkibiades.

ALKIBIADES. Nobody who ever came closer to me—on the battle plain and in the civic temple—than you — — and you don't remember?!

SOKRATES. Do I have to—

*He has unobtrusively shoved the stool out from under his
knee and cautiously sets his foot on the floor. Suppressing
a groan.*

Here—is a stool—for you.

ALKIBIADES *sits down—stares at* SOKRATES. —Why did you
alone remain behind the retreating army — — and so were
able to save me from pursuit?

SOKRATES, *not interrupting his work.* Does that concern you?

ALKIBIADES. I have had men looking for you day and night!

SOKRATES. I am an obscure maker of hermae.

ALKIBIADES. With a claim to the most extensive publicity — —
but you gave away the wreath of honor!

SOKRATES *silent.*

ALKIBIADES. I owe it to you—and my life: and you disappear
into a cubby hole in the rafters. Light from a porthole!

SOKRATES *models in silence.*

ALKIBIADES, *starkly.* One does not like to receive gifts from
hands which are knotty. One does not like to owe life
and eulogy to a hunchback—who throws it down like trash
that one must pick up—to wear as adornment and
crown! — — I am Alkibiades, on whom Greece prides and
plumes herself—and shrinks timidly from his presence, so
as not to touch him with her breath — — ! ! — — who are you,
to let fall from coarse fists what I stoop to get—hunching
my back before the hunchback who grins above me? ! ! !

SOKRATES *looks at him.* I am—Sokrates.

ALKIBIADES *reaches quickly under his cloak and holds a
dagger.* You — —

SOKRATES *does not move—smiles.* I—would be grateful to you.

ALKIBIADES, *confused.* I wanted—

SOKRATES. —to bestow on me the final liberation!

ALKIBIADES. Liberation — — ?

SOKRATES. From eulogy — — from life — —

Groaning.

— — from suffering! ! !

ALKIBIADES *puts the dagger back. Quietly—attentively.* Why did you not retreat with all the rest?

SOKRATES. We ran forward all day and rearward all night—and I was tired of the play of arms and legs.

ALKIBIADES. Our battle a play of arms and legs?

SOKRATES. Did we not march with our legs and fight with our arms?

ALKIBIADES. The playing was for Greece!

SOKRATES. Which was decided by arms and legs.

ALKIBIADES. A play with everything at stake!

SOKRATES. Then all that wasn't very important, if it was decided with such a scanty investment of arms and legs.

ALKIBIADES *silent.*

SOKRATES, *working again.* That occurred to me when I dropped down on the battlefield—and it made me thoughtful.

ALKIBIADES. You got into danger—

SOKRATES. The enemy would have killed me.

ALKIBIADES. It could have cost you your life!

SOKRATES. If it can be destroyed by arms and legs, probably its value is not worth much fuss.

ALKIBIADES. Your heroism—

SOKRATES. A little reflectiveness.

ALKIBIADES. Did the golden wreath in the civic temple mean as little to you?

SOKRATES. Had they fastened it around my arms and legs, I should have consented. But what did the golden wreath have to do with my head, on which they would have put it?

ALKIBIADES. It makes the chills run through one—to listen to you, Sokrates.

SOKRATES. Give me a rebuttal that will shake me. I accept help when I am mistaken. I am teachable, and I'll be the pupil of a child if it talks reasonably to me. But that must be reason that can be thought out in one's head—and that one does not prove with arms and legs. I will take the wreath if it annoys you—only I must not earn with arms and legs that with which I crown my head!

ALKIBIADES, *bitterly*. The playing was for Greece—

SOKRATES. Greece is a play of arms and legs!

ALKIBIADES, *hiding his face in his hands*. It will be dark in Greece — — — —

SOKRATES *looks at him a long time—then at work*. Do you see what I am doing here? — — I am making a herma. That is a monument for a person—as you are one for whom monuments will be erected. Your achievement is the victory with arms and legs—will they depict and set up your victorious arms and legs? They cut them off—shape a smooth pediment, and set your head on it. Only the head. What is there to the arms and legs? They run and strike —but the head carries out what is special. That is why I remained behind on the battlefield—and the effect showed itself right away, because my head had been at work—: I was able to save your life—and with your life your Greece—and in addition procure for you the golden wreath!
The left rear door is jerked open: the BOYS—*in gray cloaks and caps, daggers held high—crowd in.*

FIRST BOY. That is Sokrates!

OTHER BOYS. Death to Sokrates! !

ALL BOYS, *rushing toward* SOKRATES. He saved Alkibiades! ! ! !
XANTIPPE emerges at right rear—shrieks.

ALKIBIADES *confronts the* BOYS. Sokrates saved Alkibiades — — Sokrates gave the golden wreath to Alkibiades — — : only Sokrates had the right to save Alkibiades — — only Sokrates had the right to donate the golden wreath to Alkibiades! !
The BOYS *stand spellbound.*

ALKIBIADES. What do you know of Sokrates? ! — — I will tell it to you as I can tell it to you—after brief instruction which Sokrates granted me. I am already eager for tomorrow which will teach me more—as you will become eager when I instruct you. Don't bother Sokrates—I will tell

you everything that I intend to find out from Sokrates
today and tomorrow and every day! !

The BOYS *go off with him.*

XANTIPPE. — — — With you — — ? !

SOKRATES. Hush, wife — — don't speak to me — — don't disgrace yourself — — : — — I — — — I — — I — — I — —

XANTIPPE. The others — — ? !

SOKRATES, *flinging up his arms.* I — — pitied him! ! — — — —
I had to invent — — what should not be invented! ! — — —
I had to cover the sky — — and wither the earth — — ! ! — —
It was no crime of mine — — — — : Compassion! ! — — — —
Compassion! ! — — — — Compassion! !

XANTIPPE *looks at him with concern—goes off through right
rear door.*

SOKRATES *looks about—straightens up—overcomes the convulsion of pain and walks—walks off at left rear.*

XANTIPPE *comes back with a washbasin — — petrified before Sokrates' empty seat — — falling powerless on her
knees — — groaning. The — — thorn — — — —*

*Cramped fish market. Cobblestones. Alleys coming in from
right and left. From the right alley* FISHWIVES *are shoving uninterruptedly two-wheeled carts with tubs, whose
contents they pour into stout copper vats around the fish
market, returning then to the alley.* SOKRATES *stands in
the middle of the fish market.*

FIRST FISHWIFE, *stopping before* SOKRATES. Shall I make a
detour around your hunchback?

SOKRATES. My hump is a detour in my back, so that the blood
won't rise too fast into my head and flood my reason.

FIRST FISHWIFE. What is your hump to me?

SOKRATES. Just now you found it in your way.

FIRST FISHWIFE *goes around him.*

SECOND FISHWIFE, *behind* SOKRATES. Watch out, honey, you'll
get your toes flattened!

SOKRATES. Why do you tell me in advance that you're going

to run over me? I'll feel it all right when your cart rolls over my feet.

SECOND FISHWIFE. You—to one side!

SOKRATES. Or did you want to prepare me for the pain which I shall now encounter with self-control?

SECOND FISHWIFE *goes around him in a curve.*

THIRD FISHWIFE, *at a vat in the rear—spraying* SOKRATES *from her dipper.*

Has that lump taken root in the cobblestones? That's a fearfully hard ground—you got to soften it up!

The FISHWIVES *shriek.*

SOKRATES *knocks the water off his coat.* You hit too high— one doesn't water a tree trunk, it's the base one soaks.

FOURTH FISHWIFE, *at a vat in the rear—to the* THIRD FISHWIFE. Whose hide got washed by your spray, ha?

THIRD FISHWIFE, *replying shrilly.* I'll collect haddock bones for your mattress—that'll make you lively, you stockfish!

FOURTH FISHWIFE *bursts out laughing.* Put sticklebacks into your bed—otherwise nothing is going to stick you, you piddock!

FIFTH FISHWIFE, *in front of* SOKRATES *with her cart and tub.* This is a thoroughfare—gangway!

SIXTH FISHWIFE, *behind* SOKRATES *with her cart and tub.* Truck coming—step aside!

SOKRATES *turns his head to left—to right.* I can't move a foot.

FIFTH FISHWIFE. I'll teach you to run!

SIXTH FISHWIFE. I'll make you jump!

SOKRATES. I stand fast between you.

FIFTH FISHWIFE. Now—I'll shove!

SIXTH FISHWIFE. Now—I'll push!

SOKRATES. How will this end? I give way—all right—: you'll push your carts ahead and knock them together so that the tubs will burst and their contents be poured out. Did your men pull the fish out of the sea to be thrown on the pavement? I'm preventing your irretrievable loss if I stick to the spot I stand on.

SEVENTH FISHWIFE, *at a vat to the right.* He'll make you roll your carts across the moon to get to your vats!

FIFTH FISHWIFE, *curving to the front around* SOKRATES—*to the* SIXTH FISHWIFE. Do you have to trundle your cart when I come along?

SIXTH FISHWIFE, *around* SOKRATES *to the rear—retorting.* Did you lease the fish market for your finger-length herrings?

FIFTH FISHWIFE *shrilly.* I smell a stink from your tub—why don't you bring your dead flounders to market in a basket?

SIXTH FISHWIFE. You got water in your tub? Nope, it's vinegar —or your carrion would rot on the way!

FIFTH FISHWIFE *hurling water at her with the dipper.* Vinegar —see how it stings!

SIXTH FISHWIFE *spraying water back.* Rotten water—try the taste of it!

EIGHTH FISHWIFE, *at a vat.* Give that fellow a bath—till he floats off like a limp perch!

NINTH FISHWIFE, *advancing with her cart toward* SOKRATES. Forward straight ahead to the vat!

SOKRATES, *stopping the cart with both hands—bending forward.* What have you, smelts?

NINTH FISHWIFE. Whales!

SOKRATES. Do you say "whales" in order to make my ignorance of the kinds of fish clear to me with particular emphasis?

NINTH FISHWIFE. I say—straight ahead to the vat!

SOKRATES *bracing himself against the cart.* If a purchaser stepped up to your fish vat and asked you what you have to sell, would you reply with the same exaggeration if he took your pikes to be smelts?

NINTH FISHWIFE. Pikes!

SOKRATES. You would make the gullible person perplexed and injure your business.

NINTH FISHWIFE, *letting go her pushcart and clasping her hands over her head.* Now this good-for-nothing is giving me advice how to carry on my business!

SOKRATES. I am inexperienced and am using the opportunity to instruct myself.

NINTH FISHWIFE *rudely*. You want to buy fish?

SOKRATES. How can I buy a commodity when I don't know what it is?

NINTH FISHWIFE. You'll tell by the taste!

SOKRATES. Granted that I like your fish—and by all appearances they have come to the fish market fresh out of the net—how, if the appetite for just such fish comes over me again, can I get them anew, if I lack any more precise designation for the coveted object?

NINTH FISHWIFE. Come to the fish market and look in the vats!

Taking hold again.

Onward!

SOKRATES, *stopping her*. I may be prevented from leaving the house myself. How can I make clear to a messenger I send what he is to bring?

NINTH FISHWIFE *letting go again—angry*. I'll serve the booby all right!

SOKRATES. Now, are they smelts or pikes or whales?

NINTH FISHWIFE, *swinging her arms*. Whales! !

SOKRATES. Now I know that they are whales—and every day, without taking the trouble to go to the fish market myself, I'll have whales brought from your vat. You see that your business looks up as soon as you have imparted some of your knowledge to the ignorant.

NINTH FISHWIFE. Smelts—pikes—whales—!—the head of a smelt —the fins of a pike—the tail of a whale—!—: the fish market is turning around! !

TENTH FISHWIFE, *behind the* NINTH FISHWIFE *with her pushcart*. Go ahead—don't block the road!

NINTH FISHWIFE, *abusively*. Did anybody ever hear the like? It's enough to make you grow ears as big as a whale's gills! Here she comes along and takes over — — imagine a whale in my pushcart that I'm shoving in front of me with two hands!

TENTH FISHWIFE *shoving the* NINTH FISHWIFE *from behind with her pushcart.* If you've got time—I've got to make two more trips down to the wharf!

NINTH FISHWIFE, *turning around.* Are you blind, you wall-eyed pike, that you don't see where I'm standing?

TENTH FISHWIFE. Then I'd hear your croaking, you squawking old rook!

NINTH FISHWIFE. You tootle sweetly—just open your gullet good and wide—there's pay for you!

Dips water and throws it in her face.

TENTH FISHWIFE, *pouring water over her from the dipper.* Don't swallow it the wrong way!

NINTH FISHWIFE *again.* Dirt tastes bitter!

TENTH FISHWIFE *again.* Then my tub water must taste sweet to you!

ELEVENTH FISHWIFE, *bringing her cart up behind the* TENTH FISHWIFE. Watch your step—Wash your scabs at home!

TENTH FISHWIFE, *turning around.* Who's got scabs?—Look, you're gray around the muzzle!

Gives her a dipperful.

NINTH FISHWIFE, *likewise aiming at the* ELEVENTH FISHWIFE. Where's a scab?—You wait, you and your talk both need a washing!

Dipperful.

ELEVENTH FISHWIFE *briskly spraying them both.* I can dip twice—before you bend your stiff frames once!

TWELFTH FISHWIFE *spraying the* NINTH *and* TENTH FISHWIVES. Got hot, eh?—I'll cool your behinds!

THIRTEENTH FISHWIFE *spraying the* TWELFTH FISHWIFE. Who called you into this quarrel?

TWELFTH FISHWIFE *spraying back.* Must I ask your lousy whiskers for permission?

FOURTEENTH FISHWIFE *spraying the* THIRTEENTH FISHWIFE. Is somebody meddling who wants a dipperful of fish water?

FIFTEENTH FISHWIFE *spraying blindly.* There's a dousing for you out of the vat!

SIXTEENTH FISHWIFE *spraying and shrieking*. Now fish are flying with the water! !

SEVENTEENTH FISHWIFE. Anybody who sprays—gets splashed! !

EIGHTEENTH FISHWIFE. Fishes—water! !

The fight has become general: from tubs and vats water is eagerly dipped and hurled from the dippers. Amid the noise the words: "Dishes!" "Water! !" From the left alley the FORERUNNER—*half nude, resplendent trousers. He motions back into the alley defensively.*

FORERUNNER. Make way for Alkibiades! !

The FISHWIVES *lower their dippers.*

FORERUNNER *makes a sign toward the alley. In a sedan chair—on the shoulders of four nude white* BEARERS *in red boots—*ALKIBIADES *in a greenish-yellow padded cloak with bunches of blue ostrich feathers. A* BOY *follows, black flutes in a colorful, bulging belt.*

FORERUNNER *to the* BEARERS. Fish market: don't slip on wet stones and slippery fish!

The procession moves on in haste.

FORERUNNER, *stopping at* SOKRATES' *back*. Make way for Alkibiades!

SOKRATES *does not move.*

FORERUNNER *draws a short whip from his trousers*. Make way for Alkibiades!

SOKRATES *unchanged.*

FORERUNNER *lashes him*. Make way for Alkibiades! !

SOKRATES *turns slowly toward him*. You must whip in a circle if you want to go around me.

FORERUNNER *starts—lifts his whip anew.*

SOKRATES. You've just marked my back with your whip. Now I offer you my breast too.

FORERUNNER *does not strike.*

A FISHWIFE. Whip him to pieces—he started all this so that our fish are dying here on the cobblestones!

SECOND FISHWIFE. Why didn't we wash him? !

THIRD FISHWIFE. The tubs and vats are empty!

FOURTH FISHWIFE. But the dippers are whole! !

She goes at SOKRATES, *brandishing her dipper.*

ALL FISHWIVES, *rushing at* SOKRATES. The dippers are whole! ! !

ALKIBIADES, *bored—facing ahead.* What's up?

FORERUNNER. Some person does not get out of Alkibiades' way!

ALKIBIADES. Where?

He starts—slowly pushes himself up halfway—harshly to FORERUNNER.

Down!

FORERUNNER *to the* BEARERS. Down—so—so!

The BEARERS *set the sedan chair down.*

ALKIBIADES *steps out—hurries to* SOKRATES—*embraces him.* A find in the fish market!—The attic room empty—the quarter deserted—: Sokrates gone—dived down like a fish in the ocean. I cast out a thousand fishlines—not a hook drew the rare swimmer back to the light. Everything is strange about you, Sokrates—the way you disappear and the way I discover you here, the last place I expected to find you! —What are the women screaming about?

SOKRATES. I tried to get information from one of these women, and they began to quarrel.

ALKIBIADES. A fishwife should tell you more than you know yourself? You deserved the whip for such a claim!

To the FISHWIVES.

Scuffle till you're out of breath—and thank heaven that Sokrates gave you the occasion for it. What's more, he's paying you the tuition, for which you should be eternally in his debt!

He throws gold pieces among the FISHWIVES, *which they pick up avidly.*

ALKIBIADES *to the* FORERUNNER. The sedan chair in front of Sokrates!—Lift Sokrates into the seat! — — I shall walk on foot beside Sokrates!

Two BEARERS *lift* SOKRATES *into the chair.*

FORERUNNER. Up—so—so!

The BEARERS *shoulder the sedan chair.*

SOKRATES. Where do you want to go?

ALKIBIADES. A banquet, Sokrates—which will be unforgettable with you present!

The procession in rapid march off into the right alley.

NINTH FISHWIFE *stands still—eying money in one hand.* That was lightning and thunder and a shower of rain—!

Picking up a fish with the other hand.

A smelt?—a pike?—a whale?—

Shaking her head.

Who can tell that now?

Beach house. Sea pavilion: two thirds of the space, toward the back, left as open square with columns. In front, solid walls. Door openings to right and left—steps downward. The uneven plaster is painted all over in large patches of color. Irregular banquet couches with colored silk drapes—low tables alongside for crystal goblets and overfull basins of flowers. In the center of the columns a narrow object, almost man high, concealed by a drape. Ocean billowing silver below firmament of utmost blue. HOST *and* GUESTS—*in loose silk smocks—stretched out on the couches; one still vacant. Young serving* EUNUCHS—*amber chains around their ankles—busy.*

HOST, *lifting his crystal goblet toward the* FIRST GUEST. I'd like to live two thousand years and listen every afternoon to your work, Poet!

He drinks.

FIRST GUEST, *who is the only one to wear a blue ribbon about his hair.* You would outlive it by one thousand nine hundred and ninety-nine years, Host!

SECOND GUEST. It is eternal: for it was not new to me when I first enjoyed it yesterday—and yet your creation makes it new!

THIRD GUEST. They will play it above the ruins when the theater has already fallen apart!

FOURTH GUEST. Men with tongues which we do not understand will recite it—and shape it with gestures which we cannot interpret!

FIFTH GUEST. It imparts an agitation which the air does not quiet—the aroused wind transports it across zones and aeons!

HOST. That is your work, Poet—and this banquet is its celebration with your admiring friends!

FIRST GUEST *filling both hands with flowers, inspired.* Am I a poet? Does the applause hold over till today, which saluted me yesterday in the theater? Does the surge of that storm of praise not flatten out—do its waves keep pounding against me, impelled again and again by you, so that I am exalted into the brightness of midday?—I am a poet! I know that. There are visions out of me which are no one's visions but mine. Stars course for me more flaming—than stars are brightness over you. The green of box trees and the milk-white of mother-of-pearl bedew me with greater brilliance —to you they have scarce the glint of a gleam. Voices are a breath and a mighty roar in that breath—silence is eloquent. No mystery remains profound—and into the depths sinks all that is familiar. Wisdom bursts into spray —out of blood bursts emotion—blood bursts open with blossoms—and ripples down shuddering with blossoms!

He lets the flowers fall over him.

FIFTH GUEST. You are a poet!

He throws flowers at him.

THE GUESTS, *casting flowers at him.* You are a poet!

FIRST GUEST, *clutching at the rain of flowers.* Choke me in lilacs and violets and crocus—I am living! !

HOST, *loudly.* Friends—do not overspeed the feast—as yet not all are assembled!

FIRST GUEST, *carried away.* All are here who love me!

HOST. You deceive yourself in making so slight a claim!

FIRST GUEST, *half rising.* Alkibiades!—Did he promise you to

come? Inviolably? Was Alkibiades in the theater yesterday?
Did Alkibiades applaud?

HOST. He was your most eager and grateful spectator.

FIRST GUEST, *softly.* I will dedicate my work to Alkibiades.

SECOND GUEST. That will make a competition for eternity
between your name and his.

THIRD GUEST. One will keep passing the other—and the goal
will shift to infinity!

FIRST GUEST. Now it is immortal, if Alkibiades adopts it!

Outside at the right, flute music.

HOST. His flute-player—: Alkibiades!

All look toward the door at right.

HOST *to a serving boy.* Run and call your fellows to order if
they are slow in serving. You can beat them.

ALKIBIADES *already in the doorway—behind him his* FLUTE-
PLAYER, *thrusting his flutes into his belt.*

HOST. We had begun the feast, and we interrupted it because
you were missing, Alkibiades. You see that the flower-bat-
tle was already raging. Our patience acquired a bitter taste,
and we had to drink to soothe it!

ALKIBIADES *lets himself down on the vacant couch, after
the* FLUTE-PLAYER *has taken his cloak from him. Two*
SERVING BOYS *loosen his shoes—rub the bare feet with
sponge and towel.* FLUTE-PLAYER *exits with cloak and
shoes.*

ALKIBIADES. You censure my lateness, and I could not well
defend it if the occasion for it were not its own defense.

HOST. Is there such an occasion, when the celebration of the
triumph of the great poet, who is entering into eternity,
awaits you?

FIRST GUEST. Alkibiades delayed Alkibiades—or the city col-
lapsed into a mountain of stones to block his way!

FOURTH GUEST. Did the city tumble to make a wall of dust
before you?

ALKIBIADES. I met Sokrates.

Silence.

ALKIBIADES, *with great animation.* The location for your beach house was a masterful choice of yours, Host. One must cross the fish market to get here. You did not lay out your building plan without the realization that one crosses the fish market!

To the FIRST GUEST.

Or is it to you that I owe thanks, because without your triumph in the theater yesterday I should not have crossed the fish market today? As it is, your tragedy has only achieved its full success today: it brought Sokrates into my path! But you may contend with each other for the glory—only do not attack each other like fighting cocks: Sokrates would despise you for that!

He drinks hastily.

HOST, *after a pause—with an effort.* Now Alkibiades has come. Poet, the celebration of your triumph is upward bound.

He rings a tinkling bell.

Dancers!

FIRST GUEST. Dancing supple for ecstasy!

THIRD GUEST. Dancers incited by flutes!

SIXTH GUEST *lifts flowers out of his basin.*

Dancers praised with roses!

ALKIBIADES. You rang too soon, Host!

To SERVING BOYS.

Do not open yet for the dancers!—I discovered Sokrates in the middle of the fish market—and am here. Guess: did I forsake Sokrates, who had eluded me again?

FOURTH GUEST. The riddle is difficult: you are lying between us—and still you are in the fish market?

ALKIBIADES. The solution is amusing: Sokrates and Alkibiades remain together—only an open door divides them still!

SECOND GUEST. You — — are with Sokrates?

ALKIBIADES. You deserve the prize—you may be the first to cast your violets over Sokrates!

FIRST GUEST. You invited — — Sokrates?

ALKIBIADES. To honor your feast, Poet. Which is meager

without Sokrates, who donated the golden wreath to me, to make it more golden than gold itself!

To the HOST.

Does my lateness now seem rewarding?

HOST. Where — — is Sokrates?

ALKIBIADES. He is talking with the doorkeepers.

HOST, *quickly to* SERVING BOYS. Escort Sokrates to us!

ALKIBIADES, *opposing.* Don't disturb him!

To the HOST.

He will stand motionless on the threshold as long as he likes, and he yields to no force. You would not drive him away with whips—as my forerunner chastized him in vain in the fish market!

FOURTH GUEST. Why is he still talking with the doorkeepers?

ALKIBIADES. Fishwives—doorkeepers—my bearers who carried him in my sedan chair—

SECOND GUEST. How did you come here, Alkibiades?

ALKIBIADES. I walked beside him—or beneath him, for he who donated the golden wreath to me swayed along at my head—and over my head he questioned the sweating bearers!

SEVENTH GUEST. About the way?

ALKIBIADES. About their step, one going right, the other left —how one step always goes right—and one always goes left —and how without equal stepping the chair will sway and capsize: until they got confused—and didn't know what is right and what is left—and had to admit their ignorance to Sokrates, bearers who had always carried me on a run through the streets. Now they're crouching, all broken up, beside the sedan chair!

SOKRATES *has entered the doorway: he stands stiffly and is looking down before him.* HOST *and* GUESTS *catch sight of him.*

ALKIBIADES *becomes attentive—turns toward him.* Sokrates— three steps down before you—: to which foot do you grant the privilege of carrying you down twice? I bet on the left!

SOKRATES *sets one foot on the first step and draws the other after it.*

ALKIBIADES. Again figured like no one else. Two won't go into three, so two must shift three times—and left foot does not tire more than right foot, to impair the equilibrium which sustains the entire Sokrates.

SOKRATES *on the floor—again stands motionless.*

HOST. The couches are counted by the number of invited guests—

ALKIBIADES *jumps up.* Sokrates, strech out on the drape which I will yield to you. I will sit beside you—and if you again attempt to run away, I will throw myself over you with arms that embrace in love!

He pushes crystal goblet and flower basin away and seats himself on the low table.

SOKRATES, *approaching the couch one step at a time—reaches it—lays himself down.*

HOST, *half rising.* Alkibiades, it shames us to see you sitting before us—

ALKIBIADES. Tell no lies—my place beside Sokrates makes you envious!

Two SERVING BOYS *start to loosen* SOKRATES' *shoes and wash his feet.*

SOKRATES *twitching sharply—hastily.* Don't!

HOST. They are well trained.

SOKRATES. I do not accuse them of a rough grip—only I was not certain whether you should show your approval of my presence by beginning with my feet.

HOST. Your presence honors this celebration of a triumph.

SOKRATES. Then I will not prove my worthiness with the soles of my feet.

He motions the SERVING BOYS *away.*

A celebration of a triumph? Have you, Alkibiades, won another campaign?

ALKIBIADES. Should I have undertaken it without you, who interpreted for me the value of battle and war?

SOKRATES. You have not forgotten it?

ALKIBIADES. How else could I live?

SOKRATES. What other triumphs are there?

FIRST GUEST. Were you not sitting in the theater yesterday?

ALKIBIADES. You would have had to look for Sokrates in the upper rows, which one scales with an effort, and where people stand!

FIRST GUEST. Did the voices of the actors carry to the farthest rows?

SOKRATES. I was not in the theater.

SEVENTH GUEST. No citizen missed the performance!

SOKRATES. Was it a success?

FIRST GUEST. They wreathed my hair with the blue ribbon!

SOKRATES. Why did they, if your work was understood by all, and if today everyone is the creator of it, as you were yesterday?—In that case your friend is celebrating your funeral today—and the only one who still bids you live, since he does not know your work, is I. You will have to cling to me if you wish to escape with your life.

FIRST GUEST, *smiling feebly.* You have saved Alkibiades—and now you want to save me too.

SOKRATES. Had I not been prevented from mounting the steep steps in the theater—you could have no cause for laughing today. But I was hindered—and so your celebration can be held with certain limitations.—What will take place?

ALKIBIADES. Host—you must make the special offering in order to tickle the corpse of the Poet!

SOKRATES. I shall be receptive to everything and remain conscious of my unique responsibility.

HOST *with emphasis.* Poet—the point is to form the thanks which burst out in a flood to go to you. He who was poor yesterday—lives richly today—beladen with sparkling freight, which is joy that streams from your art. Laughing turns to weeping—and tears are sweetness from your work of art. You are a poet—as you transform intoxication and grief into woe and pleasure!—Voice dies away—embrace halts—no sign of love from body to body remains significant. How do thanks become visible? Only a simile elicits a testimonial which is above any doubt:—your herma will become a sanctuary in my house—and your herma will make my house holy!

He gives a sign to SERVING BOYS, *who go to the veiled object in the rear and strip off the drape: the herma of the* FIRST GUEST, *in shining bronze, stands there erected.*

FIRST GUEST *to the* HOST, *with an outcry.* You present life to me, holy and imperishable!

THE OTHER GUESTS *all throw flowers at the herma.* This herma is holy!!

ALKIBIADES *stops—hands flowers to* SOKRATES. We'll share this bunch!

SOKRATES, *gesture of rejection.*

ALKIBIADES. Herma consecration, Sokrates—you maker of hermae.

SOKRATES *turns away.*

ALKIBIADES *bends down to him.* Does not the herma stand there as holy?

SOKRATES. It — — is not complete.

ALKIBIADES *raises himself up—to the others.* Sokrates is a maker of hermae—Host, you insult the Poet. His herma has a defect!

Silence.

ALKIBIADES. A poor herma which you are setting up in your beach house, Host. Sokrates shows you the disgrace!

FIRST GUEST. My head in size and strict form!

THIRD GUEST. Who made it?

HOST. He who makes the holy hermae in the public places!

ALKIBIADES. Sokrates replies:—the valued artist failed here!

SOKRATES. I did not say that. My words were: it is not complete!

FOURTH GUEST. A casting of rare smoothness!

ALKIBIADES. Yet you detect grave faults, Sokrates!

SOKRATES. It is not complete—not because it has faults, for I discover none. I praise the herma, it shoots out light—it kindles—it is aflame — — only a small detail is lacking which is important.

FIRST GUEST. What do you miss?

SOKRATES. The blue ribbon about the metal brow.

FIRST GUEST. That is meant for the living!

SOKRATES. Did you not pass away yesterday? Did not the applause of the thousands wrest from you breath—and heartbeat—your feverish pulse in the great theater? Did you not flood your banks—to remain behind as a waterless spring—with the departure of the throngs which took with them what they took from you?—Since that hour you have been common property and dispossessed—and where a bronze casting bears your features, its life is more genuine than your throbbing breast with its blood and breath—so unchained are you from yourself! — — Enjoy enthusiasm —for now your final glory is attested:—you are forever in eternity, which knows neither life nor death!—you are imperishable without arrival or departure!—you are blessed without day and midnight! — — If therefore you will serve your true dignity—then do not leave the blue ribbon on a cadaver which will decay and eat up fine silk—but rescue the lovely symbol of honor, enter it into the duration which your herma secures!

ALKIBIADES. How hard it is for him to part with the ribbon!

SOKRATES. Nothing is gained here by little vanities—at stake are life and death!

FIRST GUEST *unfastens the ribbon from his hair.*

ALKIBIADES. His hands tremble and swerve under the light load.

SOKRATES. Only that has weight which has the appearance of being unweighty.

FIRST GUEST. Shall — — I bewreath myself?

SOKRATES. Choose the one to whom you will subject yourself.

FIRST GUEST. I − − beg you, Sokrates, to rise and go and crown my herma!

A SERVING BOY *takes the blue ribbon to* SOKRATES.

SOKRATES *holds it out—looks at all the others, who have instinctively pressed their faces into their cushions. His arms begin to waver—a groan escapes him—with enormous effort he finds words.* − − − − I gave you the golden wreath, Alkibiades, which is above the blue ribbon: − − I should offend you if I bestowed the lesser symbol with the same hands. Go—and adorn the herma on behalf of Sokrates!

Profound stillness.

ALKIBIADES *controls himself—walks hastily to the herma and puts the ribbon on it. He remains there—looks back into the room—laughs sharply.* Are you sleeping?—Already drunk?—Is this to be the roaring victory-celebration—to make the stars fall out of the night and kindle the red dawn? − − Host—do not lure into your house guests who unmask its dreariness. It is a pity of the time which is going to waste!

Rushing to SOKRATES.

You are glorious, Sokrates—no miracle of feasts and friends stuns you. You are worthy of penetrating the finest secret —and if it suffices you, my pride in the possession of it will leap up to the clouds! − − Set out from here with me— Sokrates, it will be such an evening as never was in the world!

SOKRATES *slowly props himself up—sits a moment on the edge of the couch—rises—climbs each step with both feet —exits.*

ALKIBIADES *has shoes and cloak put on by* SERVING BOYS— *exits.*

Outside, Alkibiades' FLUTE-PLAYER *moving away.*

FIRST GUEST *throws his head back—clutches his throat— hoarsely.* Dancers! !

HOST *shakes his head. To* SERVING BOYS. Loosen the curtains. It blows cold from the water—and the brightness stings.

The SERVING BOYS *let down gold-and-black tapestries be-*

tween the columns. The room melts away into semi-darkness.

HOST, *with an outcry.* Wine! !

The SERVING BOYS *in white flit amid the couches.*

Bath chamber. A frieze of animals on a bright green ground. In the center, an oval lattice made of ivory and coral surrounding the depressed bathtub. Door at left—red wood—straw seat beside it. Door at rear with shimmering curtain of glass beads. Alkibiades' FLUTE-PLAYER *is audible.* PHRYNE *pushes the bead curtain aside—behind it a room in half light with a broad couch.* PHRYNE *wears her hair like a stiff column—gold dust on it. Fingernails and toenails enameled violet. Around her torso a short embroidered coat—her legs in thin silk trousers.* FLUTE-PLAYER *silent.*

PHRYNE *quivers—takes a few steps—looks wide-eyed at the left door.*

ALKIBIADES *opens door—still outside.* Announcement is made to you—and admittance will be a happiness to you!

PHRYNE *shuts her eyes—bends her body and stretches arms out.*

ALKIBIADES *enters—remains at the door, surveying.* Seven times more brilliant than my wish conceives you; when I am far, you gain in appearance.

PHRYNE *faintly.* Beloved.

ALKIBIADES. Intoxication of friendship blown away—and the tongue of a steeper flame reaches out and touches you.

PHRYNE. Come!

ALKIBIADES. Light that glimmered is dispelled—and a night-sun suspends itself in space above your whiteness, which timidly makes your blood a secret.

PHRYNE. I—wait.

ALKIBIADES, *roughly.* I — — did not come alone.

PHRYNE *stares at him.*

ALKIBIADES, *biting his lips with a smile—silent.*

PHRYNE. Who is that?

ALKIBIADES. Who is Alkibiades? Who—with these arms—with
these legs—is Alkibiades? Who—with breathing and sleeping—is Alkibiades? Who—with his desire before you—is
Alkibiades?—A gift of Alkibiades to Alkibiades, which he
did not even give himself out of his own possessions—
but received from another treasure store, which Alkibiades
is now exploiting for Alkibiades!

PHRYNE. You are Alkibiades.

ALKIBIADES. Alkibiades, of lofty origin. Deemed worthy of
the company of one who loans away, without claim to
interest and repayment, life—the golden wreath—and you
to Alkibiades!

PHRYNE. I give myself to you.

ALKIBIADES. That loses in value—for its measure was not determined by him who puts in the weights. The scales are
indeterminate!

PHRYNE. I am—Phryne.

ALKIBIADES. A shell without air that sounds. A bell that
is not yet rung—a name that is not called up for eternity:
— — Sokrates has not yet sought you!

PHRYNE. Is Sokrates—beautiful?

ALKIBIADES. The completed beauty of a herma: — — knock
away the parts under the throat—and Sokrates will over-
whelm you!

PHRYNE. Has Sokrates so much value for you?

ALKIBIADES. Am I not a mockery without his triumph?

PHRYNE *looks at him.*

ALKIBIADES. In the midst of life, with his pulse and breath,
Sokrates is already a herma. Does he still walk the ground?
Does his step hasten over stairs in the civic temple—to
the feast in the beach house—to be admitted by you?
On the wet fish market he stands unmoving—no whip will
drive him from the spot—he does not feel the stinging
blow, which would make a horse rear, in his deceased
body: he is a herma with a head which is alive above the
pediment which is lifeless!

PHRYNE. I should like—to see him.

ALKIBIADES. Overturn this herma!—Confusion is instigated by it which makes life dead—and death alive!—Your slender arms have such power as is bestowed nowhere else. Heaven endowed you with its azure—and all shores with their green: graciously shield heaven and earth from frost and night, which will burst out if this herma disdains creation!— Overturn the herma—and on our couch—after your couching with him—pleasure shall bloom which is once more chaste! !

He reaches for the door—exit.

PHRYNE *stands still a moment—then she runs into the rear room and pulls the bead curtain to.*

ALKIBIADES *pushes open the door at left—leads* SOKRATES *in.*

ALKIBIADES. It takes less effort to move a boulder than you under the burden of your calculating head!

SOKRATES. Are you leading me into a cook-shop?

ALKIBIADES. What is the source of that guess?

SOKRATES. Odors smolder sharply.

ALKIBIADES. Vapor of rose oil and sweet distillation of cinnamon—you are penetrating the bath chamber of the shyest mistress. Nothing secret from you any more!

He goes to the bead curtain—pushes it aside.

PHRYNE—*now closely enveloped in silk scarves—lies on the couch.*

ALKIBIADES *props himself against the doorpost—his voice fails him—returns to* SOKRATES *almost out of control.* What is mortal—dies in lust—and rises again in desire!

Exit quickly.

SOKRATES *does not change his posture.*

PHRYNE *listens.*

SOKRATES *looks around. Lamenting, he lifts his arms to half height—weakness conquers him: he drags himself to the straw seat, upon which he drops heavily.*

PHRYNE, *listening with astonishment—thrusts her head forward.*

SOKRATES *clenches fists—controls himself—sits limply.*

PHRYNE, *with thin voice.* Friend of Alkibiades—your friend loves you.

SOKRATES, *silent.*

PHRYNE. The love of your friend is also my love—friend.

SOKRATES — —

PHRYNE *raises herself up—adjusts her scarves—steps into the doorway. At the sight of* SOKRATES *she starts.*

SOKRATES *looks at her.* Why does Alkibiades run out of the door? Did he not see you? Are you hiding from Alkibiades?

PHRYNE, *hesitantly.* Are you — — ? ?

SOKRATES. Did you quarrel with Alkibiades? He will repent of it when I tell him later that your face was smooth and without a trace of anger.

PHRYNE. — — the friend of Alkibiades? ?

SOKRATES. His hot blood has played him many a trick before now—but this one, it seems to me, will have the bitterest consequences.

PHRYNE, *hastily.* What will happen to him?

SOKRATES. He is making a detour and talking himself into an explanation of it—and on his return he will discover his missed opportunity, which he will have no means of recovering.

PHRYNE. He left you — — with me.

SOKRATES. Then he did not calculate the loss which, determined in one hour, bursts through the boundaries of all time.

PHRYNE. Do you love Alkibiades?

SOKRATES. I cannot escape his pursuit and by this noose I am tethered to him.

PHRYNE. Are you avoiding Alkibiades?

SOKRATES. He had me whipped on the fish market when I would not step aside for him—and as he likewise would not leave the place before me, we are inextricably connected.

PHRYNE. You despise Alkibiades?

SOKRATES. I should disgrace myself if I defamed him to whom I gave the golden wreath.

PHRYNE. You remain without love—without hate—for Alkibiades?

SOKRATES. I attempt not to prod myself to excitements which evaporate as quickly as they come: Hate burns one with a darting flame—love burns one with a darting flame. Or else hate and love were not genuine. But I cannot content myself with the moment, if I aspire to a deeper inclination.

PHRYNE. Are you inventing a new love?

SOKRATES. Were you not such a woman as your rare symmetry makes you, the words of my answer would flow glibly. But they would contain an insult—especially when uttered in your bath chamber—and since Alkibiades would call me to account and would give me no rest any more by day or night in his eagerness for an explanation, I will shut my mouth from now on, until Alkibiades returns again, and your pleasure makes it possible for me to depart unobserved.

He turns away.

PHRYNE *observes him—steps close to him—bends over him.* I—am curious.

SOKRATES — —

PHRYNE. You love—Sokrates—as others do not love.

SOKRATES — —

PHRYNE. I know—Sokrates—you will love me with your love.

SOKRATES — —

PHRYNE. You are in love with your love—as I am in love with you, Sokrates.

SOKRATES — —

PHRYNE. You will unveil your infatuated secret to me, Sokrates—when I am unveiled before you.

SOKRATES — —

PHRYNE. You will step down from the throne of your infatua-

tion — — and step by step follow me — — into the milky
flood which veils and reveals—

*She has retreated to the curved lattice, opens a door,
and descends slowly into the depths of the bath—and disappears. Keeps on saying:*

Step — — by step — — step — — by step — — step — — by
step — —

SOKRATES, *motionless.*

PHRYNE *throws out the yellow silk scarf over the lattice.*
There—a yellow birdling flutters out—that protected the
slender column of my neck!

A blue scarf follows.

There—a blue birdling flies away—that covered the low
hills of my breasts!

Green scarf follows.

There—a green birdling discloses the gentle shafts of my
thighs!

Striped scarf follows.

There—a hummingbird opens the gate into the sparkling
blood!

SOKRATES *raises himself up—bearing close to the wall he
reaches the door at rear—enters the back room—and noise-
lessly closes the bead curtain.*

PHRYNE. Darling—the waves caress with feeble force—I sink
down and am born of the swirling foam! — — — Ivory and
coral are limbs that twine to reach you—darling! — — — —
Bend down over the lattice—I want to see you, darling!
— — — — Don't bend down over the lattice—hurry in here,
darling! — — — — Darling—I am waiting — — — — darling—
you will come! ! — — — — Darling! ! — — — — you are
not coming? ? ! !

Her hands reach up.

I love you — — Sokrates! ! ! ! — — I love you — — Sokrates
— — — — I love only you — — as I never wanted to love
anyone — — you are my beloved, who will at last come in
to me! ! ! !

She lifts her head up—stares.

ALKIBIADES *rushes in from the left.*

ALKIBIADES *in blind rage.* Tell me—how he toppled over—the herma maker — —: and I'll throttle the beast with my fists! !

PHRYNE *looks into space.*

ALKIBIADES. Dump him out of the bath—I'll stamp the bloated whale to bits under my feet! !

PHRYNE, *haltingly to herself.* He—did—not—want—me — — — —

ALKIBIADES, *away from the lattice.*

PHRYNE, *as before.* He—is—gone—and—did—not—love—me — — —

ALKIBIADES *staggers—swings his arm.* The earth is bursting — — showers of sulphur hiss out of craters — — the sun is burning up — — heights and depths open the abyss — — into which we fall — — and with fall upon fall bury ourselves deeper! !

He staggers toward the lattice—reaching out for PHRYNE. Down with us — — blissful in our plunge — — and out of lust destroying each other in lust! ! ! !

PHRYNE, *hands outspread against him.* No! !

ALKIBIADES. I'll break into your cage—I'll smash the lattice bars! !

PHRYNE, *pulling the lattice door to.* Give me your cloak—I will not stand naked before you—Alkibiades! !

ALKIBIADES. Is the abyss mocking me?

PHRYNE. I do not love you—Alkibiades — — I will not have you with me! ! — — you are base—Alkibiades! ! — — you disgust me—Alkibiades! !

ALKIBIADES. Are the depths setting up a howl? !

PHRYNE. I love — — Sokrates! ! ! !

ALKIBIADES *tumbles backward—covers his eyes with his palms.* Hideous growth—seed of scorpions—rank profusion of hermae in a wilderness — — : hermae in rows — — hermae in circles—hermae coming out of niches—out of gateways—out of streets—flooding the squares — — crowds of crushing hermae that grin—that are dead and laugh — — laughter of mouths that pulse disembodied — — glaring of eyes that stare glassily — — death brought to life — — the blood dies and freezes into eternal ice which does not die and does not live — — hermae attacking — — the foe in the city — — occupies streets — — squares — — gateways — — sleep on: — — Alkibiades will save the sleeping city! ! ! !

He rushes out.

PHRYNE, *taking her hands from the lattice—pressing them to her face.* I—love—Sokrates — — — —

From the left, CITY SOLDIERS *burst in.*

LEADER, *stepping to the lattice—turning around.* Stand aside —the woman is naked and beautiful. Search in the house for Alkibiades!

SOLDIERS *pull back the bead curtain:* SOKRATES *on the couch asleep.* SOLDIERS *push in and raise him up.*

LEADER. Who is that?

SOKRATES *calmly.* Are you seeking Sokrates?

LEADER. Take him prisoner.

SOLDIERS *bind* SOKRATES.

SOKRATES. Of what am I guilty?

LEADER. Alkibiades has overthrown the holy hermae on the open square before this house.

SOKRATES. Am I Alkibiades?

LEADER. You are his friend.

SOKRATES. Does one mislead one's friend into evildoing?

LEADER. Take him to jail.

SOLDIERS *go off with* SOKRATES.

LEADER, *without turning toward* PHRYNE—*to her.* Do you know about Alkibiades?

PHRYNE. — — I—love—Sokrates — — — —

LEADER, *running to the door—shouting.* Beat Sokrates up if he talks to you on the way! !

Exit.

PHRYNE. I — — love — — you — — Sokrates — — as — — I — —
never — — wanted — — to — — love — — anyone — — — —

PART THREE

*Arena of the high court. Low circular building of red brick
with a continuous seat along the wall tightly filled by the
ELDERS—white-haired grandees in black cloaks.* SOKRATES
*stands in the middle on a square white stone set in the
floor. Endless blue sky overarching.*

THE ELDERS, *looking about—murmurs becoming audible.* The
Wrestling Master! !

WRESTLING MASTER *standing, on the left side.* Do you call
me up first—and call me: Wrestling Master? Do I give ear
and stand up between you and offend the call with my
obedience which answers you? Where does an office count
without action? Who calls himself a teacher without pupils
—how does a leader prove himself without a following?
—I am a wrestling master in an empty wrestling school.
On the track—at the jumping ground—in the throwing area,
not a foot stirs the sand—not a breast groans in the rush
of the running race—not an arm tenses its sinews to hurl
the javelin—no thigh is braced in a wrestling match.
The quiet of a graveyard steals into the wrestling school!
— — Have all the boys run away? Away from this school to
a new master who spurs them more briskly and leads them
on more nimbly? I would laugh and would praise anyone
who outdoes my claim to inspire in boys eagerness and
drive! — — Not one boy went away—all remained together
to transform the wrestling school into a court of hermae.
Motionless they stand in corners—groups of mingled older
and younger boys! Heads drooping low on the breast—
eyes half covered—mouths talkative in slow eloquence of
endless speech and response. Midday glides over it—the
evening has long since darkened distinctness—the assembly
persists in stagnation! — — I accuse him—who instigated
this transformation!—I accuse him—who led them away

from the wrestling ground!—I accuse him—who slandered
the wrestling school!—I accuse him—who made my name
as wrestling master an offense and a mockery!—

Hesitating, then powerfully.

— — I accuse Alkibiades! !

FIRST ELDER, *standing.* My son is a boy in the wrestling
school. I sent him to the wrestling school for training, to
be swift in running—bold in competition with boys!—My
son slinks limply home from the wrestling school—he is
exhausted by sleepless nights with a fever of wakefulness
which empties him out!—I accuse him—who offended
against the day and night of my son! — — : I accuse Alkibiades! !

SECOND ELDER, *standing—toward the* FIRST ELDER. My son is
a boy of the wrestling school along with your son. With
weals and stripes on his body from the pressures of wrestling bouts with your son, he used to stand proudly before
me in the evening and would put my fingers into the red
gouges in his skin and swallow his pain—now he stalks
in a gray cloak which covers him from head to shoes, as
if he were ashamed of the shape of his limbs!—I accuse
him—who defamed the body of my son! — — : I accuse
Alkibiades! !

THIRD ELDER, *standing—to the two* ELDERS. Along with
your sons my son is a boy in the wrestling school. Did he
not use to praise to me your son and your son, when one
of them, more adroit, overcame him at wrestling?—His lips
are quiet—and when praise is expressed, it is said of your
son and your son: he has made me more silent and is
pushing me nearer to the knowledge that I know nothing!
—I accuse him—who ruined for my son and your son and
your son the cry of pleasure at wrestling! — — I accuse
Alkibiades! !

THE ELDERS, *rising one after the other.* Along with your sons
our sons are boys in the wrestling school. We accuse him
—who transformed the wrestling school! — — we accuse
Alkibiades! !

They sit down.

SOKRATES *looks around.* You accuse Alkibiades. It must be an error that I am standing before you. You are getting the complaints mixed. Will you now settle first the case of Alkibiades or my case?

THE ELDERS *to each other—increasing in loudness.* The verdict!

WRESTLING MASTER, *standing.* What will become of Greece without boys who become men after you—who will bear arms for Greece?!—What is Greece without rampart and surge of warriors who bleed with a laugh and die with exultation for Greece?!—Is Greece an island—floating in the vast sea—shielded by inaccessible coasts?!—Are the foes of yesterday loving friends today and taking pains to spare us?!—Hate is aiming greedily at us from every side where the wind blows—and no towering formation will check the assault which will break loose, if we do not ward it off!—Greece will lie defenseless tomorrow if men are not trained who remain Greeks!—Greeks are the protection of Greece—no mountains and no seas ban the danger which threatens!—Greeks with pleasure in fighting for Greece which will bear Greeks after you and after your sons and other sons who are Greeks—if your sons have not ruined Greece! — — Greece is tottering before the abyss torn open by him whom you have accused: — — Alkibiades is guilty of every crime!!

THE ELDERS *stormily.* Alkibiades is guilty!!!!

They sit down.

SOKRATES. You are entangled in a remarkable deception. You do not distinguish between Sokrates and Alkibiades. And yet there is not a trace of resemblance between the unblemished Alkibiades and my bent backbone. Solve this riddle for me.

THE ELDERS *look from one to the other.*

FOURTH ELDER, *almost at center—standing.* We are sitting here in an assembly which discusses the last day of Greece. As yet the heavens' canopy is blue over us—sun pouring down on the snow of our heads, which reach up from Greece's present into the past of Greece. Our powers are small—but in our effort they swell anew to resistance and rebellion. Our shoulders are once more sustaining the burden which responsibility lays upon us. Crushed by the pressure, we are about to collapse—when we have erected Greece once more. The effort is tremendous—the reward makes it light as a feather. Death and life are entangled in the most fearful wrestling. We are defending life with inexorable strictness—and throttling death with the death to which we condemn him who violated life. Someone reached out to seize him—who is it? I

THE ELDERS *look toward* SOKRATES—*slowly and swelling the cry forms.* Alkibiades! ! ! !

FOURTH ELDER. You will find no other—he calls his own name at every reproach which condemns him! — — death to Alkibiades!

THE ELDERS, *in violent agitation.* Death to Alkibiades! ! ! !

All sit down again.

SOKRATES. Your attempt to enlighten me as to my presence here was a failure even when repeated. Perhaps your excitement forbids you to make my task clear to me—but I now believe I have discovered it. I am to conduct the defense of Alkibiades, who, as I hear, is a fugitive. It is not the first time I have made myself answerable for Alkibiades when his life was threatened.

Profound silence.

SOKRATES. You accuse Alkibiades of setting the boys against the wrestling school. How is it that Alkibiades, who is himself an excellent jumper and fencer, advises against these exercises? I should understand it if a cripple made fun of these hazardous sports—but what has Alkibiades in common with him?

FIFTH ELDER. Alkibiades left you—to go to the wrestling school!

SOKRATES. Was it chatter of mine that made him entice the boys from the sunny wrestling grounds, to put their heads together in shadowy corners?

SIXTH ELDER. He said over again—what he had heard from you!

SOKRATES. Do you take Alkibiades to be a fool who repeats

another's words without thinking?—This Alkibiades, who won your campaigns and increased your possessions—of whom you are proud?

Silence.

SOKRATES. If you will chide him for thoughtless repetition, then you must also suspect his services to Greece, for they were rendered by a blockhead. Hence you cannot utter one complaint without affronting his other deeds. But this insult would sully yourselves, since you took your advantage from his deeds. You must not despise yourselves, if you wish to be judges over Alkibiades.

Silence.

SOKRATES. You will shield Alkibiades from this reproach— that of being an irresponsible idiot.—I do not know what means he used to persuade the boys, as I have never set foot in the wrestling school. But they cannot have been clumsy, or they would not have caught on with your sons, who are favored by ancestry and education.—As to the subject which Alkibiades treated, it cannot have been unworthy of such a teacher and such pupils.—You will not condemn Alkibiades for the happenings in the wrestling school, but you must find a more genuine reason for expelling him from your community!

THE ELDERS *to each other—first muttering—then powerfully.* The hermae! !

SEVENTH ELDER, *on the right side—standing.* Does the goal not become plain in view of this crime, the overturning of the holy hermae in the public places? Does not suspicion after suspicion, first glimmering, shoot out to that flame which flares up from a crime above every other crime? What we received in veneration of fathers and forefathers, and cherished in veneration for sons and sons coming after them, Alkibiades smashed with harsh blows. He is not awed by sacred things—with the fury of destruction he rushes from herma to herma and smashes to bits what is precious to us! Our faces are struck by his blows —we are dishonored where we worship — — : are we still Greeks if we do not punish him who injures us? !

EIGHTH ELDER *stands*. My father's herma overthrown by Alkibiades! !

NINTH ELDER *likewise*. The holy herma of my race in the dust by act of Alkibiades! !

TENTH ELDER *likewise*. Along with the hermae of your fathers the hermae of our fathers and forefathers on the ground, by act of Alkibiades! !

THE ELDERS, *standing*. Overthrow of the hermae—the penalty of death for Alkibiades! !

They sit down.

SOKRATES. From my head a question falls on my tongue, which is too slippery to hold it fast:—did you take me prisoner in the house of Alkibiades' mistress to assure yourselves of a specialist for the restoration of the hermae? I am a herma-maker by profession.

Silence.

SOKRATES. You're not answering me—and I begin to worry about my standing here before you. For now I doubt that you have called me here for the defense of Alkibiades, because one does not make arrests with such a purpose. —Likewise, I wonder whether I am supposed to help you as an artisan.—Give me information, then: Do you accuse Alkibiades or Sokrates? Or Sokrates and Alkibiades? Or do you hold on to me merely because Alkibiades has escaped you?

Silence.

SOKRATES. Very well—I will take your silence as an accusation which you level against me. For certainly you would affirm my innocence loudly and joyfully. Stop chiding Alkibiades now, who cannot hear you—and let's hear your complaints against me, point by point. I shall omit no reply and shall endeavor to make everything so clear that it will be very easy for you to decide concerning good and evil!—By what fault of mine have I offended Greece?

Silence.

SOKRATES. Perhaps my general inquiry has set the boundaries too far apart, and no hard core can form for your judgment. I will recite each single happening and ask your verdict on each one.—Did I enter the campaign that time with the resolve to secure my life in every possible way, and thus to brand myself as a cowardly soldier?

Silence.

SOKRATES. You concede to me courage and loyalty.—Did I disregard a command to advance against the enemy and throw myself prematurely on the ground as if I were wounded?

Silence.

SOKRATES. You do not deny me bravery.—When the terrible retreat had to begin — — — did I not take thought how it could be stopped? Did I not remain behind when I saw an opportunity to delay the pursuer—and did I not fight until my senses left me and I was carried unconscious from the battlefield by other soldiers? Did I not achieve—what is proper for a Greek? Where lies the misdeed which brings me before the judges? How do you discover a crime so hideous that it places me here on the white stone tablet of the blackest accusation? Of what is Sokrates guilty? !

THE ELDERS, *seeking each other's eyes—swinging arms—gradually all rising—bursting out in a joint cry.* He saved Alkibiades! ! ! !

They stand rigid.

SOKRATES. Do you speak of that? I did not wish to boast of that deed and did not mention it. But since you need that for my acquittal, I will cast this weight on the scales myself: — — I saved Alkibiades!

THE ELDERS, *with arms waving.* Death to Sokrates! ! ! !

SOKRATES. I accomplished what would have exhausted a giant in stature and strength—: I saved Alkibiades — — and I demand: — — that I be given lifelong support at public expense!

THE ELDERS *take small black shards from their cloaks and hurl them upon the white stone square, where they clink and smash.* Death to Sokrates! ! ! !

SOKRATES, *looking at the floor—poking in the heap of shards with his foot.* Not one light shard? Only black tablets, splintered with dangerous edges. It would be a thorny path to freedom — — the other injury is milder—and that alone is healing for all — — — —

THE ELDERS *still erect like pillars—their arms reaching up into the azure sky.*

Prison cell—low ceiling, cramped; gray. In the center a wooden pallet. At right a high, barred porthole. In the rear wall a door closed with an iron grating—behind it, steep stone steps leading upward. SOKRATES *lies asleep.— The grating—the chain rattling—is pulled open.*

XANTIPPE, *groping her way down the steps—goes to the pallet—shakes* SOKRATES' *breast and shoulder.* Husband!

SOKRATES *awake, not stirring.* At last?

XANTIPPE. How at last? The end at the end? The end—which has no more beginning—such an end at the end? !

SOKRATES. They are mistaken: it will be a beginning without an end.

XANTIPPE. Who are "they"? What is mistaken here?—I cry out: it is I—it is you—we are not "they" — — we are man and wife—and *one* blood and *one* air in our lungs. What is there between us that throttles the one and lets the other go a cripple? ! — — Strike him dead — — bury me first in the sand! !

SOKRATES, *propping himself on his elbow.* Have they decided on that form of death?

XANTIPPE *stares at him.* Does it not snatch you up from your pallet—and drive you against walls and walls which should be crumbled by your death fury? !

SOKRATES, *smiling.* I should die a hundred deaths before that if I let myself be so misled.—You know that.

XANTIPPE, *drooping.* Your last day, husband—your last morning—your last hour—: they will kill you without mercy, without winking!

SOKRATES. Did they send you news of it?

XANTIPPE. A fellow ran up—and told me.

SOKRATES. Is it not kind of the judges? They don't like what they are doing to me—for that place where compassion has no foothold is with me. I raised my hand against something which was glorious beyond all measure—but the compulsion was too strong. The Elders will soon pass —and life, which stretches out long before the boys, is on their side.—Will they take me out of the cell today?

XANTIPPE, *weeping.* Out of light—and air.

SOKRATES. Then I'll not miss much—there's no abundance of it here—How are you living?

XANTIPPE. What I learned from your mother—is useful to me now.

SOKRATES. Midwife.—Remarkable that you resort to this occupation. Through your hands human beings will slip into that life for which I blackened a curtain. One works blindly against the other—and yet all is intertwined in love.—Will you wait for their coming?

XANTIPPE. Woe to him who intrudes—where I am! Xantippe will write her name in the history of that creature with her claws!

SOKRATES. You will soon succumb to the attack which you will provoke.

XANTIPPE. Not to the first one—hardly to the second—to the tenth with pleasure—; then you will have your death sacrifice of nine who lie cold!

SOKRATES. If it were enough — — the claims have been inflated until they are a shadow which covers the whole earth like a cloud! Are you looking forward to a busy day?

XANTIPPE. Mothers shall groan when they are in labor—I grin! !

SOKRATES. Will you let the innocent suffer?

XANTIPPE. Who is innocent—as you are without guilt and they — —

Breaks off, sobbing.

SOKRATES. I know that—but one way or the other it would

have come into the world anyway – – : sometime the others must revolt and pile one heaven on top of the other, out of which the sun will burn them awfully, so that the weaklings cannot bear it! Change would pain me—and it condemned me to steadfastness!—The new—the unbelievable is hurled out by chance—just as in cases you attend, the origin is accidental—: a child is born—was it forethought?—: only love—only that is the most uncertainly certain of all miracles! – – Neglect no duty, wife.

XANTIPPE, *irresolute.* Leavetaking – –

SOKRATES. An easy one. Are nasturtiums climbing about this window? A meager gleam—you hardly see me. Outside the brightness flows—don't mingle me with the twilight here —else you will never find me again wherever I meet you, as I remain clearly present to you.

XANTIPPE, *unsteadily to the door—suddenly screaming.* Light—!!

Hastily mounts the steps—exit.

SOKRATES *turns his face toward the round window, in which a faint gleam of the morning sun appears.*

Rushing down the steps come three BOYS—*in gray cloaks —crowding about* SOKRATES.

FIRST BOY. Sokrates—get up—

SECOND BOY. Hurry—

THIRD BOY. And flee!

SOKRATES *looks at them.* You find me ready.

THIRD BOY. No time to lose—

SECOND BOY. The plan will be revealed—

FIRST BOY. If you delay!

SOKRATES. I am neither curious nor patient—else whatever may happen is already becoming indifferent to me, as it is predestined.

SECOND BOY. You are free—

FIRST BOY. With joy—

THIRD BOY. All the boys do this for you!

SECOND BOY. Boys are up above as common guards—in the courtyard—at the gate—

FIRST BOY. Boys in the streets all the way out of the city—

THIRD BOY. Boys in the field with a cart to take you away—

SECOND BOY. Boys in the ship that will ferry you across—

FIRST BOY. All boys eager for your rescue, hot in the fight for life and death!

SOKRATES. What do you want of me?

SECOND BOY. Go out of the cell with us—up the steps—across the court—through the gate—in the street you must run with us – – run to the end of the city – – run with all your might, as we run ahead! !

SOKRATES. What street is that?

THIRD BOY. Across the fish market!

SOKRATES. With the cobblestone pavement?

SECOND BOY. In the early morning it's deserted!

FIRST BOY, *in the doorway.* The sentry is signaling!

THIRD BOY. Jump out of bed—Sokrates—run off with us!

SOKRATES, *stretching out afresh.* The journey would be too hard on me. If you wish me well, let me have my sleep out, so that later I shall be fresh to begin the great sleep which one can't endure well after a wakeful night.

FOURTH BOY *enters.*

FOURTH BOY. The guard is changing now—the last chance for us!

FIRST BOY. Upstairs—

SECOND BOY. In the court—

THIRD BOY. Out the gate! !

SOKRATES. I'm sleepy—boys—go to the wrestling school.

Two BOYS *enter.*

FIFTH BOY. Lost! !

SIXTH BOY, *collapsing beside the pallet.* Too late! !

The BOYS *stand silent.*

SOKRATES *lifts his head.* Who is sobbing? Are there women

in the room? Does one grant them entrance where men resolve to have only self-control?

He rises halfway and finds the head of the SIXTH BOY.

Silly child—did your morning soup taste salty, that tears well up?

SIXTH BOY *takes his hand and kisses it fervently.* We wanted to save you!

SOKRATES. Does the drowning man pull his rescuer to the shore? You're almost drowning in the flood of your tears —and I am calmly bedded on a solid coast.

To all BOYS.

Your forwardness had almost cost me my life.

SIXTH BOY. You will die—Sokrates!

THE BOYS *in commotion close about* SOKRATES. Why must you die—Sokrates? ?

SOKRATES. The Elders command it.

THE BOYS. You would not flee! !

SOKRATES. In order to prevent the discovery.

FIRST BOY. No one would have pursued you!

FIFTH BOY. By evening you would have been safely across the sea!

SOKRATES. Do you know that? It could have been brought to light so long as I was alive—and in a long life I might be despondent and forget—: to save Alkibiades!

SOME BOYS. Alkibiades is living with friends!

SOKRATES. In imminent danger which I am averting from him forever!

FOURTH BOY. You mean your death will soften the judges toward Alkibiades?

SOKRATES. The question is not one of a judgment for today and tomorrow—what is being founded here is the lasting stability of all of you!

SEVENTH BOY. We revere you—Sokrates—boundlessly!

THE BOYS. We love you—Sokrates—above our fathers!

SOKRATES. With such a load you burden my back? It is

hunching itself into mountains of burden—do I not cast a
shadow of a hump that blackens?

FIRST BOY, *fervently.* You are beautiful—Sokrates—and you
are beautiful — — above Alkibiades!

THE BOYS. You are beautiful—Sokrates—above Alkibiades! !

SOKRATES, *smiling.* Do you want to save me now? Who dares
save Sokrates?

THE BOYS. No one dares save Sokrates! !

SOKRATES. Only Sokrates can save Sokrates — — otherwise the
sky would collapse over Greece!

From the steps, slowly, the HEALTH-GIVER—*shorn, nude
except for a black apron—with a wooden flask and wooden
cup. Behind him* BOYS *crowd in.*

SOKRATES. Step aside with reverence—the host is waiting on
his guest with flask and cup.

To the HEALTH-GIVER.

Have I robbed you of an hour of your morning sleep?
Then I will hurry now and you will still make up the loss.

The BOYS *fill the entire cell.*

FIFTH BOY. Sokrates—according to the law you have a respite
before the cup is handed you and taken away again!

SOKRATES. Shall this man go twice, having already sacrificed
to me part of his night's sleep?

To the HEALTH-GIVER.

Excuse the boy for his zeal. Are you certain that your
poison is powerful?

HEALTH-GIVER. I grated green hemlock in the night, as it
must be prepared in order to be effective.

SOKRATES. So you never went to bed? Then there is double
reason for me to hurry. Forgive me, friend, that I have
caused you trouble. Now hurry on your part!

THE BOYS, *crowding forward.* Sokrates—go on living!

SOKRATES. Do not bump into the host!

To the HEALTH-GIVER, *who has opened the flask and is
about to empty it into the cup.*

What are you doing? A drop will be spilled—or a bit will cling to the walls of the flask, if you pour it into the cup —and I might miss it. Let me drink from the flask!

He takes the bottle and empties it in a quick draft.

Silence.

SOKRATES, *looking around.* The taste is indescribable. A mild bitterness—and already tasteless. Is that all?

HEALTH-GIVER. You must get up and walk around—until weariness sets in.

SOKRATES. Precious advice—are you a doctor?

HEALTH-GIVER. Health-Giver.

SOKRATES. A good name for the executioner. — — Are you experienced in small ministrations?

HEALTH-GIVER. What do you desire?

SOKRATES, *after a long look toward the* BOYS. Loosen my left shoe and look under the sole — — somewhere I ran a splinter into it — — which would prevent me from obeying your command. Otherwise I could not walk up and down in the cell!

HEALTH-GIVER *does so—holds the thorn.*

SOKRATES. Found it?

HEALTH-GIVER *studies the thorn.*

SOKRATES, *sitting up.* Does something surprise you?

HEALTH-GIVER. It is not a splinter, as you say — — a stiff spike — — a thorn of cactus — — which isn't common around here — —

SOKRATES. I'll bequeath it to you, since I cannot pay you otherwise.

HEALTH-GIVER. It must have pained you frightfully.

SOKRATES. Horribly, Health-Giver—and it costs a life to deaden the pain! — —

He steps down from the pallet.

But the poison in my body destroys misunderstandings. I have used my last penny for payment and should not need to shun the light!

He begins to walk.

The BOYS *retreat before him to the walls.*

SOKRATES. Am I performing a play for you? Is it a tragedy, or does laughter play a part in it? The actor up on the stage doesn't know—the curious one in the audience doesn't reveal it—how can the mixture be perfect?—Sorrow has tears—joy sheds them — — both flow into *one* blissfulness. Who distinguishes? — — Not you — — and not I — — — — : the great is hidden in the small — — and out of trifles things pile up and tower to sublime summits on which snow and sun are united!

Walking slowly.

Snow — — is coldness — — frost rising out of bone and breast — — — — sun — — fire — — circling — — in the head — — — — ice-zone — — — — desert noon — — — — cold — — warm — — trickling — — shuddering — — voluptuous — — — —

He reaches the pallet and stretches out. Murmuring.

Health-Giv—er — — you must — — sac—rifice — — for — — me — — to — — your — — patron — — — — What — — is — — the — — name — — ? ?

HEALTH-GIVER. I would do you a small service.

SOKRATES. The — — name — — ? ?

HEALTH-GIVER. Asklepios.

SOKRATES, *dying.* I — — — — owe — — — — Asklepios — — — — a — — — — cock — — — —

He stretches out—is dead.

The BOYS, *deeply moved, step in silence to the pallet.*

A BOY *at the foot—head bent upward—reaching up his arms—in a frenzy.*

THE BOYS, *attentive—pointing—whispering.* Plato — — Plato — — Plato — —

THE BOY, *with an outburst.* Did you hear? — — so Sokrates parted from life as from a long sickness — — and gives thanks to death as to a doctor who delivers him from heavy suffering! !

Through the round window comes a sunbeam and strikes the feet of SOKRATES.

THE IMMORTAL ONE*

TWO ACTS

by Yvan Goll

Translated by
Walter H. and Jacqueline Sokel

DRAMATIS PERSONAE

The musician SEBASTIAN. OLGA. BALLOON, *photographer*. LAND-
LORD LUPUS. THE BRIDEGROOM. THE BRIDE. GENTLEMAN WITH
TOP HAT. THE TAX COLLECTOR. A POLICEMAN. A SOAPBOX
ORATOR. A PASTRY-SHOP BOY. CROWDS.

* Written 1918; published 1920.

FIRST ACT

The studio of a musician and inventor of musical instruments. Musical composition books, violin cases, and other things are scattered everywhere. By the right wall, in front of a Gothic window, a large brown pianola, which looks like a harmonium. On the left, a large window overlooks a boulevard, on which people and cars pass during the entire action of the play; this action can be simulated by a film. The center wall is white and blank: upon it appear, according to directions, large filmed billboard signs, sections cut from newspapers, or actual film shots. SEBASTIAN and OLGA are standing in the studio.

SEBASTIAN. I am a beggar in heart and purse, I shall never take you to the Café Astoria! He is a scoundrel who does not angelically enjoy life.

OLGA, *holding a large bergère straw hat and waving it over-eagerly out the window. On the sidewalk, next to a lamp-post, a lieutenant is seen staring in through the window.*

I love you. But how can I stand it without iced coffee and the envious glances of little Miss Rosheim? Just think: my new blouse!

She leans out the window.

I love you. At least stop looking at me so that your kind heart won't bleed! You are after all my artist, my divine pimp.

She throws the lieutenant a kiss.

You will suffer: That's your greatness! You will write symphonies! Does my bolero fit?

SEBASTIAN. Stay, you are still my maiden. Is this a fair contest? With all the cavalrymen and all the blond elevator operators as with raving angels, the martyr must compete. I am not human! Beloved Olga!

He goes to the pianola and strikes a chord.

Can you hear the tremolo? What by comparison are hills in spring. I place you high above all mistresses, above Duse and above the Princess of Saxony and Beatrice and . . .

Meanwhile OLGA *has been waving out the window until she falls floating out.* SEBASTIAN *has worked himself into an ecstasy and is playing the following melody and singing while working the pedals: "My heart, it is a beehive." During this time a crowd gathers in front of the window; in it are the* PASTRY-SHOP BOY, *the* GENTLEMAN WITH TOP HAT *and a* POLICEMAN.

Have you heard? I am consoling you, poor pedestrian. Come and hear the sweetness of these tones of grief. Like a discus thrower, supplely I send you forth, street melody, to all mankind. Doesn't it look as if I embraced you. . . ?

PASTRY-SHOP BOY. Are you aware that your fiancée has gone to Apulia? She boarded a glowing express train. But she had a tear on her painted eyelashes when she bought these meringues which she still wished to give to you. . . .

He places pastry on the window sill.

GENTLEMAN WITH TOP HAT. I am your patron. Do you recognize me?

He throws him a purse.

I buy your genius. I buy your good digestion. I order big yellow billboard advertisements for your concerts.

*On the rear wall, big placards appear: "*THE MUSICAL GENIUS: SEBASTIAN, BACH'S NATURAL GRANDSON!*"*

You are my indivijioll

SEBASTIAN. Mercy, sir! What have I ever done to you! Have pity on me: I am a harmless artist. Leave me my unheard obscurity. Leave me the sorrow which whips me, and which my darling Olga has left me. Are you perhaps blaspheming?

POLICEMAN. In the name of the law: you belong to the state. The collective community has a claim on you, but you have no claim to starvation and loneliness.

THE CROWD. Social liberation!

On the rear wall appears a big placard in red: "SOCIAL LIBERATION! HUMAN KINDNESS!"

POLICEMAN. Loneliness is strictly forbidden! I'm giving you a reprimand! You must eat a beefsteak and take a walk in the park every day! And a minimum of work?

A man climbs upon the window sill and unfolds a newspaper as large as himself: he is the JOURNALIST. *He screams:* "Sebastian, the musician-saint of the people!"

At the same instant appears on the rear wall in fat black newsprint: "SEBASTIAN, MUSICIAN-SAINT OF THE PEOPLE!"

JOURNALIST. Hurrah!

The CROWD *shouts. Then it disperses. Through the door enters* LUPUS, THE LANDLORD.

LUPUS. Celebrated maestro!

SEBASTIAN. Pardon me, Mr. Lupus, don't underestimate me. Be frank. I know I owe you sixty marks. I slave for it day and night. I am perfectly aware that sixty marks for such a view and mice under the bed is not too much. Oh, I know everything. Just two more years of patience, Mr. Benefactor, then I shall have finished my forty-seventh opera! Mr. Lupus!

LUPUS *possesses one small ear and one as large as a hand; the latter he takes off when he speaks.* Esteemed maestro! *He pulls a sheet of paper with writing on it from the pocket of his jacket and continues, reading from it.*

I have enjoyed your startling music.

He sneezes.

Pardon me! You bestow the greatest honor upon my tenement. You . . .

He puts on pince-nez.

You, you . . . I give you my word of honor that no bailiff is waiting for you in the hall! Attention, laugh! Permit me this—joke, so to speak. Lupus comes to Orpheus, touched and weeping.

He blows his nose.

In short, we are honest men, aren't we, good businessmen, *maneschome,* so let's go into business. Tonight I am going to open the great American world-cabaret in your honor —in the basement—to consecrate your genius. Do you wish to play the new folk song of the beehive for a fee of two million?

Sneaky

Well, how about ten million? Or eleven million?

Since SEBASTIAN *does not answer, he quickly runs to the window and calls to the* CROWD:

Public! Fall into my arms! I have discovered the greatest genius! Come out of your bedrooms, offices, and telephone booths to the most heavenly of earthly hours!

Immediately a great commotion ensues. All the noises of the street invade the room: honking of horns, streetcar bells, children's shouts, clanking of chains. LUPUS's *announcement appears in glowing electric letters on the rear wall. In his zeal* LUPUS *falls out the window and the* CROWD *carries him away in triumph. The hubbub wanes.*

TAX COLLECTOR STROHHALM *enters.*

STROHHALM. I am looking for Mr. Sebastian.

SEBASTIAN. I am he.

STROHHALM *poses with a writing pad which he has dragged along on a wheelbarrow.* Your first, last, and middle name!

SEBASTIAN. Sebastian!

STROHHALM. Watch out. I am the authority. Do you want to tell me you are already as great as Charlot or Goethe, who have only one single name? Your qualities, sir!

SEBASTIAN *points at* STROHHALM's *green-and-red striped cap.* What does this uniform signify?

STROHHALM. The tax office, sir. The power that is.

SEBASTIAN *takes away the cap and puts it on his own head.* And now?

STROHHALM. You trespass against the public person that I am! Are you aware that this is *lèse-majesté* against the people's government?

SEBASTIAN. Now *I* could tax *you!*

STROHHALM. You have an income of ten million. You want to defraud the government.

He opens his leather briefcase.

Please, a small down payment of two thousand marks in advance of tonight!

SEBASTIAN *tosses the green cap out the window.* For the time being my money is still invested in Europa, Inc., in babies, beer mugs, and chemises. At the moment my capital is still in the pockets of the gentlemen Master Butchers and their Cuddle Girls.

Shows him to the window and opens it.

The public is out there!

At once the CROWD *is again in front of the window and welcomes* STROHHALM, *who climbs out the window, shouting. His cap is being tossed about, he himself is being torn to pieces.*

SOAPBOX ORATOR, *mounting the window sill, which henceforth will serve as a platform.* Comrades! Outsiders! Our workers' honor has been attacked! The petty state authority has . . . our miracle man . . .

The CROWD *jubilates, shouting:* "Sebastian! Our saint! Our comrade!"

Simultaneously these words appear illuminated on the rear wall. Meanwhile SEBASTIAN *has become absorbed in his music as if nothing had occurred, and plays on his pianola the tune of:* "My heart, it is a beehive," *accompanying himself with the words:*

The world, it is a warriors' club
And in it men are brothers!

MAN WITH TOP HAT. Hark, you people, the greatest music of the century! The fire brigade is playing a flourish!

Flourish by a few trumpets in the background. The CROWD *howls.*

He, your liberator—

A few voices: "Hurrah!"

—will appear in the world-vaudeville tonight, entrance on Rats' Alley, performance starts at eight.

Flourish.

Reduced admission for veterans' organizations and groups dedicated to the love of mankind!

Flourish. The window is closed. OLGA, *smiling, enters, her hair loose.* BALLOON *enters after her, fat, reddish crew-cut, goatee, and shiny, protruding eyes.*

OLGA, *with a gesture of embrace.* Sebastian, I love you, I have brought laurels for you from Greece. Ah, I forgot to mention, I was married in Cairo to the man who loves me most, and only for that reason! And am I not your enthusiastic fan? Your grief whipping up the seas and driving human hearts aloft to heaven?

SEBASTIAN *kisses her hand.* BALLOON *steps forward and bows stiffly.*

My husband, Balloon, is worth more for you than a nation: he is your friend!

BALLOON *bows.*

He only loves me in order to get to you. He is the greatest . . .

BALLOON *his hand on his heart.* Please, Madam, don't make the effort, I can do it myself.

To SEBASTIAN.

I am . . . I am the foremost photographer of Cairo. I am a soul-photographer, that is, I can eternalize you painlessly; you will live on in the eyes and in the memories of mankind. You yourself, however, will disappear, your sorrow, your immense, stupid artist's yearning will disappear. You will become immortal in the most chemical sense of the word—silver bromide paper and hydrogen oxide; in short: I'll film you. Painlessly—oh, how painlessly! You will live eternally and yet you will be allowed to forget; you will have the advantage that even the Homeric heroes, my noble ancestors

Bows,

lacked in Orkus—you will forget—Olga, my wife, and yourself, too, my friend. But your art I shall spread across the world. One question: You have not yet made a will?

SEBASTIAN. Well, but, must I, so to speak, die a little?

BALLOON. If you wish to put it that way, yes, perhaps a little.

OLGA *has meanwhile sat down on a couch and signals to* BALLOON. *He moves toward her.*

OLGA. Do it, Sebastian, he loves me.

BALLOON. Be understanding, my friend.

He has arrived at OLGA *and puts his arm around her waist. She embraces him.* BALLOON *continues addressing* SEBASTIAN.

I am sympathetic to all great men. Although I do despise art as such, the earth's rotation . . .

BALLOON *disengages himself from* OLGA'S *embrace, pulls a phonograph out of a small suitcase, puts on a record, winds it, and returns quickly into* OLGA'S *arms.*

PHONOGRAPH. The earth's rotation is that of an automa . . . ma . . . ma . . . rrr . . .

BALLOON. Wait a moment.

He jumps up from the couch again and rewinds the phonograph. Then back to OLGA *as before.*

PHONOGRAPH.   . . . maton. The painter paints syntheses upon the wall. The poet thinks he can reach God with verbal wings, but does the bourgeois who foots the bill ask for, ask for . . . a . . . a . . .

The phonograph stops again. BALLOON, *who meanwhile*

had become absorbed in one of OLGA's *kisses, startled, darts to the phonograph and winds it with these words:* "Wait a moment!"

. . . that? The bourgeois wants to become enthusiastic in order to sleep better. He wants machines—patented, diplomaed, prize-bedecked . . . therefore I despise art which cries to heavens and does not consider digestion . . . rrr . . .

BALLOON *gets up.* The record ends here. Too bad. So interesting! Please, one more second. Look how our mutual goddess Olga rejoices! Are you not happy with the happiness I give her? Enough now. To business!

He draws his wallet.

Incidentally, do you know that your folk song is a plagiarism? In the age of sentimentality it was sung by little whores and bees. But that is of no importance. You are a genius. The fire brigade has confirmed it with a flourish. You earn a fee of eleven million; that's not much in an age when ostriches have sold their feathers and Olga, our beloved, is without a hat. Give me your soul, your artist's soul for twenty million? Well, let's say, for twenty-five? After all, Olga does love you!

OLGA. And faithfully until the death of the soul!

SEBASTIAN. No longer to be forced to live! No longer to battle insomnia, to have to wear an overcoat whose threadbareness everyone can see. No longer to be forced to yearn, stamping on pianolas, and eating calf's feet with ragout: bliss, my sweet angel Balloon, and nameless!

He embraces BALLOON. BALLOON *takes a bundle of banknotes out of his wallet and hands them to* SEBASTIAN. *At the same instant, twenty-five brown bills flash on the screen in the rear.*

BALLOON, *stretching himself before* SEBASTIAN. Incidentally, have you already seen my new tie? Lyons silk. A bargain. And my tie pin? The biggest diamond in the world: it reflects the rainbow and all the fountains of Versailles. But this is . . . look closely . . . it's happening painlessly, how your soul is moving into this little lens of the photo camera, there underneath my shirt front. . . . A completely painless operation: please die and breathe your valuable soul into my camera. . . .

SEBASTIAN *drops feebly into* BALLOON'S *arms.*

That's it. We have inherited our freedom and his music into the bargain. We will be millionaires. . . .

BALLOON *tears the banknotes out of* SEBASTIAN'S *stiff, clenched fist.*

OLGA. Let me shed just three tears!

BALLOON. He died of a hypertrophy of the cerebellum.

OLGA. Just let me faint one more time, I owe it to him who is now forgotten, but also to the audience.

She bows gracefully.

Curtain.

SECOND ACT

The same room as in the first act, but in place of the pianola there is a gigantic photographer's box; in place of the music scores there are frames for photos, small bottles, and all the accessories of a photographer's studio. On the rear wall can be read this advertisement:

SOUL PHOTOGRAPHY
ONE MARK TWENTY PER DOZEN COPIES

The curtain rises upon BALLOON, *who is wearing a white tunic and kneeling in front of* OLGA, *who stands by the window looking out.*

BALLOON, *hand on his heart.* Well, then, love me!

OLGA. O inimitable yearning! Where is Sebastian?

BALLOON. You insult me!

OLGA. Sebastian gone! The stars are weeping. Where are you? O stranger, when will you abduct me?

BALLOON. I should not have killed him. What does possession

profit me; only in yearning does woman love. Even today prisons are too damp. And rheumatism is hereditary in my family. But what can happen to me? Killing and embezzling souls is no crime, isn't that so? I did not steal a single penny from him, I stole only his blond sweetheart, and that is no crime! Eyes averted in shame, men and the law ignore these acts.

OLGA, *dreamily, by the window.* Your dark locks like dark cedars on the Caucasus. I was the white nymph in the pool of your eyes.

Stepping to the mirror.

Am I beautiful? He who possesses me does not see my beauty! The conquered woman is merely blond, but golden is the woman one yearns for. Let me go, let me flee! Over the dead mountains of reality toward the flaming clouds of longing.

As in the first act, the rigid lieutenant appears in the street, waving. She bends out the window.

BALLOON. You want to betray me! Infidelity! Jealousy shrieks in my blood. I command you: love me!

OLGA. I would like to be sailing on the Nile 'neath the feet of the Sphinx! Is it true that Sebastian is not dead?

BALLOON. His soul is here.

He beats his shirt front.

This midget camera is my Pandora's box full of infernal doubts. Tonight I must return him to you, your Sebastian; I shall let him be resurrected in the World Variety Show.

A newly-wed couple enters, the BRIDEGROOM *in black tails and with red gauntlets, the* BRIDE *in a street dress and with merely the myrtle crown in her hair. At the same moment the poster on the rear wall flashes in a variety of hues.*

BRIDEGROOM. Can one be immortalized here?

The BRIDE *giggles.*

BALLOON. In any posture. Do you prefer one in a folder or on an easel? Do you wish a bust or a full-face or one sitting or standing?

BRIDEGROOM. Truly immortalized?

BALLOON. To the last conception and confinement!

BRIDE, *looking down on her body.* O can you see anything yet?

BRIDEGROOM. So. No full-length pictures, then. Well, but a bust looks decapitated!

BALLOON. An illusionary guillotine, so to speak! But completely painless. Besides, I sell fame; your head will hang in all shopwindows and in red plush albums. Even your grandchildren will stroke you with jammy fingers: You will be immortalized.

BRIDEGROOM. Do you also do soul photography?

BALLOON. Only of genius. Otherwise it doesn't pay.

BRIDE. Felix is a genius.

BRIDEGROOM. But I'd rather keep my soul.

BALLOON. Are you perhaps a musician?

BRIDEGROOM. All I can do is yodel.

BRIDE. Certainly! In his field he is a genius.

Meanwhile OLGA *has stepped over to the couch and is frantically signalling.* BRIDEGROOM *notices her and approaches her behind the others' backs.*

BRIDEGROOM *to his bride.* Amalia, you marvelous girl! Someday we each must die alone. We must allow ourselves to be immortalized alone. Married people sleep perhaps in the same bed, but in separate coffins. . . .

He has reached OLGA *now. She throws him a kiss. He immediately rushes at her and seizes her breasts.*

OLGA. Darling, do you wish to flee with me? One is served the best oysters in Chicago, on the terrace of the Palace Hotel. O my longing!

BRIDEGROOM. O my murmuring little angel, your dainty little arms are like fragile little wings. We could in the midst of spring-y fly upon a hill-y.

He yodels.

OLGA. I am blissful.

BALLOON *has started busying himself with his apparatus.*

*During the above scene he has ducked under the black
cloth. The* BRIDE *has stayed rigidly looking toward the
window, in the coquettish pose which he has given her.
Just before, he had fetched the phonograph, which con-
tinuously bleats:* "Smile, please! A pleasant expression,
please!"

BRIDE, *suddenly arising.* Karl, I am afraid! I don't want to!
I have been forsaken! Where are the police!

She tears the windows open.

Murder! Murder! Leave me alone, you immortalizer, you
soul-killer! You are bald!

A CROWD *assembles in the street.* LUPUS *climbs on the
window sill and starts orating.*

LUPUS. Where is Sebastian? They have taken my capital!
I have built the variety theatre in vain! He has been
killed! My eleven grand—and by now the programs are
all printed!

In the background appears the sign of the first act.
BALLOON *rapidly overturns the camera, fetches the pianola
from a corner, sits down at it, and plays the song of the
beehive. Everyone is enraptured.*

BALLOON. Gentlemen! Comrades! Envious opponents of the
status quo! Have you heard the genius play? Is he dead? I
deny it. Lupus is a defamer! And yet, perhaps he *is* dead:
but tonight I shall have the Master resurrected!

In the background appears the new advertisement: "RAIS-
ING OF THE DEAD! ART LIVES ETERNALLY! SEBASTIAN, GOD
FOR THE BOURGEOIS!"

Come, all of you, to the gala tonight! It is starting right
now! Sebastian, arise! I shall call it out three times—
as soon as all the tickets have been bought at the box
office. . . .

LUPUS, *bending over to* BALLOON's *ear.* Good business! Shall
we go into partnership?

PHONOGRAPH, *set up by* BALLOON. Performance starts! The
genius has slept till now. He has been dreaming up new
symphonies. The inspired sweetheart Olga has just come

back from her honeymoon trip to the Gaurisankar mountains!

SEBASTIAN, *appearing on a film screen on the rear wall.* Olga, beloved, give me grief! Allow me to suffer! Where is loneliness? People, people, always and everywhere!

OLGA. It was longing that has called you back, longing that will kill you again tomorrow, my eternally beloved man! *The fire brigade is playing the trumpet-flourish theme. The* OFFICER *comes in at last, kisses and carries her off.*

Curtain.

CRY IN THE STREET*

1922

by Rolf Lauckner

Translated by
Maurice Edwards and Valerie Reich

CAST OF CHARACTERS

SASHA ⎫
KONZEL ⎬ *Three Blind Men*
WOLF ⎭
MARINKA, A DRUNK, A QUAKER

Fenced-off corner of a courtyard to a Home for the Blind, leading on to a passageway into the street. Buildings, chimneys, etc., all around.

New Year's Eve. Moonlight. The bells ring out the hour of twelve. Various New Year's greetings are heard from the buildings. Three blind men have sneaked out of the Home and, overjoyed at their escape into the fenced-off courtyard, join in the New Year's greetings, mumbling first, then calling out loud: "Happy New Year!"

SASHA. And the moon! And the moon! The walls swept away. . . . And every crack resounding with the jingle of full glasses. . . .

KONZEL. Do you see? . . .

SASHA. I hear it—feel it, wrap it around my fingers like a leaf, taste it with my tongue, swallow it. . . .

* "Legend of the Periphery" (vignette from *Cry in the Street*).

WOLF. How tepid the night is, as if it were already spring. . . . People strolling! . . .

SASHA, *jubilant and loud.* Happy New Year!

KONZEL. Are you mad? . . . Do you want to wake up the old man?

WOLF. Oh, he'll make sure not to come home before sunrise. . . . He's taken the Matron along! . . . It's seething out there tonight! . . .

KONZEL. The Matron? Where?

WOLF. To bed! Into the hotbed of passion! Onto the mattress of lust!

KONZEL. The old lady? . . .

WOLF. As if *he* were a young man. . . . They sing into each other's ears in the dark until youth stirs between the sheets. . . . And besides . . .

SASHA. The whole city burns in beds of sin tonight! . . .

WOLF. Old? . . . Her hair is still long and beautiful, let me tell you. . . .

KONZEL. Who told you that?

WOLF. Nobody. I felt it with my hands. . . . After all, if she didn't sleep upstairs . . .

SASHA. You've touched her hair? . . . Tell us, Wolf. . . .

WOLF. I wouldn't think of it. . . . So that next time you'll—

KONZEL. Tell us! Tell us!

WOLF. Well, here goes! Because it's New Year's Eve . . . Though really I should keep it to myself. Still, maybe all three of us . . . Well, anyway, two weeks ago, on Saturday, she's taking a bath—I hear this very distinctly under her room. . . . Two weeks ago, the old man was out—that I knew. Why shouldn't I go up and ask her something? . . . So I dress, and, softly, up I go. . . . The door wasn't bolted yet. I grope my way through the rooms until I feel her sitting there. All the doors open. I see her clearly, and simply knock at the last door. . . . She's terrified! . . . Quickly, I tell her something I made up about the laundry, and hold a book out toward her. . . . Now she doesn't

know whether to stay or to . . . Her hair is undone, I feel
that quite distinctly! And nothing on! Only a towel! You
see, she had just taken a bath! . . . And upset! . . .
Should she put something on? . . . The head moves back
and forth. At last she can't help laughing at herself: The
blind man! she thinks. Stays seated as she is, in the nude,
and bends over the extended book! . . . I'm standing behind her and see everything. She still smells fresh from
the warm water. . . . Now cautiously I stretch out my
arms and—finger her long, beautiful hair! . . . She cries
out, just to pretend. . . . Every woman cries out a little!
. . . But just then somebody's on the stairs. . . . Excuse
me, I say simply, playing dumb; she returned the book to
me, I think. . . . Otherwise, fellows, I'd be having my
love here in the Home! . . .

KONZEL. Some guy, this Wolf! Some guy. . . And did she
say anything afterwards?

WOLF. Not a word to me. . . . But Monday morning she did
dish out something on temptation from the Bible to all of
us! . . . Of course, she continues to live her "sin"! . . .
She's aroused, that I feel. And that makes sense. Sensual,
like any woman her age. . . . Once kindled—it burns! . . .
Now she's at loose ends and fights her flesh. . . . She's
lost her poise and avoids meeting me. . . . She's completely thrown by the kiss. . . .

SASHA. You kissed her? . . .

WOLF. Kissed her? . . . I held her head in my arm—like
this—almost on my chest. . . . And am about to feel my
way further down when someone disturbs us. . . . She
hardly resisted any more! . . .

KONZEL. Some guy! Simply goes up there, picks up love in
the room, and doesn't even let us in on it. . . .

WOLF. She squawked like a loon. . . . When a woman's ripe
for love and utters a sound, half frightened and irritated,
half craving, that tickles you right down to the ass, I'm
telling you! . . . And here I wait. . . . And if you care
to, we can join forces! . . . Then each one can still have
something! . . .

SASHA. Up to now, I've always heard her only from a distance . . . One of these days I'll approach her. But first I must sniff her! . . .

WOLF. No one's begging you to come along—just keep your mouth shut, Shorty! The two of us will win her over all right, won't we, Konzel? . . .

KONZEL. Sasha wouldn't stay away!

SASHA. Just watch out I don't outsmart you! I'm the youngest; I'll say no more. . . .

WOLF. Shares will be determined right from the start. And whoever cheats and gets too passionate will be cooled off by the other two. . . .

SASHA. Barely in the saddle, he's worried already whether his love will be true to him!

WOLF. Shorty: I can still ride home without a saddle!

SASHA. So much success with women and he still can't take any ribbing!

WOLF. Why should I? . . . As if mature women would laugh! That only cuts wrinkles in the face. . . . You joke with kids. But purpose guides women! They want money or they want men.

SASHA. Then you've got money? . . .

Laughter.

WOLF. I'll show you, buddy, what I've got. . . .

They scuffle.

SASHA. Let go!

KONZEL. Quiet now! Somebody's coming! . . .

Listening. . . . Footsteps.

KONZEL. The police?

Listening.

SASHA. The police!

WOLF. Get behind the walls!

An officer in uniform slowly passes by. Then the blind men reappear.

KONZEL. That one makes an extra round on holidays. Ordinarily he'd've been sitting for some time now down in the cellar over there! . . .

SASHA. We're free! . . . Just think, we're free! Then why do we stay here? Let's clear out! Dance over the fence and celebrate New Year's on the town. . . .

WOLF. But where? . . . They know us here in the neighborhood. . . . And further down? . . .

KONZEL. Between the houses? . . . Us? . . .

SASHA. Then let's look for someone to guide us . . .

WOLF. And rob us snugly around the next corner! . . . You can't even yell for help! . . . Listen to me, Shorty, stay with us.

SASHA. But not alone! . . . Naturally, only together!

WOLF. You always get carried away! Fidgety and excited like someone out there on the street! As if you had eyes . . .

SASHA. Well, once I did see. . . .

WOLF. What you saw in those few years couldn't amount to very much. . . . The sluice with the little stretch of woods behind it, and the red fence around your yard, right? . . .

SASHA. And yet I won't ever explain to you these two—the only visual impressions that have remained with me! They certainly make me richer than either of you, and I'd rather give away anything but this bit of light behind the veils. . . .

KONZEL. How long could you see? . . .

SASHA. Until I was four. . . .

WOLF. And that keeps you hopped up all the rest of your life! . . . An old fence dangles in your mind, luring you beyond your limitations! . . . Better to have been born blind like the two of us . . .

KONZEL. Well, properly speaking, I'm not. . . . Now and then a tinge of light flashes through my brain. . . .

WOLF. Then drives you completely out of your mind! On your "light days" you're not good for anything at all!

KONZEL. The nerves take the toll!

WOLF. That's what I mean! With you it's the nerves, and with Sasha it's the memory that blinds! . . . So which is the healthy one? . . .

SASHA. Oh, Wolf, let's live tonight! . . . I never felt better! . . . Without walls! And all around—life—brimming over! . . .

KONZEL. The city celebrates—you feel it. . . . A cloud of lust hovers over the beds of stone! . . .

WOLF. Lust five flights high breaks loose on all the streets, until the New Year is sweated out! The muscles are taut with life. . . .

SASHA. The whole world swells up . . . at the bountiful tables of the night. . . .

KONZEL. Secret guests—the three of us . . .

SASHA. Out of a sleepy shaft, moon-crazy, and free as a bird, strangely awakened, suddenly plopped into light! . . . Thousandfold life foaming up! . . . The year staggers by bawling at the night. . . . We break the fence and swirl after it! Space is lust! . . . Out into space. . . .

WOLF. Are you being carried away again? . . . Just don't forget, Shorty, you walk with a cane! We blind ones . . .

SASHA. We blind ones . . .

KONZEL. We blind have it all over the others in the dark! They see only the small halos around the lamps out there! But we shovel out long stretches with our ears and find things where no beam of light ever falls! . . .

WOLF. But they find their way about town! . . .

KONZEL. And us they hide in cramped holes! . . . We should sleep during the day, and at night, lights out—*our* realm. Before long, we'd serve as guides to the seeing! . . .

SASHA. The town will never be ours. Town is light. . . . Town is like water gurgling over an abyss constantly threatening us without eyes. Town is glass-thin skin over blood-filled veins that cracks under crutches, that needs dancers!

WOLF. Well, let it crack! . . . Blood is warm! Blood shouldn't scare us—worms housed in the world's intestines!

KONZEL. Shorty is scared. . . .

WOLF. And therefore he brags. Liberty makes him anxious.

SASHA. It's just that I have better ears for the night. And every breeze brings me images. . . .

KONZEL. Not us? . . .

SASHA. Then they don't grow so big in your brain. . . .

WOLF. As if our ears weren't good enough!

SASHA. Psst! . . . Well, what do you hear? . . .

KONZEL. Now? . . . Nothing!

SASHA. I hear footsteps!

WOLF. Sure! He's right! . . .

A "loaded gentleman" comes through the passageway. The BLIND MEN *listen.*

KONZEL. Well, who's that? . . .

SASHA. He's looking in every corner. . . .

WOLF. Too much celebrating . . . *He* doesn't see us. Let's just stand silent here! . . .

KONZEL. Let's scare him! And line up quietly along the fence . . .

SASHA. He'll think it's a spook. . . .

KONZEL. Maybe this will sober him up. . . .

They line up in a row; the DRUNK *approaches. When he's about to pass them, they gently clear their throats. He stares at them, but is by no means frightened.*

THE DRUNK. Dear folks . . . dear folks . . . tonight is New Year's Eve, my dear people. . . .

He throws up.

The New Year has just come in! . . . For the third time, now! . . . A damnable year! . . . Oh, pardon me! . . . I'm just about done in! . . . I'm a Bolshist. . . . You'll treat me kindly, gentlemen!

He hands them a bottle he has taken out of his overcoat.

Here! Take it! I can't any more . . . It solves troubles, it's rather strong. . . . Take it, man, don't you want to?

SASHA. He wants to give us something? . . .

WOLF. Hand it over here! . . . We're blind! . . .

KONZEL. You see, we can't see! . . .

WOLF *has seized the bottle.*

THE DRUNK, *not noticeably impressed even by this.* I see, I see. . . . That's fine. . . . Very pleasant . . . I see exactly what's coming. . . . I'm done for. . . . Tonight—still a little drugged. . . . Tomorrow—hangover gray! . . . No, tomorrow—holiday! . . . Day after tomorrow—finished. . . . I'm a Bolshist. . . . What good's wailing? . . . You don't know the latest waltz? . . . *Pas mexicain* or *cowboy trot.* . . . You've seen it already? . . . I'll show you the steps. . . . Watch! . . .

Tries to dance a few steps for his own amusement.

SASHA. Simply break off the neck . . .

KONZEL. Careful . . .

WOLF. I have a knife. . . .

Uncorks the bottle. They drink.

KONZEL. Excellent! Fire in the bones! . . .

THE DRUNK. Simply botched . . . More or less like that . . . A rather intricate feel to it, the latest dance . . . And the key to it lies in the stomach . . . A rather intricate—

He throws up again.

Everything's going topsy-turvy! . . . Nothing doing . . . Hangover gray, as far as you can see. . . . But let 'em make their own furniture. I'm a Bolshist. . . . The entrepreneur is the pulse-beat of the body of culture, gentlemen. . . . You've cut open the arteries. The blood is tapped. . . . The taxes and wages will trumpet us to the grave. . . . I'm finished! Now let them make the furniture themselves! They won't sell a single table or chest! I'm running the business for eighteen years, and I know my way. . . . Fair and square, with ten per cent! Just work, gentlemen! . . . That's finished. . . . Drowned by the overhead. . . . Gone under little by little! . . . And nothing more to pour in! We haven't pocketed the jacked-up profits! . . . The result? . . . Bankruptcy! . . . After eighteen years of honest labor! . . . Taken over from father! . . . That's the end! . . . Gone to the devil! . . . Even though you've done your duty! . . . Built up by the father! . . . And by the son . . . Now comes the great misery . . . Hangover gray . . .

Exits weeping. The BLIND MEN *laugh.*

WOLF. So drunk, he's lost his memory!

KONZEL. Full of sweet melancholy. . . .

WOLF. The bottle bought here and lost. . . . Nothing, knows nothing any more . . .

Drinks.

SASHA. The good Lord sent him to us!

KONZEL. So tastes sweetness too. . . . And strong as arrack . . . Happy New Year!

SASHA. All that is . . . like in a dream, I feel . . . on soft ladders. . . . I'd like to set sail once again to see the setting sun, sinking into the water . . .

WOLF. Are you dreaming? . . . I'm about to wake up! As if crippled from years of sleep! . . . I lay like a ball of yarn in a corner. . . . Now the thread shoots into the weave again! . . . The half-botched life rears up and reaches far into the darkness. I lie in ambush. . . . I hover over the whole town! I touch everything as if I had eyes. . . . Off with the roofs! . . . And with fingers in the cracks of walls, I disrupt the giggling in the corners. . . . Then, all of a sudden, they lie still with terror, pale as rocks! . . . I touch everything as if I had eyes. . . . As if I had eyes in my fingertips . . .

KONZEL. The whole palate begins to tickle. Now the tongue is wild and burns with lust. A night feast! Overflowing with fruit and wine! I invite you! . . . What a climax to this night! ? . . .

SASHA. Puffing up in spurts and blowing desire into us until our poor, bloated heads rub bloody against the bars of the fence.

KONZEL. Always along fences! . . . For *once* to suck one's fill! . . . The entire city with all its churches of lust and flesh mills of sin! . . . I keep feeling the sweat on my lips like licking salt in the water! . . . Can you taste it?

SASHA. I hear it. . . . Warm waste trickles under the pavement, hot spots fester, the pavement bursts, and fever-flakes bubble up through the muck of the street. . . .

WOLF. Foaming froth! The mouth waters! And bodies in heat! . . . And up there, bare mattresses! . . .

KONZEL. Let's meet down here every night! . . . The others sleep in their gray wool. And we have flown! . . .

SASHA. Melted away! Stirred up and transformed! Where to? What for? . . . I feel only: I grew. . . . And feel: up above us there must be a heaven of enormous lust! . . . Oh, for sight tonight! More than sight! I need ten new senses to indulge! . . .

WOLF. We latch our tongues on to the moon!

KONZEL. I throw off my coat! . . . It only hampers the breathing!

Throws down the wrapper he had about him.

Why don't you undress?

WOLF. Undress? . . .

Unbuttons his shirt and takes a deep breath.

Let the air touch the bare skin so the blood won't ooze through the pores! . . . It brushes along the flesh like rays of the sun. . . .

SASHA. Rapture! . . . Profusion of blood! . . . Up to the neck in the moon! . . .

He, too, strips to the waist.

WOLF. Your dainty little neck, little one . . . Aren't you cold? You've no hair on your chest yet. . . .

SASHA. It would be scorched, too, you giant, you dark one! Don't worry! My fire burns! All the way up to the forehead. . . . In this still night, as usual? . . . Where does the dream carry us, bare-chested blind men? . . .

KONZEL. What shall we do? . . .

WOLF. We'll race each other in circles around the yard! . . .

KONZEL. We'll break down the rear wall! . . . And find a snake! . . .

WOLF. Play leapfrog! . . .

SASHA. And dance! Dance until we stagger! . . . Feel the night! . . . The night is aglow! . . . Do you hear the drums? . . . The woods have crept over the rocks! The distance roars! But what is near seems under a glass, under a cloth! . . . I claw like a scream into this soft wall! Feel night! Cry with me: we live!

ALL THREE. We live! . . .

SASHA. In the heart of stillness! . . . We see! . . .

ALL THREE. We see!

SASHA. The marvels of the Night! . . . We desire!

ALL THREE. We desire! . . .

SASHA. We're bursting with desire! We're flooded with wishes. . . .

KONZEL. Hush! . . .

Noise in the dark mixes with their submerged shouting. As if coming from a brawl. Intermittently punctuated by a woman's voice.

WOLF. That echo rebounding from the wall of a house . . .

KONZEL. Quiet there! . . .

SASHA. A girl! . . . A young lady! . . . Cover up! . . .

They put their coats back on.

KONZEL. That's a woman's voice! . . .

WOLF. A whore! Careful! . . .

They listen.

Here comes the big whore! Attention! . . .

MARINKA, *still invisible.* One more step, and I give a yell! . . .

Laughter in the dark.

Well, where are the things? Melted down, perhaps, hmn? . . . And then remolded! . . . Part still hidden in the ground, perhaps? . . .

Laughs out loud.

The rabbits: there they run! Shame on them! . . .

Spits out; then becomes visible and tries to pass by.

A gang of robbers! . . . So you have to look for other company! . . . All New Year's Eve . . .

Suddenly she becomes aware of the three silent figures on the fence, steps back, startled, and sizes them up.

What're you doing there—squatting on that fence? . . .

SASHA. Psst! . . .

MARINKA. You ravens! . . .

KONZEL. Psst! . . .

MARINKA. I guess you're on the lookout for someone to mug, too? . . .

Laughs.

Well, take a look, then! They've plucked me dry already, the gallows birds. . . .

SASHA. She's beautiful! . . . Wears thin stockings! . . .

MARINKA. And what is that? . . .

SASHA. Home for the Blind!

KONZEL. Home for the Blind!

WOLF. Home for the Blind!

MARINKA. You're blind? . . .

KONZEL. We're blind. But we hear you.

SASHA. Patter of little feet . . . She's beautiful. . . .

WOLF. Come here! . . . We won't harm you!

KONZEL. We'll protect you. . . .

MARINKA. Protect me? You? . . . I thought you were blind. . . .

SASHA. We *are* blind. . . .

MARINKA *slowly picks up a stone and acts as if she were*

going to throw it at them. The BLIND MEN *remain motionless. Then, distrustfully, she comes somewhat nearer.*
And what are you doing here?

KONZEL. We sneaked out of the Home tonight! Secretly!

SASHA. We repaired to the moon. . . .

WOLF. We were waiting for you!

MARINKA. Aren't you watched? . . .

KONZEL. The wardens are off today.

WOLF. The Old Man's sleeping with his beloved . . .

SASHA. Sh-h-h! . . . Don't drive her away!

MARINKA *laughs.* Come on out, then! . . .

KONZEL. What'll we do out there, we blind men? . . .

MARINKA. And in there? . . . What're you waiting for? . . .

SASHA. What *are* we waiting for anyway? . . . We're out in the night! . . . Actually, for us, every sound from the outside is a great event. . . . Everything we touch conveys something new to us; everything we chance upon is full of wonder and imparts life to us! . . .

MARINKA. So this is a jolly corner here? . . .

KONZEL. What was going on before? . . .

MARINKA. Wouldn't you like to know? . . . What business is it of yours? . . .

SASHA. But we only want to help. You had an argument. . . .

MARINKA. That's just what you look like! I can take care of myself! Even with you three together, I can still manage! . . .

WOLF. A strong girl! . . . Takes us three tigers on her lap . . . Such a powerful girl! . . .

KONZEL. And the others are gone? . . .

MARINKA. Of course they're gone! . . . Heaven knows who— tramps. . . .

WOLF. Oh, leave her alone! Or else she'll think we're dicks! . . . We've no eyes, so we're the police!

KONZEL. The blind servants of justice! . . .

MARINKA. How come you're blind?

KONZEL. This one's eyes were knocked out when he was four years old. The two of us were born blind . . .

MARINKA. But when the girls go by—that's something you can see yet! . . .

WOLF. We see nothing. Believe me!

MARINKA. Nothing at all? . . . I guess you think me pretty dumb! . . .

Cautiously she walks close up to the BLIND MEN *and then, all of a sudden, flashes a light or match in their faces. The heads, illuminated in the circle of light, between the fence bars, do not stir, but* MARINKA, *touched to the core by their facial expression, hastily retreats.*

SASHA. Because we know how beautiful you are? . . . Why, we can hear that! That we can smell! The whole body takes that in and absorbs it. We hear like dogs do! . . .

MARINKA. My God! . . . You poor guys . . . One really must feel sorry for you! . . . Then you probably don't even know what it looks like out here?

WOLF. Oh, that's not so bad. Whether you see these few walls around here or—

MARINKA. You're right about that! . . . Often one would be glad not to see so much. . . . My God! I still think you're making up these stories. . . . No, no! Now I know better! And I do believe! . . . You've little reason, indeed, to laugh in the dark. . . .

KONZEL. That depends on who's coming. . . .

WOLF. It can also be fun in the dark. . . .

SASHA. Entertained like that, we're quite satisfied. . . .

MARINKA. The moon is out tonight. . . .

The BLIND MEN *laugh.*

KONZEL. Oh! Really?

SASHA. We feel it, the same way you see it with your eyes. . . .

WOLF. Now she takes us for the very lowest! . .

MARINKA. But how come? . . . I can't figure out how you can see when you haven't any eyes. . . .

SASHA. That's where nose, mouth, ears, and hands come in handy.

MARINKA. You've got me there.

KONZEL. We'll explain it to you. We'll tell you about ourselves. And you'll tell us about yourself? . . . Just stay with us a little while longer. . . . Do sit down there on the corner. Here on the stone. Our visitor's stone . . .

MARINKA *complies.*

MARINKA. You live in the house back there?

SASHA. Day in and out for years . . .

MARINKA. And you're not allowed out?

SASHA. Seldom. And never alone.

KONZEL. Sometimes on Sundays from three to seven. If you've got someone to pick you up.

MARINKA. And what do you do?

SASHA. On Sundays?

MARINKA. No. In general? During the week?

WOLF. Work, naturally.

MARINKA. I can't imagine how you live. . . .

WOLF. In clothes, like you! . . . Under them, men's chests . . . We're nothing special! . . .

MARINKA. Are there many of you blind?

WOLF. A whole houseful. Men only! And all sorts—tall and short, delicate and rough, with and without beards . . .

KONZEL. Every woman can find her heart's desire there. . . .

WOLF. What's unsatisfactory is taken back. Exchange permitted . . .

SASHA. But they don't want to come to the blind because they think we can't see their beauty. . . .

MARINKA. Well, what do you expect? . . . Love without eyes? . . . You don't even know whether she pleases you. But we want to hear what you. . . .

SASHA. But that's what's so wrong! Just the opposite! Nobody could admire you women more than we—we who caress with our hands instead of our eyes! We cling to the smallest speck of your beauty, drunk in all too quickly by the eyes; we feel our way all over its wonders, and sense every tensing and slacking that ripples along the skin, like lips longing for other lips; and over the years we cannot take our eyes off every last charm of your bodies! . . .

MARINKA. And can you distinguish between us? . . . I mean, other than with your hands . . .

SASHA. We see you quite clearly, even from a great distance!

MARINKA. Do you see me, too?

KONZEL. Of course we do!

SASHA. So distinctly that we could describe you. And if we are silent, it's only because we lack *words* for your beauty, not awareness of it! . . .

MARINKA. Am I blonde or brunette? . . .

SASHA. You're blonde.

MARINKA. Right! . . . And how old do you take me for? . . . Guess!

SASHA. We see you . . . we see you as approximately twenty years old. . . .

MARINKA *laughs somewhat embarrassedly*. Why, then you see me young. . . . I'm really older. . . . I'm—I'm twenty-two already!

SASHA. Oh, really? Nevertheless, still more girl than woman . . .

KONZEL. What do we care about a girl's age!

WOLF. We care only how she kisses and how she laughs! . . . As far as that's concerned, we care nothing about age! We blind—that's the one thing we have—time! . . . We don't have to chase after the hours like those outside— sick with the need to be always on time—somewhere. . . .

KONZEL. For us the years don't run away, so we needn't curse, "There's another hour gone to the devil!" . . . No- body cheats us out of time. . . .

SASHA. With us everything flows by through the days without commotion. The years come and go. . . . And in the end, we even forget how old we are ourselves. . . .

MARINKA. Then you could really be quite content with so much time on your hands. . . . And you have food, too. . . .

KONZEL. If only something would show up more often along the fence here. . . .

WOLF. Someone like you . . .

SASHA. Who walks gracefully, swinging the hips . . .

WOLF. And smelling of mignonettes . . .

MARINKA. *That* he smells immediately!

KONZEL. And who comes just like today—when nobody can overhear us . . .

MARINKA. So many pass by here!

KONZEL. And sometimes even stop and look over this way . . . But if you approach them, they yell and off they go. . . .

MARINKA. You're probably too rough for them, I think. And then they get scared. . . .

SASHA. We're so gentle, anyone can play with us. . . .

MARINKA. Then most likely you just don't know how to handle them. . . .

WOLF. *We'd* know just how! . . . If only *they* wouldn't know we're blind . . .

MARINKA. You poor fellows! . . .

SASHA. And what's your name? . . .

MARINKA. Minka . . . That is to say, Marinka is my real name . . .

WOLF. Marinka? . . . I've never heard that name before . . .

MARINKA. Don't you like it?

KONZEL. Oh, yes! It's a beautiful name. . . .

SASHA. And strange, just like this whole night . . . Deep-sounding, broad in scope, and all earth; but tonight the moon is shining down on it and—

KONZEL. So your name's Marinka. And what's your lover's name? . . .

MARINKA. Who could that be?

SASHA. Your lover! The one who's waiting for you at night.
The one who walks you through town, with whom you
like to be alone, who's in your thoughts, the one who
looks after you . . .

MARINKA. He died.

KONZEL. And now? Now you have no one? . . .

WOLF. One? . . . No one? . . . What ideas you have about
women! I bet she has three sweethearts! And maybe room
for three more! And because they're all nice to her, she
says she's got no lover. Right, Marinka?

SASHA. After all, we don't want to let anything leak out either!
Of course, she won't talk about her love! . . .

MARINKA. What nonsense you dream up! . . . My God!
Maybe back there in your house . . . But out here on the
street we've got other things to worry about. . . .

WOLF. And no lover? Girls no longer have lovers? . . .

MARINKA. What do *you* know about lovers! . . . They're
animals, let me tell you, you dumb oafs! They suck the
last drop of blood out of you, and drag you down deeper
into the dirt! Be happy if you can do without! You and
your lovers! . . . I have a Pekingese at home. That's
all. His name is Pulex—my sweetheart. . . .

Silence.

You're not so badly off there in your dark cradle, after all.
. . . And now—good night!

KONZEL. Do stay with us, Marinka! . . .

MARINKA. But I can't stay out here all night. . . .

SASHA. You must stay awhile yet! . . . Are you cold?

WOLF. We'll give you our coats.

MARINKA. So that *you* catch cold? . . . No. It's quite mild
out tonight.

SASHA. We won't catch cold! We'd taken off half our clothes
before you came. We were so hot!

MARINKA. What makes you so hot, I wonder? . . .

SASHA. You! The night and the moon! The Festival of Liberty!

The frenzy of voices! The year just past and our secret sins! . . .

MARINKA. You little lambs! But you're so pure of all sin! . . .

SASHA. You think so? . . . You don't know us! Often we burn with passionate greed, driven by consuming lust! . . .

MARINKA. Maybe in dreams. Yet the fence protects you! Here, outside, with every wish out in the open, stand the wretched and the souse! Here time flies; inside there, it only rocks you to sleep, and cools off every sin where there still is longing in you, you blind! . . . Now, then, are you rich or are you poor? . . . I don't know. . . .

SASHA. Tonight we're rich! So rich! . . .

MARINKA. In this little corner of moonlight—between these walls? And one hour out of your cubbyholes? . . . My God! . . . Beside yourselves already! . . . Have you never burned before? There's still another kind of lust! Once led there, I think the fire that warms you now would consume you. . . .

WOLF. Then pour your fires into our blood!

MARINKA. So you could wallow again on the ground and shoot straight up to heaven without farewell!

SASHA. Woman, help us up to heaven! . . .

MARINKA. Better hold your horses. Take it easy! . . You've the calm of twilight—the blind man's holiday!

SASHA. We are cursed! You shall be the blessing!

MARINKA. How shall I do this? . . .

KONZEL. If only once we could—could kiss you. . . .

MARINKA. Here? Through the fence? . . . I can't even get my hair between the bars.

WOLF. Have you so much hair?

MARINKA. Of course! . . . Besides, then my head would get stuck in the iron. Just reaching for me would break my neck. . . . I'd be afraid! . . .

SASHA. Rest assured, we'd be very careful with your little head! . . .

KONZEL. We want only our lips to touch it. No one will lay hands on you! . . .

MARINKA. But then your kisses would miss me! For you can't see! . . . No, no . . .

WOLF. Enough to kiss! Then the whole body stretches—as if it had tentacles—eye on eye, lip on lip . . .

KONZEL. Why not try it! . . . Let us kiss you! . . .

SASHA. You shall drown in our kisses. You'll dream about them all your life! . . .

MARINKA. Don't you see, I can't even squeeze my head through the bars. . . .

SASHA. Then lend us your arm! Only your arm . . .

KONZEL. Give us your hand! . . . We want to kiss your arm just once. . . .

MARINKA. And what good would that do you?
Puts her arm through the bars. The BLIND MEN *hold it firmly, fondle it, and kiss it.*

SASHA. Never were my lips more softly bedded! You sweet venom! . . . Minka, you nimble— Minka, you really don't know how beautiful you women are! Only men, starving behind bars, know. . . .

WOLF. Woven! . . . The tiny bones of the fingers . . . Woven like a sparrow's breast! . . .

KONZEL. And soft as a carpet! You can feel the veins within! . . . As though it might turn into milk! . . .

MARINKA. They hang there like leeches! . . . Let go, now! . . .

KONZEL. But why? You let the tenderness in you go to waste! Three men drink of it here till lost in rapture! . . .

WOLF. And we treat it so fondly! We kiss with our teeth drawn back so as not to rip the daintiest little blue vein— so no blood will flow . . .

SASHA. Which makes us all the hungrier! All the more aroused! . . . We have your arm; now give us your neck! . . . Let us touch your sweet bosom. . . .

WOLF. We want to touch your bosom. . . .

KONZEL. Come closer, Minka!

MARINKA. You'd tear me to pieces! . . . My arm hurts already! . . .

SASHA. Soft and gentle, as though no one had courted you yet, or cooled his ardor on your flesh, so soft and tender we coax every caress from you! . . . Flakes of foam on your fingertips, our hands shall purl over your body so you'll hardly perceive the pressure, and will float on a cloud of lust until everything within you quivers and quakes: Take more! . . . Give more! . . .

MARINKA. You hot little dog! . . . You hot—

WOLF. Come on! . . . Come over here, you! . . .

KONZEL. No moon back there! . . . Climb over the fence here and— Oh, you beautiful, beautiful . . .

MARINKA. What an idea! . . . Do you think—

SASHA. We think: bliss for once in a year! We think: memories for our old age! And think: tonight on New Year's Eve women are free, driven deep in their blood, to open up where men go, where stream rushes to join stream. Celebrate the embrace . . . Year melting into year . . . Why not do something nice for a few blind men! . . .

MARINKA, *stroking* SASHA's *head at the fence.* You've never touched a woman. . . . Oh, you bearded children! . . . I almost pity you. . . . Never felt a woman yet . . . and never seen day. . . . How you must moan through the nights. . . .

WOLF. At night each hanging on to any odd skeleton he can sink his teeth into—though tied down to iron cots. . . . And in the morning finding his mouth stuffed with wool. . . . So come on, then! Come on over! . . .

MARINKA. And you could call that a blessing? . . .

SASHA. Come, sin—come, blessing! . . .

MARINKA. I think you're much too excited. . . .

SASHA. Come, Woman! Come, Mother! . . . Sweet Darling! . . .

MARINKA. I'm afraid of you. . . .

WOLF. Of blind tigers? . . . Only don't scream . . . We'll burn down on you still as candles. . . .

MARINKA. Not tonight! Another time! . . . You're—

KONZEL *very loud.* Blind cripples, you mean! Us, cripples! . . . To cripples she doesn't want to—

MARINKA. Who says so? . . .

SASHA. Our empty eyes disgust you? . . . Then, to please you, we'll prick them with needles until the blood brings them back to life. . . .

MARINKA. Don't shout so. . . . Then you'd better take. . . . It's New Year's tonight. . . . Take! . . . Maybe this will please the good Lord. . . .

With these words she climbs over the fence.

KONZEL. Hush! . . .

WOLF. She's coming! . . .

SASHA. Quiet! . . .

Huddled close together, the three stand somewhat aside, staring with their dead eyes and tense faces, breathing heavily. None of them dares step forth.

MARINKA. Well . . . here I am. . . .

SASHA, *whispering.* Nobody saw you? . . . Listen! There she stands! Not since I was a kid, a woman so close . . .

KONZEL, *whispering.* Say something. . . . Wolf! . . . Two must stand guard! . . . I'll do it, and . . .

WOLF, *silent at first, finally deciding.* Now let's draw lots! . . .

SASHA. Let's draw lots!

KONZEL. Draw lots!

MARINKA. Are you all stupid? . . . Now, why don't you throw your arms around my neck, you blind ravens? . . . What are you up to? . . .

WOLF. First we draw lots. . . .

SASHA. We draw lots . . . strange woman . . . for who's to sizzle. . . .

KONZEL. We draw lots for the first to get your kisses. . . .

MARINKA. How do you do that?

Steps closer.

WOLF. Hands! . . .

They interlock hands.

One, two, three . . . Sasha out! . . . Once more: one, two, three! . . . Me out? Myself? . . . Then Konzel's left! Konzel drew it. . . .

MARINKA. Which one is Konzel?

KONZEL. Me. . . .

WOLF. We'll wait. . . .

KONZEL. May I take your hand, Marinka? . . .

MARINKA. Here! . . .

KONZEL. I'll lead you. . . . Just follow me. . . .

WOLF. Quick! . . . Blood throbbing in the throat . . .

The two exit. SASHA *kneels at the fence.* WOLF *paces up and down behind him.*

SASHA. I don't know . . . I'm dizzy. . . .

WOLF. He's lifting her, the dog! For us, the empty husk . . .

SASHA. Leave him alone! Don't you see, he's burning up? . . . He's burning up. . . .

WOLF. Yes, and we'll have to drink the stale dregs. . . .

Listens intently.

They left the door open, so we can hear them squealing, those cats. . . . They'll skin each other alive! . . .

SASHA. Leave them alone! Listen! Come here! . . Tell me. . . . We must be quiet now, as if asleep! . . . Or else the whole miraculous bundle will blow up in flames, and the next morning there'll be nothing more left than any other night, right? You can't even remember—yet we must hold on to that inside for a long time. Therefore cool, absolutely cool—whatever may happen tonight—all the senses clear . . . Wolf, are you listening? . . . There's nothing whatever to get excited about. . . . A female, like a thousand others who walk by during the night, stopped for a while at the fence, and finally let herself be kissed by some blind men. . . . What of it? . . . Three left, three follow—that's it: Every day has its program. . . . And you, you get all worked up. . . .

Noise is heard from the rear of the courtyard.

WOLF. Hey! Hey, listen! She's groaning. . . .

SASHA. Hush! Here, hold on to the fence, like me! . . . The moon has moved on. . . . By now the courtyard must be almost dark. . . . What if the old man comes back earlier! . . . And next week when the others are asleep— We wanted to discuss that. In the end we'll be so experienced in matters of love, we'll wind up as blind "men-about-town." . . .

Laughs.

I'll let you have the second turn without a draw—I'm not so bent on taking turns. . . . In the end, I'll give up altogether. . . . 'Cause I'm also . . .

Again muffled sounds out of the dark.

WOLF. Hey! Hey, listen to the cats! . . . The little lobes of her ears, I want to . . . I want to . . . .

SASHA, *shouting.* Stay here, you! . . . Don't do anything to her! . . . Are you still here? . . .

A moment of silence.

There's a red fence in front of the garden. . . . My God! A red fence . . . I no longer catch the image! . . . I'd rather split open my dome and pick my fence out of my brain with my fingers. . . . My fence . . .

Voices pop up intermittently, then a shrill scream. SASHA *staggers up, totters back and forth.*

they'll kill each other, of course . . . They'll—beat themselves bloody. . . .

Silence. He kneels down again.

Mercy! Mother . . . Protect her now, Mother. . . .

The other two return carrying MARINKA.

KONZEL. Help, please, Sasha, we've got to get away.

SASHA. What have you . . . done?

KONZEL. Get going! We've got to get away. . . .

WOLF. But the little dove is bleeding. . . . The little dove is bleeding. . . .

SASHA. You must have—beaten her—to death. . . . You really must have—beaten her! . . .

They lift MARINKA *over the fence and, after laying her on the ground, hastily beat a retreat. Her bosom is still uncovered. . . . Red silk underwear shows beneath the skirt, as though she were lying in a pool of blood. The flickering shadow of the moon plays over the prone figure for a short time. . . . Then a* QUAKER *passes by.*

THE QUAKER. A drunk! . . . From New Year's Eve . . .

Bends down.

A girl? . . . In blood? . . .

Examines her.

Murder! . . . A doctor's no use here. . . .

MARINKA, *coming to once more.* Who—are you? . . .

THE QUAKER. A Quaker . . .

MARINKA. Must I die now? . . .

THE QUAKER. Die, like all . . . What's your name? . . .

MARINKA. Now?

THE QUAKER. Only God knows when . . .

MARINKA. They . . . they stabbed me . . . the cowardly dogs. . . .

THE QUAKER. Who?

MARINKA. Three men . . . Three blind men . . . over there. . . .

THE QUAKER. And are you innocent?

MARINKA. I didn't do . . . anything . . . to them. . . . No guilt. . . . I had only pity for . . . and so they . . .

THE QUAKER. They wanted to rob you? . . .

MARINKA. No, no . . . not rob! . . . Only . . . I gave of my own . . . They never had a woman. . . . Such hot eyes . . . empty . . . the Blind! . . . Until pity made me . . .

I wanted to give them what I have. . . . That's when they stabbed me, I think. . . .

THE QUAKER. They stabbed you? Why? In a fight? . . .

MARINKA. In lust! . . . The beasts . . . Are they—are they gone? . . .

THE QUAKER. They escaped. But God sees everything! . . . Rest assured! They'll be judged for it. They'll atone their crime under the sword. . . . God has led me this way to avenge the murder. . . . God sees everything. . . .

MARINKA. Oh, Quaker . . . I think . . . I'm not much good. . . . I'm . . . from the street. . . . I . . . I'm also . . . tired. . . . And blind myself . . . my whole life . . . Quaker, let them . . . the blind creatures . . . Don't let them . . . die . . . I— Guilt! . . . And after all . . . quite content . . . with . . . Marinka's my name. . . . Just carry me . . . home . . .

She dies.

THE QUAKER. Marinka! . . . My child!

Listens to her heart and slowly removes his hat.
The end! . . .
     Take her Life! . . .
Many a person will have died more sinfully!—
But Heaven will forgive you much, I believe,
You little Saint of the gutter. . . .

Curtain.